Product Standards for Internationally Integrated Goods Markets

Integrating National Economies: Promise and Pitfalls

Barry Bosworth (Brookings Institution) and Gur Ofer (Hebrew University)
Reforming Planned Economies in an Integrating World Economy

Ralph C. Bryant (Brookings Institution)
International Coordination of National Stabilization Policies

Susan M. Collins (Brookings Institution/Georgetown University)
Distributive Issues: A Constraint on Global Integration

Richard N. Cooper (Harvard University)
Environment and Resource Policies for the World Economy

Ronald G. Ehrenberg (Cornell University)
Labor Markets and Integrating National Economies

Barry Eichengreen (University of California, Berkeley)
International Monetary Arrangements for the 21st Century

Mitsuhiro Fukao (Bank of Japan)
Financial Integration, Corporate Governance, and the Performance of Multinational Companies

Stephan Haggard (University of California, San Diego)
Developing Nations and the Politics of Global Integration

Richard J. Herring (University of Pennsylvania) and Robert E. Litan (Department of Justice/Brookings Institution)
Financial Regulation in the Global Economy

Miles Kahler (University of California, San Diego)
International Institutions and the Political Economy of Integration

Anne O. Krueger (Stanford University)
Trade Policies and Developing Nations

Robert Z. Lawrence (Harvard University)
Regionalism, Multilateralism, and Deeper Integration

Sylvia Ostry (University of Toronto) and Richard R. Nelson (Columbia University)
Techno-Nationalism and Techno-Globalism: Conflict and Cooperation

Robert L. Paarlberg (Wellesley College/Harvard University)
Leadership Abroad Begins at Home: U.S. Foreign Economic Policy after the Cold War

Peter Rutland (Wesleyan University)
Russia, Eurasia, and the Global Economy

F. M. Scherer (Harvard University)
Competition Policies for an Integrated World Economy

Susan L. Shirk (University of California, San Diego)
How China Opened Its Door: The Political Success of the PRC's Foreign Trade and Investment Reforms

Alan O. Sykes (University of Chicago)
Product Standards for Internationally Integrated Goods Markets

Akihiko Tanaka (Institute of Oriental Culture, University of Tokyo)
The Politics of Deeper Integration: National Attitudes and Policies in Japan

Vito Tanzi (International Monetary Fund)
Taxation in an Integrating World

William Wallace (St. Antony's College, Oxford University)
Regional Integration: The West European Experience

Alan O. Sykes

Product Standards for Internationally Integrated Goods Markets

THE BROOKINGS INSTITUTION
Washington, D.C.

Library of Congress Cataloging-in-Publication data:
Sykes, A. O.
Product standards for internationally integrated goods markets /
Alan O. Sykes
p.   cm.—(Integrating national economies)
Includes bibliographical references and index.
ISBN 0-8157-8296-9—ISBN 0-8157-8295-0 (pbk.)
1. Nontariff trade barriers.   2. Standardization.   3. Commercial
Products—Quality control.   4. International economic integration.
5. Foreign trade regulation.   I. Title.   II. Series.
HF1430.S95   1995
382'.5—dc20   94-42146
                                                                       CIP

9 8 7 6 5 4 3 2 1

The paper used in this publication meets the minimum requirements of
American National Standard for Information Sciences—Permanence of Paper
for Printed Library Materials, ANSI Z39.48-1984

Typeset in Plantin

Composition by Princeton Editorial Associates
Princeton, New Jersey

Printed by R. R. Donnelley and Sons Co.
Harrisonburg, Virginia

Foreword

*I*N 1947, twenty-three nations ratified the General Agreement on Tariffs and Trade. Since then, tariffs and quotas have been progressively reduced throughout much of the industrialized world, resulting in greatly expanded international trade. The Uruguay Round negotiations, concluded in December 1993, extended GATT's reach to agriculture, services, and intellectual property and clarified policies toward other aspects of trade. What steps remain to carry international economic integration beyond the impressive accomplishments already attained?

In this book, Alan O. Sykes analyzes "technical barriers" to international trade in goods. These include impediments to trade created by divergent national product standards and regulations, and by the systems that trading nations use to verify conformity with applicable standards and regulations. He traces the history of the problem and sets out the available empirical evidence on its importance. He then uses economic theory to suggest when differences in standards and regulations may be desirable or undesirable and explains how an ideal conformity assessment system should operate. The book also contains a survey of the legal response to the problem of technical barriers in the World Trade Organization system, the European Union, the North American Free Trade Agreement, and the U.S. federal system, as well as an overview of the operation of international standardization entities such as the International Organization for Standardization and the Codex Alimentarius. Finally, the author assesses the adequacy of the existing international response to technical barriers and makes a number of recommendations on what might be done to address the problem.

Alan O. Sykes is professor of law at the University of Chicago Law School. He is grateful to Robert Lawrence, Kalypso Nicolaïdis, Jacques Pelkmans, the participants in a Brookings review conference, and the participants in the University of Chicago law faculty workshop for their comments and suggestions. Peter Barot, Donna Cote, and Audrey Lee provided valuable research assistance.

Princeton Editorial Associates edited the manuscript and prepared the index, and David Bearce verified the factual content of the manuscript. Lisa Guillory provided word processing assistance.

Funding for the project came from the Center for Global Partnership of the Japan Foundation, the Curry Foundation, the Ford Foundation, the Korea Foundation, the Tokyo Club Foundation for Global Studies, the United States–Japan Foundation, and the Alex C. Walker Educational and Charitable Foundation. The author and Brookings are grateful for their support.

The views expressed in this book are those of the author and should not be ascribed to any of the persons or organizations acknowledged above, or to the trustees, officers, or staff members of the Brookings Institution.

BRUCE K. MACLAURY
President

February 1995
Washington, D.C.

Contents

Preface to the Studies on Integrating National Economies

ECONOMIC interdependence among nations has increased sharply in the past half century. For example, while the value of total production of industrial countries increased at a rate of about 9 percent a year on average between 1964 and 1992, the value of the exports of those nations grew at an average rate of 12 percent, and lending and borrowing across national borders through banks surged upward even more rapidly at 23 percent a year. This international economic interdependence has contributed to significantly improved standards of living for most countries. Continuing international economic integration holds out the promise of further benefits. Yet the increasing sensitivity of national economies to events and policies originating abroad creates dilemmas and pitfalls if national policies and international cooperation are poorly managed.

The Brookings Project on Integrating National Economies, of which this study is a component, focuses on the interplay between two fundamental facts about the world at the end of the twentieth century. First, the world will continue for the foreseeable future to be organized politically into nation-states with sovereign governments. Second, increasing economic integration among nations will continue to erode differences among national economies and undermine the autonomy of national governments. The project explores the opportunities and tensions arising from these two facts.

Scholars from a variety of disciplines have produced twenty-one studies for the first phase of the project. Each study examines the heightened competition between national political sovereignty and increased cross-border economic integration. This preface identifies background themes and issues common to all the studies and provides a brief overview of the project as a whole.[1]

Increasing World Economic Integration

Two underlying sets of causes have led nations to become more closely intertwined. First, technological, social, and cultural changes have sharply reduced the effective economic distances among nations. Second, many of the government policies that traditionally inhibited cross-border transactions have been relaxed or even dismantled.

The same improvements in transportation and communications technology that make it much easier and cheaper for companies in New York to ship goods to California, for residents of Strasbourg to visit relatives in Marseilles, and for investors in Hokkaido to buy and sell shares on the Tokyo Stock Exchange facilitate trade, migration, and capital movements spanning nations and continents. The sharply reduced costs of moving goods, money, people, and information underlie the profound economic truth that technology has made the world markedly smaller.

New communications technology has been especially significant for financial activity. Computers, switching devices, and telecommunications satellites have slashed the cost of transmitting information internationally, of confirming transactions, and of paying for transactions. In the 1950s, for example, foreign exchange could be bought and sold only during conventional business hours in the initiating party's time zone. Such transactions can now be carried out instantaneously twenty-four hours a day. Large banks pass the management of their worldwide foreign-exchange positions around the globe from one branch to another, staying continuously ahead of the setting sun.

Such technological innovations have increased the knowledge of potentially profitable international exchanges and of economic opportunities abroad. Those developments, in turn, have changed consumers' and producers' tastes. Foreign goods, foreign vacations, foreign financial investments—virtually anything from other nations—have lost some of their exotic character.

1. A complete list of authors and study titles is included at the beginning of this volume, facing the title page.

Although technological change permits increased contact among nations, it would not have produced such dramatic effects if it had been countermanded by government policies. Governments have traditionally taxed goods moving in international trade, directly restricted imports and subsidized exports, and tried to limit international capital movements. Those policies erected "separation fences" at the borders of nations. From the perspective of private sector agents, separation fences imposed extra costs on cross-border transactions. They reduced trade and, in some cases, eliminated it. During the 1930s governments used such policies with particular zeal, a practice now believed to have deepened and lengthened the Great Depression.

After World War II, most national governments began—sometimes unilaterally, more often collaboratively—to lower their separation fences, to make them more permeable, or sometimes even to tear down parts of them. The multilateral negotiations under the auspices of the General Agreement on Trade and Tariffs (GATT)—for example, the Kennedy Round in the 1960s, the Tokyo Round in the 1970s, and most recently the protracted negotiations of the Uruguay Round, formally signed only in April 1994—stand out as the most prominent examples of fence lowering for trade in goods. Though contentious and marked by many compromises, the GATT negotiations are responsible for sharp reductions in at-the-border restrictions on trade in goods and services. After the mid-1980s a large number of developing countries moved unilaterally to reduce border barriers and to pursue outwardly oriented policies.

The lowering of fences for financial transactions began later and was less dramatic. Nonetheless, by the 1990s government restrictions on capital flows, especially among the industrial countries, were much less important and widespread than at the end of World War II and in the 1950s.

By shrinking the economic distances among nations, changes in technology would have progressively integrated the world economy even in the absence of reductions in governments' separation fences. Reductions in separation fences would have enhanced interdependence even without the technological innovations. Together, these two sets of evolutionary changes have reinforced each other and strikingly transformed the world economy.

Changes in the Government of Nations

Simultaneously with the transformation of the global economy, major changes have occurred in the world's political structure. First, the number of governmental decisionmaking units in the world has expanded markedly, and political power has been diffused more broadly among them. Rising nationalism and, in some areas, heightened ethnic tensions have accompanied that increasing political pluralism.

The history of membership in international organizations documents the sharp growth in the number of independent states. For example, only 44 nations participated in the Bretton Woods conference of July 1944, which gave birth to the International Monetary Fund. But by the end of 1970, the IMF had 118 member nations. The number of members grew to 150 by the mid-1980s and to 178 by December 1993. Much of this growth reflects the collapse of colonial empires. Although many nations today are small and carry little individual weight in the global economy, their combined influence is considerable, and their interests cannot be ignored as easily as they were in the past.

A second political trend, less visible but equally important, has been the gradual loss of the political and economic hegemony of the United States. Immediately after World War II, the United States by itself accounted for more than one-third of world production. By the early 1990s the U.S. share had fallen to about one-fifth. Concurrently, the political and economic influence of the European colonial powers continued to wane, and the economic significance of nations outside Europe and North America, such as Japan, Korea, Indonesia, China, Brazil, and Mexico, increased. A world in which economic power and influence are widely diffused has displaced a world in which one or a few nations effectively dominated international decisionmaking.

Turmoil and the prospect of fundamental change in the formerly centrally planned economies compose a third factor causing radical changes in world politics. During the era of central planning, governments in those nations tried to limit external influences on their economies. Now leaders in the formerly planned economies are trying to adopt reforms modeled on Western capitalist principles. To the extent that these efforts succeed, those nations will increase their economic involvement with the rest of the world. Political and economic alignments among the Western industrialized nations will be forced to adapt.

Governments and scholars have begun to assess these three trends, but their far-reaching ramifications will not be clear for decades.

Dilemmas for National Policies

Cross-border economic integration and national political sovereignty have increasingly come into conflict, leading to a growing mismatch between the economic and political structures of the world. The effective domains of economic markets have come to coincide less and less with national governmental jurisdictions.

When the separation fences at nations' borders were high, governments and citizens could sharply distinguish "international" from "domestic" policies. International policies dealt with at-the-border barriers, such as tariffs and quotas, or responded to events occurring abroad. In contrast, domestic policies were concerned with everything behind the nation's borders, such as competition and antitrust rules, corporate governance, product standards, worker safety, regulation and supervision of financial institutions, environmental protection, tax codes, and the government's budget. Domestic policies were regarded as matters about which nations were sovereign, to be determined by the preferences of the nation's citizens and its political institutions, without regard for effects on other nations.

As separation fences have been lowered and technological innovations have shrunk economic distances, a multitude of formerly neglected differences among nations' domestic policies have become exposed to international scrutiny. National governments and international negotiations must thus increasingly deal with "deeper"— behind-the-border—integration. For example, if country A permits companies to emit air and water pollutants whereas country B does not, companies that use pollution-generating methods of production will find it cheaper to produce in country A. Companies in country B that compete internationally with companies in country A are likely to complain that foreign competitors enjoy unfair advantages and to press for international pollution standards.

Deeper integration requires analysis of the economic and the political aspects of virtually all nonborder policies and practices. Such

issues have already figured prominently in negotiations over the evolution of the European Community, over the Uruguay Round of
GATT negotiations, over the North American Free Trade Agreement
(NAFTA), and over the bilateral economic relationships between
Japan and the United States. Future debates about behind-the-border
policies will occur with increasing frequency and prove at least as
complex and contentious as the past negotiations regarding at-the-
border restrictions.

Tensions about deeper integration arise from three broad sources:
cross-border spillovers, diminished national autonomy, and challenges
to political sovereignty.

Cross-Border Spillovers

Some activities in one nation produce consequences that spill
across borders and affect other nations. Illustrations of these spillovers abound. Given the impact of modern technology of banking
and securities markets in creating interconnected networks, lax rules
in one nation erode the ability of all other nations to enforce banking
and securities rules and to deal with fraudulent transactions. Given
the rapid diffusion of knowledge, science and technology policies in
one nation generate knowledge that other nations can use without full
payment. Labor market policies become matters of concern to other
nations because workers migrate in search of work; policies in one
nation can trigger migration that floods or starves labor markets
elsewhere. When one nation dumps pollutants into the air or water
that other nations breathe or drink, the matter goes beyond the
unitary concern of the polluting nation and becomes a matter for
international negotiation. Indeed, the hydrocarbons that are emitted
into the atmosphere when individual nations burn coal for generating
electricity contribute to global warming and are thereby a matter of
concern for the entire world.

The tensions associated with cross-border spillovers can be especially vexing when national policies generate outcomes alleged to be
competitively inequitable, as in the example in which country A
permits companies to emit pollutants and country B does not. Or
consider a situation in which country C requires commodities, whether
produced at home or abroad, to meet certain design standards, justified for safety reasons. Foreign competitors may find it too expensive

to meet these standards. In that event, the standards in C act very much like tariffs or quotas, effectively narrowing or even eliminating foreign competition for domestic producers. Citing examples of this sort, producers or governments in individual nations often complain that business is not conducted on a "level playing field." Typically, the complaining nation proposes that *other* nations adjust their policies to moderate or remove the competitive inequities.

Arguments for creating a level playing field are troublesome at best. International trade occurs precisely because of differences among nations—in resource endowments, labor skills, and consumer tastes. Nations specialize in producing goods and services in which they are relatively most efficient. In a fundamental sense, cross-border trade is valuable because the playing field is *not* level.

When David Ricardo first developed the theory of comparative advantage, he focused on differences among nations owing to climate or technology. But Ricardo could as easily have ascribed the productive differences to differing "social climates" as to physical or technological climates. Taking all "climatic" differences as given, the theory of comparative advantage argues that free trade among nations will maximize global welfare.

Taken to its logical extreme, the notion of leveling the playing field implies that nations should become homogeneous in all major respects. But that recommendation is unrealistic and even pernicious. Suppose country A decides that it is too poor to afford the costs of a clean environment, and will thus permit the production of goods that pollute local air and water supplies. Or suppose it concludes that it cannot afford stringent protections for worker safety. Country A will then argue that it is inappropriate for other nations to impute to country A the value they themselves place on a clean environment and safety standards (just as it would be inappropriate to impute the A valuations to the environment of other nations). The core of the idea of political sovereignty is to permit national residents to order their lives and property in accord with their own preferences.

Which perspective about differences among nations in behind-the-border policies is more compelling? Is country A merely exercising its national preferences and appropriately exploiting its comparative advantage in goods that are dirty or dangerous to produce? Or does a legitimate international problem exist that justifies pressure from other nations urging country A to accept changes in its policies (thus

curbing its national sovereignty)? When national governments negotiate resolutions to such questions—trying to agree whether individual
nations are legitimately exercising sovereign choices or, alternatively,
engaging in behavior that is unfair or damaging to other nations—the
dialogue is invariably contentious because the resolutions depend on
the typically complex circumstances of the international spillovers
and on the relative weights accorded to the interests of particular
individuals and particular nations.

Diminished National Autonomy

As cross-border economic integration increases, governments experience greater difficulties in trying to control events within their
borders. Those difficulties, summarized by the term *diminished autonomy*, are the second set of reasons why tensions arise from the competition between political sovereignty and economic integration.

For example, nations adjust monetary and fiscal policies to influence domestic inflation and employment. In setting these policies,
smaller countries have always been somewhat constrained by foreign
economic events and policies. Today, however, all nations are constrained, often severely. More than in the past, therefore, nations may
be better able to achieve their economic goals if they work together
collaboratively in adjusting their macroeconomic policies.

Diminished autonomy and cross-border spillovers can sometimes
be allowed to persist without explicit international cooperation to
deal with them. States in the United States adopt their own tax
systems and set policies for assistance to poor single people without
any formal cooperation or limitation. Market pressures operate to
force a degree of de facto cooperation. If one state taxes corporations
too heavily, it knows business will move elsewhere. (Those familiar
with older debates about "fiscal federalism" within the United States
and other nations will recognize the similarity between those issues
and the emerging international debates about deeper integration of
national economies.) Analogously, differences among nations in regulations, standards, policies, institutions, and even social and cultural
preferences create economic incentives for a kind of arbitrage that
erodes or eliminates the differences. Such pressures involve not only
the conventional arbitrage that exploits price differentials (buying at
one point in geographic space or time and selling at another) but also

shifts in the location of production facilities and in the residence of factors of production.

In many other cases, however, cross-border spillovers, arbitrage pressures, and diminished effectiveness of national policies can produce unwanted consequences. In cases involving what economists call externalities (external economies and diseconomies), national governments may need to cooperate to promote mutual interests. For example, population growth, continued urbanization, and the more intensive exploitation of natural resources generate external diseconomies not only within but across national boundaries. External economies generated when benefits spill across national jurisdictions probably also increase in importance (for instance, the gains from basic research and from control of communicable diseases).

None of these situations is new, but technological change and the reduction of tariffs and quotas heighten their importance. When one nation produces goods (such as scientific research) or "bads" (such as pollution) that significantly affect other nations, individual governments acting sequentially and noncooperatively cannot deal effectively with the resulting issues. In the absence of explicit cooperation and political leadership, too few collective goods and too many collective bads will be supplied.

Challenges to Political Sovereignty

The pressures from cross-border economic integration sometimes even lead individuals or governments to challenge the core assumptions of national political sovereignty. Such challenges are a third source of tensions about deeper integration.

The existing world system of nation-states assumes that a nation's residents are free to follow their own values and to select their own political arrangements without interference from others. Similarly, property rights are allocated by nation. (The so-called global commons, such as outer space and the deep seabed, are the sole exceptions.) A nation is assumed to have the sovereign right to exploit its property in accordance with its own preferences and policies. Political sovereignty is thus analogous to the concept of consumer sovereignty (the presumption that the individual consumer best knows his or her own interests and should exercise them freely).

In times of war, some nations have had sovereignty wrested from them by force. In earlier eras, a handful of individuals or groups have questioned the premises of political sovereignty. With the profound increases in economic integration in recent decades, however, a larger number of individuals and groups—and occasionally even their national governments—have identified circumstances in which, it is claimed, some universal or international set of values should take precedence over the preferences or policies of particular nations.

Some groups seize on human-rights issues, for example, or what they deem to be egregiously inappropriate political arrangements in other nations. An especially prominent case occurred when citizens in many nations labeled the former apartheid policies of South Africa an affront to universal values and emphasized that the South African government was not legitimately representing the interests of a majority of South Africa's residents. Such views caused many national governments to apply economic sanctions against South Africa. Examples of value conflicts are not restricted to human rights, however. Groups focusing on environmental issues characterize tropical rain forests as the lungs of the world and the genetic repository for numerous species of plants and animals that are the heritage of all mankind. Such views lead Europeans, North Americans, or Japanese to challenge the timber-cutting policies of Brazilians and Indonesians. A recent controversy over tuna fishing with long drift nets that kill porpoises is yet another example. Environmentalists in the United States whose sensibilities were offended by the drowning of porpoises required U.S. boats at some additional expense to amend their fishing practices. The U.S. fishermen, complaining about imported tuna caught with less regard for porpoises, persuaded the U.S. government to ban such tuna imports (both direct imports from the countries in which the tuna is caught and indirect imports shipped via third countries). Mexico and Venezuela were the main countries affected by this ban; a GATT dispute panel sided with Mexico against the United States in the controversy, which further upset the U.S. environmental community.

A common feature of all such examples is the existence, real or alleged, of "psychological externalities" or "political failures." Those holding such views reject untrammeled political sovereignty for nation-states in deference to universal or non-national values. They wish to constrain the exercise of individual nations' sovereignties through international negotiations or, if necessary, by even stronger intervention.

The Management of International Convergence

In areas in which arbitrage pressures and cross-border spillovers are weak and psychological or political externalities are largely absent, national governments may encounter few problems with deeper integration. Diversity across nations may persist quite easily. But at the other extreme, arbitrage and spillovers in some areas may be so strong that they threaten to erode national diversity completely. Or psychological and political sensitivities may be asserted too powerfully to be ignored. Governments will then be confronted with serious tensions, and national policies and behaviors may eventually converge to common, worldwide patterns (for example, subject to internationally agreed norms or minimum standards). Eventual convergence across nations, if it occurs, could happen in a harmful way (national policies and practices being driven to a least common denominator with externalities ignored, in effect a "race to the bottom") or it could occur with mutually beneficial results ("survival of the fittest and the best").

Each study in this series addresses basic questions about the management of international convergence: if, when, and how national governments should intervene to try to influence the consequences of arbitrage pressures, cross-border spillovers, diminished autonomy, and the assertion of psychological or political externalities. A wide variety of responses is conceivable. We identify six, which should be regarded not as distinct categories but as ranges along a continuum.

National autonomy defines a situation at one end of the continuum in which national governments make decentralized decisions with little or no consultation and no explicit cooperation. This response represents political sovereignty at its strongest, undiluted by any international management of convergence.

Mutual recognition, like national autonomy, presumes decentralized decisions by national governments and relies on market competition to guide the process of international convergence. Mutual recognition, however, entails exchanges of information and consultations among governments to constrain the formation of national regulations and policies. As understood in discussions of economic integration within the European Community, moreover, mutual recognition entails an explicit acceptance by each member nation of the regulations, standards, and certification procedures of other members. For example, mutual recognition allows wine or liquor produced in any European Union country to be sold in all twelve member countries even if production standards in member countries differ. Doctors licensed in France are permitted to practice in Germany, and vice versa, even if licensing procedures in the two countries differ.

Governments may agree on rules that restrict their freedom to set policy or that promote gradual convergence in the structure of policy. As international consultations and monitoring of compliance with such rules become more important, this situation can be described as *monitored decentralization*. The Group of Seven finance ministers meetings, supplemented by the IMF's surveillance over exchange rate and macroeconomic policies, illustrate this approach to management.

Coordination goes further than mutual recognition and monitored decentralization in acknowledging convergence pressures. It is also more ambitious in promoting intergovernmental cooperation to deal with them. Coordination involves jointly designed mutual adjustments of national policies. In clear-cut cases of coordination, bargaining occurs and governments agree to behave differently from the ways they would have behaved without the agreement. Examples include the World Health Organization's procedures for controlling communicable diseases and the 1987 Montreal Protocol (to a 1985 framework convention) for the protection of stratospheric ozone by reducing emissions of chlorofluorocarbons.

Explicit harmonization, which requires still higher levels of intergovernmental cooperation, may require agreement on regional standards or world standards. Explicit harmonization typically entails still greater departures from decentralization in decisionmaking and still further strengthening of international institutions. The 1988 agreement among major central banks to set minimum standards for the required capital positions of commercial banks (reached through the Committee on Banking Regulations and Supervisory Practices at the Bank for International Settlements) is an example of partially harmonized regulations.

At the opposite end of the spectrum from national autonomy lies *federalist mutual governance*, which implies continuous bargaining and joint, centralized decisionmaking. To make federalist mutual governance work would require greatly strengthened supranational institutions. This end of the management spectrum, now relevant only as an analytical benchmark, is a possible outcome that can be imagined for the middle or late decades of the twenty-first century, possibly even sooner for regional groupings like the European Union.

Overview of the Brookings Project

Despite their growing importance, the issues of deeper economic integration and its competition with national political sovereignty were largely neglected in the 1980s. In 1992 the Brookings Institution initiated its project on Integrating National Economies to direct attention to these important questions.

In studying this topic, Brookings sought and received the co-operation of some of the world's leading economists, political scientists, foreign-policy specialists, and government officials, representing all regions of the world. Although some functional areas require a special focus on European, Japanese, and North American perspectives, at all junctures the goal was to include, in addition, the perspectives of developing nations and the formerly centrally planned economies.

The first phase of the project commissioned the twenty-one scholarly studies listed at the beginning of the book. One or two lead discussants, typically residents of parts of the world other than the area where the author resides, were asked to comment on each study.

Authors enjoyed substantial freedom to design their individual studies, taking due account of the overall themes and goals of the project. The guidelines for the studies requested that at least some of the analysis be carried out with a non-normative perspective. In effect, authors were asked to develop a "baseline" of what might happen in the absence of changed policies or further international cooperation. For their normative analyses, authors were asked to start with an agnostic posture that did not prejudge the net benefits or costs resulting from integration. The project organizers themselves had no presumption about whether national diversity is better or worse than international convergence or about what the individual studies should conclude regarding the desirability of increased integration. On the contrary, each author was asked to address the trade-offs in his or her issue area between diversity and convergence and to locate the area, currently and prospectively, on the spectrum of international management possibilities running between national autonomy through mutual recognition to coordination and explicit harmonization.

HENRY J. AARON   SUSAN M. COLLINS
RALPH C. BRYANT   ROBERT Z. LAWRENCE

Product Standards for Internationally Integrated Goods Markets

Chapter I

Introduction

A S TARIFFS have diminished pursuant to the General Agreement on Tariffs and Trade (GATT) and other international agreements, the significance of nontariff impediments to international trade has increased relatively and, in some instances, absolutely. Diverse standards and regulations governing the sale of products in national markets are a potential source of these nontariff impediments and, in modern parlance, may become "technical barriers to trade."

It is ironic that product standards and regulations should create trade barriers, as many of them evolved for the purpose of promoting trade.[1] Familiar weights and measures were developed to facilitate the description of goods in commerce and to obviate problems of fraud. Voltage standards allow electrical products to operate satisfactorily in different geographic areas. Standardized television broadcast formats enable programs of varying origin to be viewed on receivers of varying manufacture, a similar function being performed by standard operating systems for microcomputers. Regulations governing the wholesomeness of foodstuffs serve in part to reassure consumers of their safety and thus to expand the market of willing buyers. Innumerable other examples might be offered.

Yet it is not difficult to appreciate how these same measures can diverge across national markets and become trade impediments. Standards and regulations may be deliberately crafted to impose a cost disadvantage on foreign competitors. They may also differ across

---

1. For general historical accounts of standardization, see Cochrane (1966); Perry (1955); Stephens (1983); Verman (1973).

1

jurisdictions as a result of divergent tastes, because of variations in technology, income, or resource endowments, or even chance. It is thus common for goods that conform to all pertinent standards and regulatory requirements in their country of origin to fail to conform elsewhere. And even when conformity to foreign standards and regulations is not difficult, the burden of *demonstrating* conformity to the satisfaction of consumers or regulators abroad can still be considerable. "Technical barriers" thus arise both from the divergence of standards and regulations across nations and from the burden of establishing conformity with them whether or not they are divergent.

Definitions

A product *standard* is defined here as a specification or set of specifications that relates to some characteristic of a product or its manufacture. It may relate to its size, its dimensions, its weight, its design, its function, its ingredients, or any number of other product attributes. It may or may not be formally promulgated by a private or public standard-setting entity. The distinguishing feature of a standard is that compliance is *voluntary*. Thus products that do not conform to a standard are legally permitted to be sold, and any penalty for nonconformity is a market one. A "regulation" differs from a standard only in this key respect—it, too, may relate to any aspect of product characteristics or manufacture, but compliance with a regulation is legally *mandatory*. It is not uncommon for standards to be converted into regulations by government fiat.

Within the broad categories of standards and regulations, it is useful on occasion to draw some further distinctions. First, virtually all standards or regulations within the scope of this study are readily classifiable as relating either to product "compatibility" or to product "quality." *Compatibility* refers to the capacity of products to function in association with others—VHS cassettes are only compatible with VHS players, computer software may require a particular operating system, and the like. *Quality* refers to any *other* attribute of a product that well-informed users care about—wholesomeness, safety, durability, proper labeling, and so forth. Matters of compatibility tend to be the subject of standards rather than regulations, whereas matters of quality are somewhat more often the focus of regulation. Plainly, however, many aspects of product quality are left entirely to the market, and compatibility is sometimes achieved through government fiat.

It may also prove useful at times to distinguish "product" standards or regulations from "production" standards or regulations. Roughly, standards in the former group specify attributes of the finished product, whereas standards in the latter group specify attributes of the process by which it is manufactured or created. The difference is unimportant for many purposes, but has at times had legal significance. A further distinction may be drawn between standards or regulations governing "design" and those governing "performance." The design category encompasses standards and regulations that specify precisely how a product must be made ("the door must be of steel, one-inch thick"). The performance category encompasses standards and regulations that require the product to meet a certain objective but permit it to do so through alternative designs ("the door must be fire resistant with a 30-minute burn-through time").

Finally, the term *conformity assessment* refers to the process through which products are evaluated for compliance with standards and regulations. It encompasses the certification requirements imposed on product manufacturers, testing and certification by third-party laboratories, inspections by customs authorities or other regulatory officials, and so on.

Scope of the Study

This book explores the problem of technical barriers to trade in international goods markets and the possible policy responses. Among the questions that it addresses are, When is international heterogeneity in standards and regulations economically desirable or undesirable? When heterogeneity is unjustified, is international harmonization a desirable and achievable solution? To what extent can and should the consequences of heterogeneity be ameliorated through "mutual recognition" covenants? How well do the legal principles of the WTO/GATT system (as enhanced by the Uruguay Round) function to address technical barriers, and how might they be improved? How well do international standards organizations such as the International Organization for Standardization (ISO) and the

Codex Alimentarius (Codex) perform? What can the global community learn from the "old," "new," and "global" approaches to technical barrier problems in the European Union?

Several limitations on the scope of the study should be noted at the outset. As the remarks thus far suggest, the focus is exclusively on technical barriers to trade in goods markets and thus excludes services. This is not meant to suggest that heterogeneous standards and regulations are unimportant to international trade in services but express attention to those markets is omitted simply to make the study more manageable. Likewise, little attention is devoted to government procurement specifications even though they may be understood as "standards" for many purposes and even though it is also clear that they have profound trade significance, especially in certain sectors (telecommunications, railroads, broadcasting, air transport, and electric power generation, to name a few). Discussion of certain regulatory measures that fall in part within the definition of product regulations yet are addressed directly by other books in this series has also been omitted. In particular, production regulations concerning the environmental impact of manufacturing processes or concerning labor market practices, such as the use of child labor or the level of a minimum wage, are not considered.[2] Finally, again for reasons of manageability, discussion of certain laws and regulations governing terms of sale, such as those created by the law of tort and warranty, is omitted. Much of the analysis to follow is quite general, however, and applies in substantial measure to these omitted topics.

Chapter Summary

Even with this narrowed focus, the scope of the technical barrier problem is vast, and this book cannot begin to survey all the particular instances in which technical barriers prove important. Indeed, little systematic evidence exists regarding the significance of technical barriers, sector by sector, and much of what is known is by anecdote or example. Chapter 2 discusses the available evidence on the scope and magnitude of technical barriers in international goods markets, making the argument that technical barriers are extensive and important

---

2. See Cooper (1994); Ehrenberg (1994).

even though their quantitative effect on the volume of trade is usually unknown and often unknowable as a practical matter.

The analysis of technical barriers is further complicated by theoretical uncertainty in many cases about their effects on economic welfare. Technical barriers are, in this respect, quite unlike traditional impediments to trade, such as tariffs and quotas, which can be shown to be economically inefficient in almost all cases from the global perspective. Chapter 3 develops some of the economic considerations that bear on the efficiency of heterogeneity in standards and regulations and on the optimal design of conformity assessment systems. It considers the adequacy of market solutions and sources of market failure, as well as the proper scope for government intervention.

The extant and proposed policy responses to technical barriers are the topic of chapter 4. These responses include multilateral cooperation to develop international standards and to harmonize national regulations and treaty-based legal restrictions on the conduct of national policies. Examples of the first type of response include the standardization efforts of the ISO and the Codex and recent initiatives of the European Commission. Examples of the second include the Uruguay Round agreements on technical barriers and sanitary and phytosanitary measures, articles 30 and 36 of the Treaty of Rome, the dormant commerce clause under the U.S. Constitution, and portions of the North American Free Trade Agreement. Each approach is surveyed in some detail, with attention to its strengths and failings.

The main conclusions and recommendations are in chapter 5. The strengths and weaknesses of the policy responses discussed in chapter 4 are analyzed, and some options for reform are offered.

Overview of Principal Conclusions

One inescapable conclusion is that the trading community needs more information about technical barriers. Their importance, sector by sector, is generally unknown, as is their impact on economic welfare. Additional systematic research into their incidence and magnitude would be immensely beneficial. And because information about the problem is so scant, the remaining conclusions of this study must be viewed as tentative.

With that caveat, many problems of potential technological *incompatibility* appear to be handled adequately by existing institutions. Decentralized market forces suffice to avoid unproductive incompatibilities (not all are undesirable) in a considerable percentage of cases. Other problems are averted through the work of international standardizing bodies such as the ISO that facilitate cooperative activity among national standardizers and do much to avoid unproductive incompatibilities that might otherwise arise by accident.

Nevertheless, some notable compatibility problems have arisen that market forces and international standardizing bodies have not averted. Most of these problems fall into two categories. The first involves incompatibilities that predate extensive international trade or modern international standardization efforts, such as those due to differences between the imperial and metric systems. The second involves incompatibilities associated with new proprietary technologies, when the selection of a standard necessarily favors one producer group over another and national or subnational interest groups may block the consensus needed for the adoption of an international (or even national) standard. Historical controversies over television broadcast format standards are illustrative of this problem.

Little can be done at the global level about most problems that fall into the first category. The essential question is whether the nations that adhere to a minority standard would benefit on balance from switching, given all the costs involved, a question that is not always easy to answer (consider the debate in the United States over metric conversion). If the answer is yes, government action will be necessary to make the change for many different reasons. But these are primarily matters of national rather than international policy and are not discussed here at length.

As for the second group of incompatibility problems, it is not easy to imagine any reform of international institutions that would eliminate them and that would also be politically feasible. Outside the European Community, nations have shown no willingness to cede sovereignty to a central authority with the power to compel them to follow a particular technological standard. Treaty covenants to use international standards such as those in the GATT system are also unlikely to be effective, either because the adoption of an international standard can be blocked by a lack of consensus or because nations will opt out of the standard (as GATT allows). Therefore when divergence of producer interests threatens to create inefficient incompatibilities in global markets, the best hope for solution may lie in explicit or implicit side payments among producers, as through joint ventures or mergers.

Turning to matters of product *quality*, it is helpful to distinguish between technical barriers that result from a divergence of national goals and preferences regarding quality and barriers that result from a divergence in the means selected to achieve similar goals and preferences. This line is not always easy to draw, but it can be operationalized easily in many cases and is a useful analytical construct.

Legal constraints on national sovereigns such as those in the GATT system—an approach termed policed decentralization—can respond fairly well in principle to the barriers that result from divergent means to the same end. The most important legal constraint here is the "least-restrictive means principle." Related or corollary principles include nondiscrimination requirements, generality requirements, an obligation to use existing international standards and to afford mutual recognition when adequate to meet domestic objectives, and an obligation to justify a refusal of mutual recognition. Adherence to these principles can readily avert technical barriers that result from chance differences in national standards and regulations and, to a lesser extent, can police problems of capture by exposing them and subjecting nations that use quality measures for protectionist purposes to reputational penalties or retaliation. In the end, however, the effectiveness of the GATT system or any other legal system for policing these technical barriers also depends on diligence in enforcement and compliance efforts. On this score, GATT is apparently less successful to date (although systematic information is again lacking). Recent improvements in GATT dispute resolution as a result of the Uruguay Round have the potential to strengthen considerably the effectiveness of the system, as does the extension of GATT obligations to matters not previously covered (such as process and production standards). Hence, much of the necessary legal framework to police this class of technical barriers already exists as to the activities of national governments, although possibilities are suggested for modest changes that would strengthen the Uruguay Round accords. The greater task at hand, however, is to extend GATT principles to the activities of subsidiary governments and private entities that affect trade and to ensure that national governments take their legal obligations seriously. The not inconsiderable costs of enforcing international obligations must also be considered in policy formulation, and some problems will no doubt arise that are simply not worth fixing.

When technical barriers result from genuine differences in national goals and objectives regarding quality, general legal obligations such as those in the GATT system can accomplish much less. Indeed, it is precisely here that "technical barriers" may be economically efficient, and it becomes difficult to know whether anything should be done about them at all. The reduction of technical barriers in this category will likely come primarily from international cooperation to achieve complete or partial harmonization. More should be done to explore opportunities for profitable harmonization, either through the WTO/ GATT or the ISO and related entities, perhaps drawing on the model developed in Europe as part of the single-market initiative. In particular, to help prioritize harmonization efforts, more should be done to identify the technical barriers with the greatest impact on trade. To increase the likelihood that national governments and standardizing bodies will adopt international quality standards once they are developed, more should be done to ensure high-level participation by national regulators and standardizers in the work of international bodies. The trading community should also consider the possibility of agreements to harmonize only the "essential objectives" of regulation for categories of products, delegating the task of producing detailed standards, product by product, to technical experts in international standards organizations and promising mutual recognition when national standards and regulations subsequently diverge in unimportant ways. Similarly, the trading community should consider the possibility of "deregulation" agreements, which would provide that certain matters be left entirely to market forces or that a particular form of regulation (such as labeling requirements) be used in preference to another (such as mandatory ingredient regulations).

One issue that cuts across problems of compatibility and quality concerns the need to anticipate the effects of new standards and regulations on trade and to use that information to avert unnecessary new technical barriers. In general, it is easier for the international community to agree on compatibility or quality issues before producers have made sunk investments to comply with a particular standard or regulation. Notification systems that bring proposed standards and regulations to the attention of trading partners before they are cast in stone have an important role to play here. Although notification requirements are contained in existing GATT rules, it is questionable whether they have been observed diligently or conscientiously. If indeed these notification obligations are not taken terribly seriously, this problem should be remedied. The trading community should also consider whether notification of *all* new product-related regulations at the national level should be made mandatory, rather than simply those that, in the judgment of the notifying country, will have a significant impact on trade (as presently required by GATT). The latter phrasing of the notification obligation tends to invite careless-ness and abuse.

Finally, with regard to *conformity assessment,* some of the technical barriers that arise can also be policed through international legal constraints that emphasize use of the least restrictive means. The application of such principles to conformity assessment can be found to a considerable extent in the WTO/GATT system, especially as it has been extended by the Uruguay Round accords. But much more can be done to induce greater reliance on testing and certification conducted in the country of exportation, which often reduces the costs of conformity assessment immensely. In particular, govern-ments can do more to devise systems to guarantee the reliability of self-certification and foreign testing, perhaps cooperatively through the WTO/GATT or the ISO. Once confidence in certification and testing abroad is developed, nations can then enter stronger cove-nants to accept it. The use of existing world standards for quality control, such as the standards in the ISO 9000 series, can help in building confidence cost-effectively. Aspects of the "global approach" to certification and testing in the European Union can serve as a model.

Chapter 2

Nature and Scope
of the Problem

*T*HE PURPOSE of this chapter is threefold: (1) to illustrate the myriad of ways that standards, regulations, and conformity assessment procedures impose barriers to the free flow of goods in international markets; (2) to provide some further classification of technical barriers that will prove useful to later discussion; and (3) to offer a general assessment of the importance of the problem to trading nations. The latter task has proven especially difficult.

Efforts to assess the scope of the problem are hampered considerably by a lack of hard information about the consequences of technical barriers, a difficulty that does not arise to the same degree in studies of more conventional trade barriers. The effects of tariffs, for example, can usually be estimated from the tariff rate itself, coupled with plausible assumptions about pertinent supply and demand elasticities. Estimates of the impact of quantitative restrictions such as quotas are likewise straightforward. The empirical economic literature is thus replete with estimates of the welfare losses from conventional protectionist measures and the benefits of liberalizing them. By contrast, the effects of technical barriers are typically hard to measure. They are often hidden in the firm-specific costs of modifying a product to meet a standard or regulation, in the costs of testing and certification procedures and their attendant delays, or in the ways that noncompliance with a standard may affect consumer purchasing decisions. Broad systematic studies of technical barriers are generally lacking, and the available information tends to be limited to particular markets and industries in which disputes have arisen or in which case studies have been undertaken. Even then, much of what we know is impressionistic and anecdotal.

Nevertheless, there is no lack of consensus to the proposition that technical barriers have been and remain a substantial barrier to the increased international flow of goods. The problem cuts across a wide array of industries, from motor vehicles to computers to consumer electronics to beef to wines and beverages.

Perhaps the most ambitious effort to assess the effects of technical barriers was undertaken in the European Community as part of the impetus for "EC 92," the recent single-market initiative. The project was directed by Paolo Cecchini at the request of the Commission of the European Communities. The study produced a wealth of material, including extensive surveys of business executives and a handful of sectoral case studies in which the effects of technical barriers were examined. These larger studies are summarized in a widely circulated volume known as the "Cecchini Report," and several of its findings warrant mention.[1]

In the survey of business leaders in the twelve member states, eleven thousand respondents ranked the importance of divergent national standards and regulations, along with seven other general categories of trade impediments, as a source of barriers to intra-Community exports by their company. In the aggregate, survey respondents from France, Germany, and the United Kingdom all ranked divergent standards and regulations as the most important source of trade impediments.[2] The ten industry classifications for which technical barriers were said to be the most important, in descending order, were motor vehicles, electrical engineering, mechanical engineering, pharmaceuticals, nonmetallic minerals, other transport equipment, food and tobacco, leather, precision and medical equipment, and metal articles.[3] The report also conveys a general sense that trade in capital goods is somewhat more affected by technical barriers than trade in consumer goods.[4] The six case studies examined intra-Community barriers to trade in telecommunications equipment, automobiles, foodstuffs, building products, textiles and

---

1. Cecchini and others (1988).

2. Cecchini and others (1988, p. 5). The other items to be ranked were government procurement practices, "administrative barriers," border costs and delays, value added tax differences, freight transport regulation, capital movement restrictions, and existing Community laws.

3. Cecchini and others (1988, p. 27).

4. Cecchini and others (1988, p. 28).

clothing, and pharmaceuticals. The only one of these in which technical barriers were not mentioned as a significant problem was textiles
and clothing.[5]

Inferences about the world as a whole must be made cautiously
from the European experience, but it seems likely that technical
barriers in the world economy generally are even more significant
than were those in the Community before the EC 92 initiative. This
conjecture is based on the fact that the Community had already
pursued several legislative and judicial initiatives directed at technical
barriers (discussed in later chapters of this book) and on the fact that
intra-European trade was already so extensive. That so many technical barriers remained is highly suggestive as to the widespread existence and significance of technical barriers in general.

A few other bits of evidence are worthy of note, this time from the
U.S. experience. In the early 1970s, Saudi Arabia formed the Saudi
Arabian Standards Organization (SASO) as part of a broad initiative to
introduce product standards into the Saudi Arabian market. The Saudi
government requested technical assistance from abroad, but the United
States did not respond for about fifteen years. The Europeans and others
did, however, with the result that standards for a wide range of products
were drafted to favor foreign products over those of the United States. As
a consequence, the U.S. share of Saudi imports fell from 30 percent in
1980 to 19 percent in 1987, "largely because of the inability of U.S.
industry to meet SASO standards."[6] The value of the decline in U.S.
exports was estimated to be as much as $500 million annually.[7]

The importance of technical barriers was also addressed in a recent
report from the Office of Technology Assessment. Among other things,
it attributes a serious decline in the competitive position of the U.S.
machine tool industry to its failure to participate effectively in international standard setting activities.[8]

To be sure, it would be wrong to suppose that every measure
regarded by exporters as a "technical barrier" is problematic from a

---

5. Cecchini and others (1988, pp. 50–68). Additional detail may be found in Emerson
and others (1988, pp. 39–46).

6. U.S. House of Representatives, Committee on Science, Space, and Technology (1992,
p. 116) (testimony of Gilbert P. Tupper, Standards Advisor, American/Saudi Roundtable).

7. U.S. House of Representatives, Committee on Science, Space, and Technology
(1992, p. 124) (testimony of Gilbert E. Dwyer, President, American/Saudi Roundtable).

8. Office of Technology Assessment (1992, pp. 8, 80).

policy standpoint. Heterogeneity of standards and regulations may, in many instances, be desirable and, in others, uneconomic to remedy. Take an obvious example—Japanese companies that wish to sell their products in the United States would be well advised to provide product literature and labeling in English (the language "standard" in the United States). U.S. companies confront the reciprocal problem in selling to the Japanese market, and the costs of obtaining translations and printing literature in multiple languages can, no doubt be considerable. But it hardly follows that the United States and Japan, or trading nations generally, should undertake to eliminate language differences. The resistance to metric conversion in the United States is perhaps another example of a divergence that *may* not be worth correcting, at least entirely, given the costs of converting or replacing signs, measuring rods, machine tools, scales, mechanics' tools, and innumerable other items.[9]

These issues are discussed much more extensively in later chapters. Before that discussion, however, it may be helpful to be somewhat more specific about particular ways in which technical barriers may arise, and how each has, at times, become a significant issue within the trading community.

Standards

Most of the government-to-government disputes over technical barriers concern mandatory government requirements, "regulations" in the terminology here. Nevertheless, voluntary "standards" are often an important source of technical barriers, even when they are not adopted by reference in government regulations.[10]

The reasons why noncompliance with standards may impede efforts to sell abroad are many. Compliance with compatibility standards may be essential because consumers require compatibility with complementary products or services. Examples abound: Videocassettes manufactured for the U.S. market are generally incompatible with European videocassette players due to the difference in broadcast formats (PAL or SECAM in Europe, NTSC in the United

9. See General Accounting Office (1978).
10. Emerson and others (1988, p. 40).

States). Computer software producers must ensure that their products are compatible with the operating system on the user's computer. Differences between the imperial and metric systems of weights and measures create a variety of incompatibilities in products and the tools used to assemble them.[11] Different voltage standards make electrical appliances manufactured in some countries unusable in others without an appropriate adapter.

Compliance with quality standards may also be important to the marketing of products because of consumer preferences. In the United States, the Underwriters Laboratory (UL) seal of approval affords an excellent illustration. Testing and certification by UL is generally voluntary, and the fact that the manufacturers are willing to incur the cost of meeting UL standards and securing the UL approval demonstrates their conviction that such costs will be recouped in the marketplace.[12] Another illustration is provided by a widely publicized dispute among Japan, the European Community, and the United States over a Japanese safety standard governing the thickness of downhill skis. European and American skis did not meet the standard and were thereby denied the "safe goods" (SG) seal of approval thought by many companies essential to consumer acceptance in Japan.[13] Other voluntary standards in Japan, such as the Japan Industrial Standards (JIS) and Japan Agricultural Standards (JAS), are also said to be crucial to consumers—"even when a product could be sold without the JIS or JAS mark to non-government customers, products without the mark face consumer resistance and distributors and retailers are reluctant to stock them."[14]

Also, government procurement is often undertaken with reference to voluntary standards. The problem surfaced in a recent case study

11. Anne O. Krueger has recently suggested that the persistence of the imperial system in the United States is the most important standards-related problem for American competitiveness. U.S. House of Representatives, Committee on Science, Space, and Technology (1992, p. 31). The metric requirements in various U.S. export markets are surveyed in International Trade Administration (1982).

12. See generally, Peach and Wilson (1980). The significance of the UL mark in international trade is evidenced by Taiwanese manufacturers sending their products to UL for testing certification. C. Y. Chen, "Conquering Uncertainty; Loss Control," *Best's Review*, October 1985, p. 84.

13. Carla Rappoport, "Japanese Ski Makers Freeze Out the Opposition," *Financial Times*, September 4, 1986, sect. 1, p. 1.

14. Lecraw (1987, p. 33).

of trade barriers within the European Community. French producers of building tiles prevailed on a national standards body, the Association Française de Normalisation, to set thickness standards that Italian and Spanish competitors did not meet. Although building tiles that did not meet the new standard could legally be sold, 40 percent of the market was for public building contracts that invariably incorporated the new standard by reference.[15] The problem is also illustrated by a recent case in which a procurement specification for steel pipe required compliance with the Irish Standard Mark Licensing scheme, effectively excluding foreign competition.[16]

Compliance with standards may also be encouraged by insurers and insurance underwriters. The French building tile standards are also illustrative here, as French insurers evidently refused to insure against any hazards materializing to or from any tiles that did not meet the national thickness standard.[17] In the United States, theft policies with burglary coverage routinely rely on the standards to determine the adequacy of the insured's alarm system.[18]

Finally, noncompliance with standards may have adverse legal consequences in the event of product-related accidents. In the United States, a product alleged to be defective in design may well be judged against industry standards, and civil liability can then turn on compliance or noncompliance.[19]

Therefore, it is evident that voluntary standards respecting compatibility and quality can, at times, become important as technical barriers. They may be less likely to become contentious in international economic relations because they are frequently not the product of government action, and there has perhaps been a tendency to leave the solution, if any, to the private sector. But their importance should not be underestimated, and as will be seen, they are receiving increasing attention in government-to-government negotiations.

15. Center for European Policy Studies (1992, p. 12).

16. *EC Commission* v. *Ireland,* [1987] E.C.R. 1369. The European Court of Justice struck down the contract provision.

17. Center for European Policy Studies (1992, p. 12).

18. Joseph F. Mangan, "Burglar Alarm Systems That Do the Job," *Best's Review,* December 1990, p. 93.

19. See *Nesselrode* v. *Executive Beechcraft, Inc.,* 707 S.W.2d 371 (Mo., 1986); *Jeng* v. *Witters,* 452 F. Supp. 1349 (1978).

Health and Safety Regulations

Health and safety regulations are ubiquitous, at least in the developed nations. They apply to foods, drugs, cosmetics, electrical appliances, building materials, automobiles, toys, and innumerable other products. The exact volume of international trade that must comply with overseas health and safety regulations is unknown, although a recent Department of Commerce estimate suggests that some $48 billion in annual U.S. manufactured exports are subject to the product safety requirements of the European Community alone.[20] Given their widespread application and mandatory character, it is no surprise that many of the most publicized disputes over technical barriers relate to these regulations.

The European harmonization effort standing to some degree as an exception, there seems little disagreement that national governments are entitled to promulgate *reasonable* safety and health regulations to protect their citizens. Thus disputes tend to arise over the reasonableness of the regulations in question, and most seem to fall into one of three categories. First, when regulators have taken affirmative action that results in a prohibition on the sale of an imported product on health or safety grounds, disputes arise over the regulators' interpretation of the available evidence on product risks or, similarly, over the tolerable risk level. Second, when the regulatory structure requires positive approval of a product before it can be marketed, disputes arise because regulators have, through accident or indifference, omitted the imported product from the approval list. Finally, whether the regime is one of prior approval or subsequent prohibition, the suspicion arises, in some cases, that announced concerns about health and safety are mere pretense for regulation that is motivated by protectionist ends.

A good example of the first category of dispute, much publicized, is a recent ban by the European Community on the importation of beef treated with growth hormones. In celebrated incidents during the early 1980s, the ingestion of beef treated with the hormone DES produced serious adverse reactions (such as the development of breasts in infants). These incidents set in motion a process that culminated in a decision by the Council of Agricultural Ministers in

20. Office of Technology Assessment (1992, p. 8).

1985 to pursue a "zero-risk" policy, banning the use of all growth hormones in beef cattle within the Community and likewise prohibiting imports of beef from jurisdictions that did not observe the same standards. Most important, the zero-risk policy extended to various hormones that had never been shown to produce any adverse reaction in humans. The import restrictions were made effective at the beginning of 1989 and resulted in the cessation of imports from the United States, which had previously exceeded $100 million annually. The United States took the position that the ban, even if motivated by legitimate public health concerns, was, in fact, unnecessary to the protection of public health because it was overbroad and scientifically unsound. It thus violated Community obligations under the General Agreement on Tariffs and Trade (GATT) and the GATT Standards Code in the view of the United States. But the Community insisted, among other things, that it was entitled to make its own judgments about the scientific evidence and the tolerable risk levels without outside interference. The Community blocked efforts by the United States to pursue dispute resolution options within GATT, and the United States ultimately retaliated with punitive tariffs on more than $100 million in Community exports pursuant to Section 301 of the Trade Act of 1974. The matter is not fully resolved to this day, although an agreement in principle has been reached that may eventually put the matter to rest.[21]

Other examples of this type of dispute through the years include prohibitions by several countries on the importation of uncooked meat from countries where foot-and-mouth disease was present in cattle, an issue of great concern to Uruguay some years ago, and restrictions within the European Community on the importation of beef from countries with "mad cow" disease in its herds, a regulation

---

21. In July 1992, the United States concluded an agreement in principle with the Community that sets out a plan for the resolution of differences over meat inspection procedures, provides for requirements for determining the eligibility of U.S. slaughtering facilities to supply the Community, and seeks to improve communication and cooperation between the U.S. and Community veterinary services. See Office of the United States Trade Representative, "Determination Concerning European Community Third Country Meat Directive," 57 Fed. Reg. 47508 (October 16, 1992); "US Announces Agreement with EC in Dispute over Meat Exports," *BNA International Trade Reporter,* October 21, 1992, pp. 1806–07. Useful histories of the dispute, from various perspectives, may be found in Meng (1990); Hammonds (1990); Froman (1989).

that has affected imports from the United Kingdom.[22] Agricultural products are not the only products at issue, as illustrated by a recent Organization of Economic Cooperation and Development report discussing technical barriers to trade in toys attributable to disparate product safety regimes.[23] In each of these examples, the essential question is whether national authorities have gone too far in the pursuit of legitimate health and safety objectives by restricting the sale of products that pose no real risk.

The second important category of disputes, arising out of regulatory inaction rather than action, is well illustrated by two recent cases before the European Court of Justice. In one, a Belgian national was prosecuted for importing fish roe that had been colored with a food colorant not on the list of food additives approved by the Belgian authorities.[24] In another, a French national was prosecuted for the importation of a pastry product containing an emulsifier that had not been authorized for such use in France.[25] In both instances, the product in question could be marketed legally in its country of origin (Germany, as it turns out), and there was no suggestion that officials in the country of importation had made any affirmative judgment that the additives at issue were dangerous. They had simply omitted to consider the safety of the additive at issue because no one had asked them to do so in timely fashion before the importation of the goods in question.

The third type of dispute, involving alleged sham in the use of health and safety regulation, is unfortunately all too common. Typical is the recent clash between the United States and Thailand over cigarette imports, in which the government of Thailand asserted that a variety of taxes and restrictions applicable to imported cigarettes *only* were justified by a campaign to reduce the incidence of smoking.[26] As another example, the governor of South Dakota—a major pork-producing state—recently prohibited the importation into the

22. See GATT, "Uruguayan Recourse to Article XXIII: Report Adopted on November 16, 1962," Basic Instruments and Selected Documents (BISD), 11S (March 1963, p. 95). For a discussion, see Tillotson (1990).

23. Organization for Economic Cooperation and Development (1991, pp. 59–61).

24. *Criminal Proceedings against Léon Motte,* [1985] E.C.R. 3887.

25. *Ministère Public* v. *Muller,* [1986] E.C.R. 1511.

26. GATT, "Thailand: Restrictions on Importation of and Internal Taxes on Cigarettes: Report of the Panel Adopted on November 7, 1990," BISD, 37S (July 1991, p. 200).

state of pork from animals raised in a jurisdiction where the antibiotic chloramphenicol could be used for veterinary purposes, even though a threat to human health from animals treated with chloramphenicol has never been established. The announcement followed shortly after a negative countervailing duty determination by the International Trade Commission in an investigation of pork imports from Canada. Not surprisingly, chloramphenicol was widely used for veterinary purposes in Canada but not in the United States.[27]

These types of disputes are distinguished not out of any affinity for classification but because the principles for resolving them, if acceptable ones are to be found, will, to a degree, vary. Genuine disagreements over scientific evidence and differences in risk tolerance must be distinguished from mere regulatory inaction and from capture or sham. Indeed these distinctions are already to be found in aspects of the international legal regime governing technical barriers.

Other Consumer Protection Regulations

"Other consumer protection regulations" means any mandatory requirements respecting the characteristics of a product or its production process, other than those enacted for safety and health purposes, that nevertheless find purported justification in the protection of purchasers. Most commonly, the justification offered is some need to protect consumers against deception or confusion or against the imprudent purchase of a product that is "inferior" by some measure other than its safety.

Disputes over such regulations have been especially frequent in Europe.[28] For example, for many years Italy maintained "pasta pu-

---

27. "General Developments," *BNA International Trade Reporter,* May 29, 1985, p. 745; "Canada Appears to Favor Trade Pact with U.S.: Talks May Begin in Fall, Trade Minister Says," *BNA International Trade Reporter,* June 26, 1985, p. 845; "Agriculture Can Set Example for U.S.–Canada Free Trade Agreement, Secretary Block Says," *BNA International Trade Reporter,* January 22, 1986, p. 142.

28. In the United States, similar consumer protection regulations regularly become a subject of litigation when imposed at the state level. For example, a Wisconsin law prohibiting the sale of a chocolate milk substitute was recently challenged by an Illinois company. *Dean Foods v. Wisconsin,* 478 F. Supp. 224 (W.D. Wis. 1979). Washington State challenged a North Carolina statute that prohibited the sale of apples in containers bearing a grade in

rity" regulations, prohibiting the sale of any product labeled "pasta" that was not made entirely from durum wheat—durum wheat was grown extensively in Southern Italy and not much elsewhere within Europe, so that potential German and British competition in the pasta market did not satisfy the requirement.[29] The Netherlands prohibited the sale of liqueur labeled "jenever" with an alcohol content of less than 35 percent, making the sale of Belgian jenever with an alcohol content of 30 percent illegal.[30] Greece and Germany both maintained "beer purity" regulations, precluding the sale of any product labeled "beer" that was not brewed from enumerated ingredients, precluding imports from nations such as France.[31] Germany also prohibited the sale of beverages in champagne-style bottles other than sparkling wine and certain other nongrape products, thereby excluding a French product known as Petillant de Raisin.[32] Belgium required that margarine be sold only in cube-shaped containers, thereby prohibiting the sale of German margarine in a truncated cone-shaped container.[33] Germany prohibited the sale of sausages containing certain nonmeat additives (such as egg or milk protein), as well as the marketing of many milk substitutes that resembled milk in appearance.[34] France maintained a similar regulation.[35] Italy banned the sale of cheese with an excessively *low* fat content.[36]

A common thread in most of these cases is a judgment by the regulatory authority, sometimes genuine and sometimes pretense, that labeling requirements are not an adequate solution to the problem of

---

accordance with the stringent Washington State grading standards. *Hunt* v. *Washington State Apple Advertising Commission*, 432 U.S. 333 (1977). A Wisconsin company challenged an Ohio regulation that prohibited the sale of "Hebe," a product that resembles pure condensed milk but contains 6 percent coconut oil, on the grounds that it was an "adulterated" product even if its label disclosed its ingredients. *Hebe* v. *Calvert*, 246 F. Supp. 711 (S.D. Ohio 1917).

29. Center for European Policy Studies (1992, p. 12).

30. *Criminal Proceedings against Miro BV,* [1985] E.C.R. 3731.

31. *EC Commission* v. *Greece* (Re Beer Purity Standards), [1987] E.C.R. 1193; Clark (1988).

32. *EC Commission* v. *Germany* (Re Champagne-type Bottles), [1988] 1 C.M.L.R. 135.

33. *Walter Rau Lebensmittelwerke* v. *De Smedt PvbA,* [1982] E.C.R. 3961.

34. *EC Commission* v. *Germany,* [1989] E.C.R. 229. *EC Commission* v. *Germany,* [1989] E.C.R. 1021.

35. *EC Commission* v. *France* (Case 216/84), February 23, 1988.

36. *State (Italy)* v. *Nespoli,* [1992] 2 C.M.L.R. 1.

consumer deception or confusion. The result is a mandatory product design or content regulation that results in the exclusion of some products from the market that can lawfully be marketed elsewhere.

The soundness of the decision to regulate the product rather than the label in these cases may often be questioned. Indeed the issue also arises in the health and safety cases—When is the provision of information to the consumer preferable to regulating the characteristics of the production process or the product itself? At the international level, the parallel inquiry concerns the extent to which nations can and should accept constraints on their ability to elect between consumer information and other regulatory alternatives.

The issue is a difficult one. It can be conjectured that most thoughtful observers would find exclusive use of consumer information remedies unsatisfactory. For example, the proposition that children's pajamas should meet some mandatory flammability standard, in preference to bearing labels that read "will burn readily if exposed to lighted flame," would likely be accepted by many. If a general principle is to be found, it is perhaps that product regulations instead of labeling regulations are more palatable and may even become preferable when the societal interest at stake is great and there is no suspicion of sham. On the first criterion, health and safety issues are more likely to qualify than other consumer protection objectives. The question of whether these other objectives should *ever* qualify is discussed later.

Labeling Regulations

Although some technical barrier disputes could be averted by the use of labeling regulations instead of other regulatory options, labeling regulations themselves can become a source of friction. The essence of the problem is a simple one—if labeling requirements differ from market to market, manufacturers must not only incur the costs of producing different labels for the same product but must often maintain distinct inventories for each market, and so on. The added costs can become considerable.

As one example, the U.S. Food and Drug Administration nutrition labeling requirements require the labels for a wide variety of food products to list the contents per serving of fourteen specific nutrients. It has been argued that the U.S. label will be the most detailed in the world and has the potential to become a substantial obstacle to the importation of foodstuffs from foreign suppliers. Compliance costs for U.S. industry alone have been estimated at $1.5 billion.[37] In this instance, the costs for foreign sellers will encompass not only the relabeling and inventory-related costs noted above but also the costs of obtaining an accurate analysis of the nutritional contents of each product.[38] The problem is by no means a new one—differences between U.S. food labeling standards and those promulgated elsewhere have long been a source of trade impediments.[39] Disputes over disparate labeling requirements have also arisen with some frequency in the European Community.[40]

Conformity Assessment Procedures

Just as the costs of complying with foreign product regulations may impede trade so may the costs of demonstrating compliance with such regulations. Issues relating to the costs of conformity assessment also arise with voluntary standards. These costs are, to a degree, unavoidable as long as independent national standards and regulations persist, but their magnitude can vary greatly according to the product at issue and according to how conformity assessment is conducted.

In general, the conformity assessment process raises many of the same trade issues as the substantive standards and regulations themselves. Difficulties in securing approval for a product may result from differences of opinion about scientific evidence, from regulatory in-

37. "Industry Groups Oppose Food Label Format, Call New Rule International Trade Barrier," *BNA International Trade Daily,* December 28, 1992, p. 7.

38. Similar issues have arisen with regularity within the U.S. federal system. For example, California's Safe Drinking Water and Toxic Enforcement Act of 1986 prohibits the exposure of an individual to any chemical known to cause cancer or reproductive toxicity "without first giving clear and reasonable warnings." The governor is required to compile a list of the chemicals requiring warnings and to update the list annually. (California Health and Safety Code, §25,249.) This law and others have been criticized in Bork (1991, p. 5).

39. A point-by-point comparison of U.S. labeling standards to those recommended by the international Codex Alimentarius Commission may be found in Lister (1987).

40. See, for example, *Kommanditgesellschaft Eau de Cologne & Parfümerie–Fabrik Glockengasse No. 4711 v. Provide Sarl,* [1989] E.C.R. 3891. Italy required, among other things, that the label of cosmetic products bear the name of the Italian producer or person responsible in Italy for marketing the product.

action and bureaucratic inertia, and from capture or manipulation of the process by protectionist interests. Likewise, heterogeneity in conformity assessment procedures, which assuredly tends to raise the costs of conformity assessment to producers who sell in multiple markets, may result from honest disagreement about optimal procedures, chance, or anticompetitive purpose.

But conformity assessment also raises some distinct issues. Perhaps most obviously, when each nation sets up a separate procedure for sellers to pursue in securing approval of their products, a duplication of effort will exist across markets even if the standards or regulations themselves and the conformity assessment procedures are identical everywhere. Also, the conformity assessment process raises issues relating to the choice between ex ante and ex post enforcement and to the trade-off between the probability of detecting nonconformity and the magnitude of penalty. At one extreme, each unit sold might be subject to inspection or testing. At the other extreme, sellers might be permitted to certify compliance, with applicable standards and regulations themselves subject to limited spot inspection or even only to ex post litigation in the event that their certification proves false or inaccurate. Finally, conformity assessment raises the problem of how to develop trust between parties with a stake in its accuracy. Even when there is no disagreement about the method of testing, the standards to be used, and so forth, how can parties abroad feel confident that it is conducted honestly?

Without going into any of these points in great detail at this stage, a few of the studies and disputes relating to conformity assessment that have come out in recent years will be mentioned to illustrate the importance of the problem in practical terms. Theoretical issues are discussed in later sections.

In conjunction with the EC 1992 initiative, several case studies of technical barrier issues were undertaken at the request of the European Commission, some already discussed. With regard to conformity assessment, pharmaceuticals were identified as an area of particular concern, understandably so given the elaborate nature of the drug approval process in most developed nations. The study confirmed that the necessity of separate approval proceedings in each European nation adds greatly to the costs of intra-European trade in pharmaceutical products, with direct costs of the approval process and opportunity costs attributable to delays in approval adding up to tens of millions of European Currency Units. Reform in the drug approval process was thus advanced as an important priority for the 1992 initiative by the authors of the study.[41]

An issue related to the problem of multiple approvals concerns the willingness of regulators to accept information generated by foreign laboratories, such as safety test data. It is not uncommon for regulators to refuse to do so, adding to the costs of multiple regulatory regimes.[42] Further, when testing in the country of importation is necessary, problems concerning equal access to testing facilities often arise. If the testing facility is run by domestic competitors of the exporter, for example, as is apparently the case in Japan for some products, the danger of exclusionary tactics is obvious.[43]

In addition, the conformity assessment process for imports may be made more burdensome than for domestic products, either deliberately or simply through disregard for the costs of regulatory compliance. The long story behind the efforts of U.S. baseball bat manufacturers to secure regulatory approval for the sale of their bats in Japan affords a classic example, in which years were invested in first trying to understand the certification process and then to gain access to it.[44] Indeed the extensive literature on U.S.–Japan trade relations is replete with instances in which the conformity assessment process in Japan became a major obstacle to efforts by U.S. manufacturers to sell there. Examples exist in which certification authorities simply refused to allow U.S. products to be tested, at least temporarily (as in the baseball bats controversy). Other examples arose in which Japanese producers could establish compliance with regulations by having their factory inspected once and thereafter having a few units of output

41. The pharmaceutical case is discussed explicitly in Center for European Policy Studies (1992, p. 12).

42. The United States has long complained over the refusal of the European Community to accept its test data for telecommunications equipment. International Trade Administration (1989, p. xv); "F.C.C. Ban on Electronic Testing by E.C. Labs May Provide Leverage to US Negotiators," *BNA International Trade Reporter*, May 9, 1990, p. 672. Similar problems have arisen within the Community itself. Differing French and German standards for building products means that it can take as long as five years for French producers to obtain the technical certification necessary to sell its product on the German market. International Trade Administration (1989, p. xi). See also Gorski (1991) for an analysis of the problems associated with the acceptance of foreign clinical data in new drug approval and the regulations that determine when such data are acceptable.

43. Edelman (1988, p. 401).

44. Edelman (1988, pp. 406–10); Coccodrilli (1984, p. 137).

tested periodically, whereas foreign suppliers had to have each shipment of product tested at the time of importation.[45]

The Japanese are by no means the only offenders in this area. In a
well-known GATT dispute, the European Community lowered tariffs
on high-quality beef as a Tokyo Round trade concession. It provided
that U.S. Department of Agriculture (USDA) "choice" or "prime"
beef automatically qualified and agreed to accept the grading process
of USDA inspectors as conclusive. But for other countries, beef could
not qualify for the tariff concession without being graded in Europe,
putting other foreign suppliers in the position of having to ship their
beef to Europe before its tariff treatment could be ascertained. Canada claimed that the resulting uncertainty effectively denied its producers the benefits of the tariff concession, and also violated the most
favored nation obligation.[46]

The essential lesson from these studies and disputes is that conformity assessment procedures are fully as important as the underlying
standards and regulations with which conformity is to be assessed. It
does no good to comply with a voluntary standard if a seller cannot
demonstrate that fact to the satisfaction of the buyer, and it does no
good to comply with a regulation if the regulatory authorities cannot
be convinced of it at reasonable cost. Finally, because conformity
assessment is so often laden with bureaucratic discretion and industry
influence, opportunities for calculated barriers to trade arise with
great regularity.

Conclusion

This chapter has identified various kinds of technical barriers to
trade. Most result from heterogeneity across national markets in
standards, regulations, and conformity assessment procedures, but
other important barriers arise because of the duplication of effort
associated with separate conformity assessment procedures with or

45. Edelman (1988, p. 402).

46. GATT, "European Economic Community: Imports of Beef from Canada, Report
of the Panel Adopted on March 10, 1981," BISD, 28S (March 1982, p. 92). Several
disputes within the United States federal system are also illustrative of the problem. See, for
example, *Farmers' Grain Co. of Embden* v. *Langer,* 273 F.2d 635 (8th Cir., 1921) (challenge
to state grading agency in agricultural sector); *Miller* v. *Williams,* 12 F. Supp. 236 (1935)
(challenge to city inspection requirements for milk producers).

without underlying substantive heterogeneity and because of unnecessarily costly conformity assessment mechanisms. Each of these problems in turn results from a mixture of benign and not-so-benign forces, ranging from honest differences in tastes and judgment to bureaucratic indifference to unabashed protectionist manipulation.

The total costs to the world economy attributable to these technical barriers are unknown and no doubt unknowable as a practical matter. Case studies, surveys, and bits of anecdotal evidence tend to support the claim that these costs are "large," however, and suggest that greater international attention to the problem would be productive.

Among the many difficulties in assessing the costs of technical barriers is the absence of an obvious baseline against which the "cost" is to be measured. Perhaps implicit in the term *technical barrier* is the suggestion that the "barrier" in question is undesirable and would not exist in an ideal world. Although this is no doubt true for many things to which the label "technical barrier" attaches, it is also evident that heterogeneity in standards and regulations is not always undesirable and that greater centralization and harmonization of standards, regulations, and conformity assessment procedures can be costly in a variety of ways. Thus although the conventional wisdom that technical barriers are costly in the aggregate is no doubt correct, some so-called technical barriers are likely to be economically desirable given the set of feasible alternatives. It thus remains to explore principles for sorting cases. The next chapter begins to explore these matters by developing some of the theoretical considerations that bear on the desirability of heterogeneity versus harmonization in standards and regulations and on the optimal design of conformity assessment mechanisms.

Chapter 3

Some Economics of Product Standardization, Regulation, and Conformity Assessment

M UCH HAS BEEN written about the economic process through which the market generates product standards, and untold volumes have been written about government regulation of product safety, quality, and labeling. A comprehensive survey of this literature is not attempted here; this chapter will simply draw from it various ideas and principles of relevance to aspects of the technical barriers problem. The goal is to identify the reasons why heterogeneity in standards and regulations may arise across jurisdictions and, in the process, to provide insight into the positive and normative economics of heterogeneity. A further objective is to assess the need for third-party verification and enforcement mechanisms and the optimal design of those mechanisms.

Market Solutions and Market Failures

The process of ensuring product compatibility and policing aspects of quality has always entailed a mixture of public sector and private sector initiatives. Yet great variation exists across nations in the matters that have been left to the market and those that have been subjected to regulation, and debates continue both in political assemblies and in the academy as to the appropriate role of government in regulating product characteristics.

Whatever the appropriate scope of government intervention, it is indisputable that the market alone regularly generates solutions to compatibility problems and quality problems within industries.[1] These private sector efforts are by no means confined to national boundaries. The International Organization for Standardization (ISO), the International Electrotechnical Commission (IEC), and other international organizations regularly produce global standards as a result of private sector initiatives.[2] For some technical barrier "problems," therefore, the best public policy response may be to leave the matter to the private sector, perhaps with some government encouragement in the form of subsidy to overcome collective action problems. In other cases, however, market failure may be anticipated. The issues tend to divide, with some overlap, between compatibility measures and quality measures.

Compatibility and the Market

Because only *in*compatibilities give rise to "technical barriers," the emphasis here is on the causes of incompatibilities and the question whether they are economically inefficient. The possibility that inefficient compatibility may arise is largely ignored here.[3] The central question, then, is what inference to draw when the market has not produced compatibility on its own, at least to the degree that some observers believe appropriate and within a time frame that they believe appropriate. One possibility is that the absence of greater compatibility in the marketplace reveals that it is undesirable. The other possibility is that market failure in the economic sense has arisen. Which is the case in a given instance may be unclear. Consider first the various welfare issues that arise with incompatibilities, and next the question of whether the market will sort things out optimally.

WELFARE EFFECTS OF INCOMPATIBILITY. The economic consequences of any product incompatibility, whether market- or govern-

1. Useful histories of market-driven standardization in the United States, containing many examples, are Hemenway (1975) and National Industrial Conference Board (1929).
2. See the discussion of these organizations and their functioning in chapter 4.
3. There are various reasons why markets may generate economically inefficient compatibility. It has long been said that product standardization may be valuable to a cartel, for example, as it facilitates policing violations of its price structure. See Scherer (1980, pp. 170–71). The market may also be inefficiently slow in switching from a widely adopted standard to a new and superior one because of collective action problems, or it may inefficiently switch to a new standard when the old one is superior socially—the network externality literature, cited below, develops this possibility.

ment-generated, turn on much the same issues—the extent to which incompatibility is a result of valuable product heterogeneity in the market or an impediment to it, the extent to which the incompatibility affects costs of production, the extent to which it affects competition, the extent to which it precludes the attainment of "network externalities," and the extent to which efforts to eliminate it would prove costly for reasons other than an attendant reduction in product variety.[4] Regarding the first set of issues, much of what is regarded as choice in the marketplace entails a lack of compatibility and may, in some sense, create technical barriers to commerce. As an example, consider the introduction of the compact audio disc (CD) technology. It immediately resulted in several incompatibilities between long-playing records and CD players, between analog recording equipment and CD production, and so on. Yet these incompatibilities lay at the heart of the difference between the new and old technologies, and it was not possible to avoid them and still embrace the benefits of the new technology. Likewise, the availability of choice among different makes and models of televisions, automobiles, washing machines, and innumerable other products logically necessitates incompatibility between at least some of their components—if the components were all identical, the products would not be different. When incompatibility is of this type, efforts to reduce it will obviously entail a significant cost in the form of restrictions on consumer choice.[5]

These sorts of incompatibilities, however, are rarely viewed as technical barriers. When incompatibility necessarily results from product differentiation by manufacturers driven by the development of superior technology, by heterogeneity in consumer preferences, and so on, it tends to emerge within nations as well as across them. Therefore any problems that it creates are typically not perceived as international trade problems.

When incompatibility does become an issue in international trade, the usual concern is that nations or national industries will converge

4. Informal surveys of the welfare economics of compatibility standards may be found in Farrell and Saloner (1987); Besen and Saloner (1989); Besen and Johnson (1986).

5. I do not mean to suggest that product differentiation and attendant incompatibilities are always socially optimal. There is a rich industrial organization literature, for example, concerned with the question of whether the degree of product differentiation in the market is socially appropriate. A leading paper is Schmalensee (1987). The literature is surveyed in Scherer (1980, pp. 393–401); Tirole (1988, pp. 277–303).

or have converged on a particular compatibility standard for convenience or for strategic reasons and that resulting international incompatibilities serve little or no useful function. Examples include the international divergence between the metric and imperial systems, the present difference in color television broadcast formats between the United States and Europe, the divergence between left-hand drive and right-hand drive vehicles, divergence in railroad gauge standards, and differences in voltage standards.

In such cases, the likely effect of incompatibilities is to *reduce* variety in the marketplace. Many electrical appliance manufacturers that might otherwise be inclined to export may be discouraged from doing so by the difference in voltage standards. Television manufacturers that serve the U.S. and Japanese markets, with the NTSC broadcast format, may not attempt to manufacture for the French market with its SECAM format or other European markets with their PAL formats. The reduction in choice that these international incompatibilities can produce, therefore, is one of their welfare costs.

Similarly, incompatibilities can increase production costs and thus prices. Costs can rise, for example, because the need to produce different products for different markets prevents the realization of economies of scale in manufacturing. It may also necessitate costly changes in inventory policies and distribution systems. In some cases, the increase may be trivial, and incompatibility may not pose much of a problem, whereas in other cases, market segmentation may have a significant effect on costs.[6]

The segmentation of markets due to incompatibilities may also create competition problems. If a market is small relative to the minimum efficient scale of operation for producers, only one or a few firms may serve it. Incompatibilities may thus function as a barrier to entry, with the possibility of welfare losses due to the exercise of market power.

Incompatibilities can also prevent the attainment of network externalities. When a new user joins a telephone or computer network, for example, other users may receive a nonpecuniary benefit.[7] To the extent that compatibility standards facilitate larger networks, the exis-

6. The different television broadcast format in Europe is said to have prevented the achievement of significant scale economies in the manufacture of televisions for the European market. Pelkmans and Beuter (1987).

7. The network externality literature is cited extensively below. For a critique of that literature, suggesting that many of the purported externalities are strictly pecuniary and thus not a source of potential market failure, see Liebowitz and Margolis (1991).

tence of network externalities in some settings suggests an additional benefit to these standards. This issue has obvious significance for telecommunications and computers.

For a variety of reasons, therefore, most of the incompatibilities that are viewed as technical barriers in the trading community are likely to have some significant economic costs associated with them, rarely offset by any valuable heterogeneity in the product market that incompatibility facilitates. It does not follow that these incompatibilities should be eliminated, however, for at least two reasons. First, to eliminate incompatibilities, a choice must be made among the competing options. Often it will not be clear which option is superior. Second, once incompatibilities emerge, it is not costless to correct them. The divergence in television broadcast formats is a useful example once again. If the world as a whole, or even Europe alone, were to convert to a single format, broadcast facilities using the discarded format would have to incur significant costs to replace equipment, and consumers with television receivers incompatible with the new format would have to purchase new ones. Such difficulties of conversion are sometimes referred to as the "installed base" problem, and it is an empirical question whether the costs of conversion would exceed the benefits.

This last point suggests the importance of distinguishing incompatibilities that already exist from those that may arise in the future. It may, at times, be worth avoiding incompatibilities in the first instance but not be worth fixing them after they have arisen.

VIABILITY OF MARKET SOLUTIONS. If product incompatibilities result in a significant increase in production costs and prevent firms from taking advantage of profitable opportunities to sell to consumers in other markets, an incentive to eliminate incompatibility will arise at least on the part of some market participants. Even when profits will be competed down to a competitive level in the long run, opportunities to expand sales and reduce costs yield at least transitory gains that justify efforts to attain them.

Incompatibilities may be eliminated in various ways. Firms may elect on their own to make their products compatible with those of the industry leader (the decision to make IBM-compatible software and hardware by firms in the computer industry was largely a "follow the leader" approach).[8] Alternatively, the developer of a proprietary

8. See Hergert (1987); Gabel (1991, pp. 19–53).

technology may license it cheaply with the objective of making it the industry standard (the triumph of the VHS standard for video-cassettes is said to be an example).[9] Yet another alternative is merger among the firms with the need to cooperate on compatibility matters (the history of the railroad industry in the United States is suggestive).[10] Incompatibilities may also be remediable through various forms of interfaces or adapters, a familiar item in the suitcases of world travelers who must cope with voltage differences.

A further way that the private sector eliminates undesirable in-compatibilities is through cooperative efforts to promulgate compatibility standards. The creation of standards organizations such as the American Society of Testing and Materials, the American Society of Mechanical Engineers, the American Society of Automotive Engineers, and others, established and funded privately, reflects effective market responses to profitable opportunities for standardization.

Thus theory suggests and empirics confirm that market incentives exist to eliminate many compatibility problems. It does not follow, however, that the market produces "optimal" compatibility. In reflecting on the reasons why, it is instructive to recollect some basic price theory regarding the circumstances under which market allocations achieve optimality. One requisite for efficiency is the absence of "nonpecuniary" externalities to the decisions of market participants. Another is the presence of competition.

As for externalities, among the most obvious ones are collective action problems. These problems prove unimportant when convergence on an appropriate standard is possible through strictly non-cooperative behavior, as when it is clear that a particular standard will prevail in the end because of strong consumer preferences or cost advantages.[11] Noncooperative behavior may also suffice when the returns to establishing a standard can be internalized by a firm with property rights in the standard.[12] But property rights in a standard

9. Gabel (1991, pp. 65–89).

10. Carlton and Klamer (1983).

11. Formal treatment of a related idea may be found in the discussion of the "complete information" case in Farrell and Saloner (1985) and in Farrell and Saloner (1988). Cases in which firms simply follow the standard chosen by the market leader (such as IBM) are illustrative.

12. Competition between standards that may or may not be promoted by an entity with property rights to the standard is the subject of Katz and Shapiro (1986a).

may be impossible to establish, and the outcome of noncooperative behavior in their absence may be difficult to forecast so that convergence does not occur. The consequence is a need, in many instances, for cooperative undertakings.

Cooperative activity is not costless, however, and the question arises as to how it will be organized and financed. Firms will prefer to let others bear the costs if possible. When only a few firms exist with an interest in the matter, they may be able to communicate fairly cheaply and negotiate a cooperative funding arrangement that meets their needs. But when the numbers involved are large, the coordination costs rise and the "free rider" problem may stand in the way.[13] The consumer side of the market is similar. Rarely will any one consumer have sufficient incentive to undertake cooperative standardization efforts.[14]

The privately funded standards organizations mentioned earlier are a partial solution to the collective action problem. Instead of confronting the free rider problem on a case-by-case basis every time the need for standardization arises, industries can create a standards-setting entity with general authority to investigate the need for standardization and to act when appropriate. Firms contribute to their financing based on market share or some other equitable formula, each firm realizes that it receives a net benefit from participation in the organization, and the agreement to fund the activity is made self-enforcing by a mutual implicit threat to withhold contributions if others do the same.[15] When the standards promulgated involve detailed technical specifications, these organizations can also recoup some of the costs of creating standards by selling them to newcomers.

But problems may still arise. A common difficulty is that supporters of an organization have divergent preferences among competing possible standards, most likely because firms find that one

13. The positive externalities that may be associated with the standard-setting process are central to the discussion in Kindleberger (1983); Lecraw (1984); Link (1983); Dybvig and Spatt (1983).

14. Yet another kind of externality is the network externality, as noted. A considerable literature exists on the question of whether noncooperative behavior will generate the socially optimal network in the presence of such externalities. See Farrell and Saloner (1985); Katz and Shapiro (1985); Farrell and Saloner (1986b). A nice summary of the issues may be found in Tirole (1988, pp. 404–09).

15. See, for example, Martino (1941, p. 6) (discussing funding structure of ASTM).

standard is cheaper for them to meet than another. Absent a side-payment system, which itself may be costly to orchestrate, socially valuable standardization can be impeded by infighting, and the voting rules become relevant. Many of these organizations operate by consensus, and hence disagreement can delay the standardization effort greatly.[16]

A further difficulty with private sector solutions arises in international markets. Even when the collective action problem could be overcome in an open trading system, there may be little incentive to do anything about emerging incompatibilities before the opening of trade. Under autarchy, to use the familiar construct, differences across nations in technology or resource endowments can lead to different methods of production for the same or similar products. It is no surprise that compatibility standards might evolve in national markets that differ from country to country, yet the present value of their effects on firms abroad can be negligible because trade is minimal or the opening of trade is well in the future. Conceivably, inaction under these circumstances is efficient because the present value of the gains from efforts to resolve international incompatibilities fall short of the current period costs. But this need not be the case, and the fact that the gains lie in the future may simply compound the free rider problem when cooperative action is desirable.

The result is that the opening of trade may reveal incompatibilities previously ignored in the trading community. This prospect raises another question—To what extent will the market eliminate such incompatibilities over time when it is efficient to do so? In many cases, the market will do well. Consumers will switch to superior products, albeit slowly in some cases as they wait for incompatible products to depreciate and require replacement. A possible source of market failure in some instances, however, is again the possibility of collective action problems. When the decision by one consumer to switch to a new standard has nonpecuniary consequences for other consumers (the network externality problem), efficient switching may not occur

---

16. A formal model incorporating such concerns is developed in Farrell and Saloner (1988). As an example of when divergent preferences thwarted industry consensus, leading to government intervention in the end, see the discussion of the decision by the Federal Communications Commission to adopt the NTSC broadcast format in Besen and Johnson (1986, pp. 89–93).

(because no one wants to take the risk of moving first under conditions of imperfect information) and inefficient switching may occur (because those who switch "strand" those who do not, a negative externality that they do not consider in their decisions).[17] Further, when firms in different nations are already producing in accordance with different standards, the opening of trade may reveal a strong divergence in preferences over the best standard. Infighting during the course of international cooperative efforts may become intense and consensus impossible to reach.

An additional problem is the capture of private standards setting entities by a subset of interested firms. The result may be an effort to establish standards that yield *incompatibility*, the motivation being an anticompetitive one. It has long been suggested that large firms may, at times, prefer to make their products incompatible with others to maintain market power over pricing in a market segment and, in extreme cases, to drive out rivals altogether. The creation of such technological "tie-ins" and their consequences has been the subject of a considerable strand of industrial organization literature.[18] It is only a modest extension to imagine that groups of firms may prefer to insulate themselves from competition at times through coordinated incompatibilities, at least when installed base problems give them the leverage to succeed. Even when competition will eventually erode their market position, the transitory gains may justify the effort.

Similarly, the timing and transparency of the standardization process may be subject to manipulation. Inside information about the development of a new standard is potentially valuable. Firms that know about new standards sooner will have a lead in retooling to meet them. Not only may they enjoy a transitory period of market power before others enter the market, but when economies of scale and learning by doing are important, the advantage may be permanent.

In summary, both theory and experience suggest that market incentives to eliminate undesirable incompatibilities are often powerful and that much will be accomplished when the private sector is left to its own devices. Collective action problems and competitive im-

17. See Farrell and Saloner (1986a).
18. See Ordover and Willig (1981); Ordover, Sykes, and Willig (1983); Braunstein and White (1985); Farrell and Saloner (1986b); Matutes and Regibeau (1988); Katz and Shapiro (1986b); Katz and Shapiro (1985).

perfections, however, are a source of potentially important market failures.

Having acknowledged the possible inefficiencies of markets, however, it is difficult to offer many persuasive examples of when market activity *alone* has resulted in persistent, inefficient incompatibilities that have come to be perceived as technical barriers internationally. Incompatibilities can be found, to be sure, but most are at least arguably efficient due to the consumer choice with which they are associated (such as incompatibilities in the computer industry) or, in part, the product of government intervention in the establishment of compatibility standards (such as the incompatibility of television broadcast formats). This is not to say that benefits might not result from an acceleration of private standardization activity, both within nations and internationally, but does suggest that concerns about market failures are easy to exaggerate.[19]

Further, to the extent that persuasive examples of market failure may be identified by others, it does not follow that government intervention is appropriate, as governments often fail worse than markets. Before turning to such issues, however, the market response to issues of product quality will be discussed.

Quality and the Market

Market incentives to generate product quality, and the possible imperfections in those incentives, are by now too well known to require much exposition.[20] Aspects of quality, whether relating to the healthfulness or safety of a product, to its suitability for a particular taste or purpose, or to its durability or performance in relation to competing products, are all matters of interest to consumers. When consumers are well informed about these aspects of quality and capable of appreciating their significance, better-quality products can command a premium. As a first approximation, sellers in a competitive market will then be induced to supply quality to the point at

19. An oft-cited "market failure" in the standards area, albeit not a source of incompatibility, is the persistence of the QWERTY keyboard for typing in preference to the Dvorak keyboard that is said to be demonstrably superior. See David (1985). Yet the assertion that QWERTY is demonstrably inferior has recently been challenged forcefully. Liebowitz and Margolis (1990).

20. For a similar discussion, see Viscusi (1984, pp. 2–16).

which the marginal cost of further improvements in quality begins to exceed the marginal benefits, and the market equilibrium will be efficient.

The claim that markets have a considerable incentive to produce quality is not mere theoretical construct. Whether one looks at the growth of Japanese market share in the U.S. automobile market during the 1980s, the introduction of low-fat food products and health foods, the voluntary procurement of the Underwriter's Laboratory certification by most U.S. electrical appliance manufacturers, or the promulgation of quality standards by any number of private sector standard-setting entities, the conclusion is inescapable that consumers respond to perceptions of quality and reward it; the market responds by supplying it.

As in the case of compatibility, however, there are various reasons why the market may not supply "optimal" quality. Although perhaps the least important, the problem of imperfect competition has been studied at length. The uninformed intuition that firms with market power will respond by systematically producing suboptimally low-quality products (rather than extracting the surplus on better-quality products through higher prices) is surely wrong. But it is equally clear that even with perfect information, the seller's marginal conditions for optimal quality choice can differ from the social marginal conditions, resulting in an undersupply or oversupply of quality relative to the first-best.[21]

The much greater problem is imperfect information. If purchasers do not know and cannot cheaply ascertain the quality of what they buy, willingness to pay will not adjust to improvements in quality, and the economic incentive to produce them can be lost. Likewise, because quality is generally costly to produce, poor-quality products can outcompete high-quality products, and the market equilibrium may entail the production of suboptimally low-quality products exclusively.[22]

Yet there are many market responses to consumer information problems. The first is simply to remedy them by providing informa-

21. A simple model of quality decisions under single-price monopoly making this point may be found in Tirole (1988, pp. 100–02). An aspect of quality that has been studied at great length under imperfect competition is durability. See, for example, Coase (1972); Swan (1970). See also Spence (1975).

22. The seminal paper is Akerlof (1970).

tion, perhaps through advertising if it can be made credible and perhaps through the development by consumers or producers of reputable independent testing and evaluation organizations such as Consumer Reports and Underwriter's Laboratories.[23] When consumers will reward quality with repeat purchases, sellers may also compete on quality to retain customers.[24] The development of marketwide reputation through word of mouth and through investment in brand-name capital is a related way that manufacturers gain a stake in maintaining quality.[25] Yet another mechanism is the issuance of a warranty, which will typically be cheaper for sellers of high-quality products and is thus a viable signaling device.[26]

Regulatory intervention is not necessary, in many cases, to induce firms to supply quality products, therefore, even when consumers are poorly informed at the time of purchase or would be without market-generated information. Further, when the market performs well, its ability to satisfy diverse preferences regarding quality is an important virtue. Not all consumers are willing to pay the same for particular attributes of quality due to differences in underlying tastes or to differences in wealth. It should come as no surprise that some consumers select lower quality than others, therefore, or that quality may vary across an international cross section of markets.

This is not meant to suggest that market solutions to information problems will work well in every case. Advertising and independent testing will do poorly at ensuring quality when products only occasionally pose problems (the defectively manufactured automobile or contaminated meat). The provision of information as to attributes of quality that are highly complex may also prove excessively costly. As noted, the problem of assuring consumers that information is credible exists.[27] Repeat purchasing is not always likely, and many products

23. See Nelson (1974).

24. End-game problems and the associated unraveling are likely avoided through the possibility that the game can always continue and the fact that sellers' agents do not attempt to discriminate in the quality of goods provided to likely repeat customers versus others.

25. On this set of issues generally, see Klein and Leffler (1981); Kreps and Wilson (1982); Shapiro (1982); Shapiro (1983); Grossman (1981). A nice survey is by Tirole (1988, pp. 106–14).

26. See Priest (1981).

27. A further point is that information produced by a seller benefits not only those who buy a product but those who do not, and thus there is likely an underincentive to produce it even when it is completely credible.

(particularly those such as foodstuffs) are unbranded. Warranties may themselves be a source of inefficiencies (moral hazard on the buyer's side), solvency problems may undermine their value as may the costs of enforcing them, and in any case consumers need a good sense of the nature and magnitude of the risks covered by them to price warranties (or their absence) properly. For these reasons, it is widely accepted that market solutions to the information problem may fall short of what is needed.

A further concern about markets relates to consumers' cognitive capacities—much has been written in recent years about the ability of the consumer to assess risks correctly. Even well-informed consumers may overvalue or undervalue product risks, and either type of error can be associated with inadequate incentives at the margin to supply quality.[28]

Externalities are also of some significance. The purchaser of an automobile, for example, may not take account of risks to pedestrians and other motorists. There is also some doubt that family members always take proper account of risks to each other, as when parents purchase items for children.

Finally, as with compatibility issues, the possibility arises that the process of setting quality standards or certifying compliance with them will be captured by producer interests and manipulated to anticompetitive ends. When compliance with market-generated quality standards becomes important, as when they are essential to consumer acceptance or when they are incorporated into building codes, insurability requirements, and the like, the standards selected may be chosen because particular firms have a cost advantage in meeting them rather than because of any genuine superiority. Likewise, the conformity assessment system can be manipulated to deny certification to the products of competitors—precisely such allegations were made in an antitrust suit against the American Society of Mechanical Engineers in the early 1970s.[29]

In the end, therefore, markets will generate optimal product quality only some of the time, and even when they do so, in the long run they

---

28. The literature is voluminous. Representative selections include Viscusi (1979); Arnould and Grabowski (1981); Tversky and Kahneman (1974); Arrow (1982).

29. The case is discussed in "The Restrictive Effects of Industrial Standards on International Commerce," *Law and Policy in International Business,* vol. 4 (1972), pp. 613–14.

may be slow at it. The reader will not be burdened with examples of arguable market failures in this regard, as the literature cited previously is replete with them.

Once again, however, the possibility of market failure does not by itself establish that government intervention will improve matters, nor does it say anything about the best option for government intervention.

Government Intervention

The difficulties with government regulation in the product market are also too familiar to require lengthy exposition. Here, as elsewhere, concerns about information and capture arise, as well as concerns about the appropriate choice of policy instruments. With particular regard to the problem of technical barriers in international markets, additional issues arise with respect to the choice between centralized or cooperative international action and decentralized or noncooperative action (whether by national governments or private sector entities).

Closed Economy Issues

For many decades, welfare economics focused intently on the myriad of circumstances under which markets might fail. Government, by contrast, was typically viewed as a faithful agent of the public interest, with the capacity to design and administer effectively all manner of sophisticated corrective policies. At best, this view of the role of government was naive.[30] The modern perspective is far more balanced, acknowledging that government intervention is not the solution to all market failures and that the real issue is one of comparative institutional competence—Will government perform worse than the market, or vice versa? With particular reference to government regulation of the product market, the essential difficulties with any form of government intervention are two: (1) a lack of information, and (2) a divergence between the incentives of regulators and the social interest.

30. This is the essence of Coase's critique of Pigou in an article often said to be the most cited in the history of economics. I will add to its lead in the citation competition. Coase (1960).

INFORMATION AND INCENTIVES. The informational requirements for constructive government intervention are potentially great for both compatibility and quality issues. As to compatibility, it is far easier to identify compatibility problems attributable to divergent standards than it is to solve them appropriately. First, there is the sometimes difficult question of whether the incompatible standards ought survive in the long run because they are differentiated in the marketplace and appeal to different consumer needs—incompatibilities in the computer industry, for example, are typically of this sort. Once the determination is made that the incompatibility should be eliminated, there is the question of which standard should prevail. The choice is rarely obvious, and governments can be assured that much of the information that they receive about the relative merits of competing standards will be tainted by self-interest. When governments act, therefore, they may well make the wrong choice (the decision of the French government to promote the domestically produced SECAM broadcast format is at least arguably an example).[31] Thus even when it seems likely that only one standard will or should prevail in the end, government should sometimes leave the problem to the market rather than attempt standardization by fiat.[32]

Information problems may also be substantial with respect to quality issues. Questions arise as to the magnitude of the risks associated with products and their proper valuation, the costs of remedying those risks, and the issue of whether consumer tolerance of such risks in the absence of intervention reflects a favorable market judgment about them or a market failure for one or more of the reasons noted above. When government acts, the suggestion is often made that action was unnecessary or counterproductive and that regulation has had little beneficial impact on the problem that it purported to address.[33]

Failures of regulatory policy may also result from calculated departures from the social interest. The notion of regulatory "cap-

31. Pelkmans and Beuter (1987).

32. That view was embraced by the U.S. Federal Communications Commission in the ongoing battle in the United States over AM stereo broadcast formats and over videotext and teletext standards. See Besen and Johnson (1986, pp. 32–57, 72–86); Berg (1987).

33. See Peltzman (1987); Peltzman (1975); the papers in Poole (1982), especially Clarkson and Muris (1982), Weimer (1982), and Meiners(1982); Grabowski and Vernon (1983).

ture," whereby producer groups that are subject to regulation exert considerable influence on the process, dates back to the earliest work on public choice. The sources of capture are varied—the possible monopoly of the regulated over information, the "revolving door" between the public and private sectors, and the prospect that legislatures may design regulatory agencies to be responsive to well-organized interest groups. Hence the notion that regulators will confine themselves to the selfless pursuit of economic efficiency or some other high-minded conception of the public interest appears fanciful.[34]

The kinds of perversities that may result from the regulation of product markets are obvious. Compatibility standards may be embraced not because of any thoughtful conclusion about their overall economic superiority, but because of the influence of well-organized producer interests that have a cost advantage in meeting them. Quality standards may be chosen for the same reason, with the standard-setting process becoming a device for the exclusion of rivals rather than for the protection of consumers. These problems can be particularly acute when only some of the interested parties have effective access to the regulatory process (as when foreign producers are excluded).

SOME POLICY INSTRUMENT ISSUES. Beginning with compatibility, recall that collective action problems are an important reason why market standardization efforts may prove deficient. When the sole problem is one of free riders, as distinguished from private sector gridlock due to disputes over the appropriate standard, a natural choice of policy instrument is a subsidy for standardization. The government might provide aid for the establishment of private sector standardization organizations or for new standardization initiatives by existing organizations. When the failure of private activity in the absence of government intervention is the result of divergent preferences, by contrast, government fiat *may* become the best option, notwithstanding the aforementioned risks of error.

Turning to standards of quality, the fundamental choice is not so much between subsidy and fiat as between information remedies and fiat. From the economists' standpoint, the information option will often have great appeal. As noted, the economic perspective tends to

34. Stigler (1971); Peltzman (1976); Becker (1976).

emphasize information failures as the source of quality problems within the market, and it is then natural to view the provision of information as the solution to most market failures.[35] The externality problem remains, and when the buyer does not sufficiently internalize the consequences of inferior quality, information remedies will not work. The other caveat relates to the possible absence of much heterogeneity in consumer preferences—when all consumers desire the same level of quality, it may be cheaper to require its provision than to place consumers in the position of having to investigate quality at the time of purchase even when information is good. With heterogeneous preferences, however, information remedies have the virtue of allowing the market maximal flexibility to satisfy them.

The economists' arguments for information remedies may not persuade those who see the need for regulation as resting on cognitive failures as much as information failures. I cannot hope to resolve the tension between paternalistic and consumer sovereignty perspectives here and must acknowledge that reasonable persons may conclude that fiat can dominate information remedies with some regularity.

Nevertheless, something may be said about the relative costs and benefits of the information and fiat alternatives under different circumstances. Fiat tends to foreclose opportunities to serve different tastes and may further injure consumers through adverse effects on competition. Two questions to ask about the wisdom of fiat, therefore, are, To what extent are consumers homogeneous or heterogeneous in their tastes?, and To what extent will a mandatory quality standard create market power? A third question relates to the putative benefits of fiat—If information remedies are deficient because of externalities or cognitive problems, what are the stakes in permitting the externality to persist or in risking the cognitive error? Other things being equal, risks to life and limb may provide a better case for fiat than most other sorts of risks (such as the risk of inadvertently consuming low-alcohol jenever or low-fat cheese).[36]

Open Economy Issues

In international product markets, the decision to intervene on matters of compatibility or quality is almost invariably made in the

35. Beales, Craswell, and Salop (1981).
36. Recall the examples in chapter 2.

first instance by national governments (certain decisions by the European Commission being the exception). It is inevitable that national governments acting independently will develop distinct policies in some areas, and the question for the international community is whether the resulting heterogeneity in policies is a virtue or a vice. This question is not often easy to answer.

JUSTIFICATIONS FOR POLICY HETEROGENEITY. Just as the market may respond to heterogeneous consumer preferences with a menu of imperfectly substitutable product choices, so may heterogeneity in tastes, wealth, or income distribution across nations justify different regulations respecting the same facet of product quality and perhaps even compatibility. Consider safety and health regulations as an example. It is invariably costly for producers to comply with such regulations, and the extent to which citizens in an economy will wish to see resources devoted to improvements in health and safety will assuredly be a function of national wealth (per capita wealth is perhaps the best proxy here) and its distribution. Health and safety are, no doubt, normal goods, and in general, we might expect products to be safer in wealthier nations whether safety levels are government- or market-determined.

Even for nations at comparable levels of per capita income, differences in the shared experience of the citizenry may lead to different preferences and different regulatory initiatives. Inevitably, the decision about how much risk to tolerate with products, to continue with the health and safety illustration, is a political one that balances the interest group pressures on all sides. In some nations, product risks materialize and become widely publicized, whereas in others they may not, with the result that interest group pressures for regulation will vary. The hormone-beef regulations of the European Community are perhaps illustrative—given the unfortunate experience in Europe with the ingestion of beef treated with DES, it is not surprising that the zero-risk policy might emerge there but not elsewhere.[37] The recently announced labeling initiative in the United States, concerning the need to cook beef thoroughly before ingesting it, is another example driven by the unfortunate *Escherichia coli* cases in children in Washington State.[38]

---

37. See the discussion in chapter 2.

38. Department of Agriculture, Food Safety and Inspection Service, "Heat-Processing Procedures, Cooking Instructions, and Cooling, Handling and Storage Requirements for Uncured Meat Patties," 58 Fed. Reg. 41138 (August 2, 1993); Department of Agriculture,

To be sure, if interest groups in each nation all shared the same experience and information, the degree of heterogeneity in policy would likely diminish considerably (although it would by no means disappear as there are other reasons for heterogeneity). In this sense, much of the heterogeneity that exists might be difficult to justify on grounds of a "perfect information" cost-benefit analysis. But it is also clear that national governments do not operate in an environment of equally informed polities and that some of the diversity in regulatory initiatives that emerge in actuality have unquestioned democratic legitimacy.

In short, regulatory heterogeneity will sometimes emerge in response to genuine international variations in the preferences of citizens. Except for the possibility that these variations result from poor information rather than variation in underlying tastes or income, regulatory heterogeneity in response to them is defensible and indeed desirable.[39]

The other important justification for heterogencity, operative even when preferences do not vary, is honest disagreement about how best to satisfy preferences. Well-informed regulators may disagree over the magnitude of the risks associated with a product, the question of whether information remedies are sufficient, and so on. In the face of such disagreements, policy heterogeneity is not only expectable but potentially desirable, as differences across national markets become a source of cross-sectional data for resolving uncertainties.

COSTS OF HETEROGENEITY. The fact that a high-minded justification for regulatory heterogeneity can be adduced in some cases does not end the inquiry. Policy heterogeneity invariably comes at some price to the international community, as the need for producers to comply with multiple regulatory regimes can only increase their costs. Sometimes this cost increase is plausibly small or even negligi-

---

Food Safety and Inspection Service, "Mandatory Safe Handling Statements on Labeling of Raw Meat and Poultry Products," 58 Fed. Reg. 43478 (August 16, 1993); "U.S. Orders Safety Tags on Meats, Poultry in October," *Chicago Tribune*, August 12, 1993, p. N7; "U.S. Orders Care Labels on Raw, Rare Meat. Decision Was Motivated by Cases of Food Poisoning," *Dallas Morning News*, August 12, 1993, p. 1A.

39. It has long been recognized in the public finance literature, for example, that decentralized government policymaking can promote welfare by adapting to variations in preferences across jurisdictions. The classic paper is Tiebout (1956). An excellent recent survey is that of Rubinfeld (1987).

ble—scale economies may be fully exploited, inventory and distribution costs may be largely unaffected, and so on, notwithstanding regulatory heterogeneities. But in other instances, the added costs of compliance with multiple regulatory regimes can exceed their benefits. It is not enough to attribute heterogeneity to differences in tastes, wealth levels, or expert assessments of risk, therefore, because a question remains as to its *net* consequences.

Any assessment of these consequences can be exceedingly difficult. It requires that the existing state of affairs be compared to counterfactual worlds without heterogeneity and to worlds with other types of heterogeneity, in which costs, prices and surplus to buyers and sellers would differ. The magnitude of these differences will typically be uncertain and controversial.

Consider the European ban on beef treated with growth hormones as an example once again. Assume that there indeed exists a strong aversion on the part of many consumers in Europe, shared by few consumers elsewhere, to the actual or perceived health risks of hormone-treated beef. Would welfare in Europe or in the world as a whole rise if the disparity in regulatory policy were somehow eliminated or modified? The answer is not at all clear. There is the question of whether Europe itself benefits from the ban, taking into account the intensity of consumer preferences, its effect on beef prices in Europe, and the possibility that the European beef industry exercised undue influence in securing it. If we *assume* that Europe comes out ahead relative to a world in which growth hormones are legal everywhere, that external effects on other nations are strictly pecuniary, as seems likely, and that there are no competitive issues, then the hormone ban has probably raised global welfare as well as European welfare relative to a world in which growth hormones are legal everywhere. But that is not the end of the issue, as one must consider alternative regulatory possibilities and their global effects. An obvious candidate is a labeling policy, whereby hormone-treated beef can be sold everywhere but its label must disclose that it has been produced in a jurisdiction that permits growth hormones. To evaluate this alternative, we come full circle to the choice between information remedies and fiat remedies, with all the arguments on both sides. One might also inquire whether the international divergence in consumer preferences is the product of imperfect information in Europe or elsewhere, so that policies to educate consumers about the true risks of hormone-treated beef are in order and might ultimately generate pressures for policy convergence. No doubt other issues and alternatives warrant attention as well.

Such difficulties can lead commentators to throw up their hands. In the economic literature on federalism, for example, some commentators have argued that differences in regulatory policies should be *presumed* justifiable unless they impose costs principally on other jurisdictions or facilitate the extraction of monopoly rents from citizens of other jurisdictions.[40] By this standard, most international technical barriers would be presumed justifiable—standards and regulations that impede trade do not often facilitate the extraction of monopoly rents from those outside, and much of the costs of those standards and regulations will be borne by consumers within the jurisdiction who must pay higher prices.

For reasons that will become clear in a moment, I find this view of regulatory heterogeneity overly charitable. But the task of identifying undesirable heterogeneities more broadly is assuredly a difficult one. For many cases in which heterogeneity serves some arguable purpose, it is essentially impossible to ascertain as a practical matter whether its benefits exceed its costs. It is then equally difficult to say whether the absence of harmonization and the technical barriers that result are on balance desirable or undesirable. But not all cases are so difficult.

UNJUSTIFIED HETEROGENEITY. Instances assuredly arise in which high-minded arguments for regulatory heterogeneity are inapplicable. Suppose, for example, that the regulatory goal is to ensure fire safety—say, for concreteness, to ensure that items of children's sleepwear are adequately fire-resistant. Assume that this goal may be met in a variety of ways, through the application of a variety of flame retardant chemicals. A national regulatory authority specifies, however, that children's sleepwear must be treated with one chemical in particular, thus excluding equally safe products from the market.

The welfare costs of such a policy are neutral at best and likely adverse. Consumers are foreclosed from the purchase of products that meet their needs. In the most optimistic scenario, the allowable treatment is no more costly for any supplier than the disallowed alternatives, and so prices are unaffected. But the more likely scenario

40. See Easterbrook (1983); Levmore (1983).

is that some suppliers are barred from the market or can only comply at increased cost, so that consumers are no better served, yet prices rise and the lowest-cost supplier of a satisfactory good is sometimes excluded from the market.

The principle that this example illustrates is both simple and general. When a legitimate objective of regulation can be attained in a variety of ways, as through different production processes and product designs, welfare will be greater if regulation is undertaken in such a manner as to allow its objectives to be achieved in the cheapest way possible. Often the cheapest solution will vary across suppliers or across products subject to the regulation, and hence regulations that require a particular design, manufacturing process, or the like can be greatly inferior to those that simply require the seller to meet the objectives of the regulation in whatever manner the seller prefers. An important class of cases that raises this issue concerns the choice between "design" and "performance" regulations. The former specifies some feature of performance that a product must attain, whereas the latter specifies how it must attain it. Hence performance regulations will often dominate design regulations. The caveat relates to the possibility that conformity assessment may be more costly for performance regulations, but in the absence of this complication, a preference for performance regulation is appropriate, and a proliferation of disparate design regulations is likely to reflect economically indefensible heterogeneity.

A further source of unjustified heterogeneity, although more difficult to spot in practice, results from manipulation of the regulatory process by producer interests. Even in a closed economy, the notion that "capture" may produce serious regulatory failure is familiar. The problem is likely greater in international markets because foreign producer interests typically have little input into domestic political processes. The regulatory process may then be manipulated in various ways to disadvantage foreign competitors.

Domestic interests will prefer to manipulate the process to impose costs exclusively on foreign rivals. Regulations that apply only to foreign products are the obvious choice, but these may run afoul of various legal constraints discussed later. When discriminatory substantive regulations are infeasible, discrimination may instead be introduced into the conformity assessment system. Foreign products may be subjected to undue testing, inspections, and delays that greatly increase their costs of distribution even if substantive regulations on their face apply evenhandedly.

A third option is substantive regulation that imposes costs on all parties but is relatively more burdensome for foreign suppliers. An interesting result in the industrial organization literature, for example, is that a dominant firm can increase its profits through actions that increase its own costs, as long as those actions also increase the costs of competitors to a sufficient extent—the intuition is that as the costs of rivals rise, the residual demand at any price facing the dominant firm, increases, and if this demand curve shifts upward by more than average cost for the dominant firm, then the dominant firm benefits.[41] The basic idea generalizes beyond the dominant firm model. Whenever regulation raises the costs of rivals, their prices tend to rise for any quantity sold, and the increased residual demand to the firm or firms that procure the regulation *may* offset the effect on their profits of whatever direct cost increase they suffer as a result of regulation. Obviously, such strategies are more likely to be profitable when the compliance costs for domestic firms are modest and when the disparity in compliance costs between foreign and domestic firms is large. Thus for example, regulation designed to raise foreign rivals' costs may have particular appeal when compliance requires access to some proprietary technology over which domestic firms have control. More generally, it will have appeal when international differences in technology, or in factor endowments, give domestic firms a distinct cost advantage in compliance (recall the pasta purity regulations and the concentration of durum wheat farmers in Italy).

However, it can again be exceedingly difficult to ascertain whether the motive for regulation is anticompetitive. The general lesson here is perhaps that significant disparities in compliance costs between domestic and foreign firms are suspicious and at times serve as a marker for instances of regulatory heterogeneity that are economically counterproductive.

NOTE ON MUTUAL RECOGNITION. I wish to underscore that when heterogeneity in regulatory policy is desirable or at least potentially so because the "optimal" policy is unclear, it does not follow that domestic and imported products must be subject to the same require-

---

41. See Salop and Scheffman (1983).

ments in each market. Rather, importing nations may elect to permit the importation of goods that do not conform to the requirements imposed on domestic producers—"mutual recognition."[42]

Mutual recognition is not always an attractive policy, to be sure. For example, suppose that a developing nation tolerates the use of a dangerous pesticide because of its effectiveness in the face of food shortages. Consumers in developed countries may well desire protection from imported goods with substantial residues of the pesticide, and thus a prohibition on imports of foodstuffs treated with it may be quite sensible even though they may legally be sold in the country of exportation. To take another example, when regulatory heterogeneity is the result of uncertainty about the dangers of a particular product, mutual recognition may make it difficult to ascertain the extent of those dangers over time by examining the experiences of different countries—international trade can introduce the potentially hazardous product everywhere, which sometimes (although by no means always) can complicate efforts to draw inferences about its dangerousness.

Yet mutual recognition has obvious advantages at times. It tends to make the costs of regulation more transparent, as foreign producers with any cost advantage abroad due to a lesser degree of regulation can pass it through in their export prices. It also makes it impossible for domestic producers to use regulation to "raise rivals' costs" abroad and obviates one form of regulatory capture. Concomitantly, it tends to reduce the costs of inefficient regulation to the domestic economy by allowing consumers to circumvent it by purchasing cheaper products from abroad.

More generally, mutual recognition has some tendency to "drive out" regulations that raise prices when consumer willingness-to-pay for the regulatory protection is less than the attendant price increase. Not only will consumers switch to cheaper, less-regulated foreign products, but capital will migrate to the country with the regulatory policy that consumers prefer. Eventually regulators may be forced to abandon unpopular policies to avoid destroying their domestic industries Indeed the mobility of capital may engender regulatory competition among jurisdictions to attract investment.

On the one hand, the process of regulatory competition will tend to promote consumer welfare *if* consumers make well-informed judg-

42. See Nicolaïdis (1989); Nicolaïdis (1993b).

ments in their own best interests. On the other hand, if consumers are poorly informed or incapable of appreciating risks properly, regulatory competition can reduce consumer welfare. Put differently, it may induce either a "race to the bottom" or a "race to the top," evoking familiar debates about federalism.[43] Thus perhaps rather trivially, the wisdom of affording "mutual recognition" to foreign products that do not comply with domestic regulations may turn on the question of whether the importing nation's regulatory policy is a good one or a bad one.

Once again, the stakes for consumers who may err in their purchases seem pertinent. When the hazards to life and limb are small and ill-informed purchases are of minor consequence, mutual recognition may be relatively attractive for its assistance in policing capture and anticompetitive activity. But when the dangers are great and national regulators have a high degree of confidence in their own judgments about matters, mutual recognition may appear undesirable.

Economic Issues in Conformity Assessment

Conformity assessment is costly but so is nonconformity, and the central issue is how to balance the two sets of costs sensibly. Little has been written directly on this issue, but it is closely analogous to the general problem of optimal law enforcement and control of externalities, about which a great deal has been written.

For obvious reasons, formal conformity assessment is usually unnecessary for matters of compatibility. When compatibility is important and a purportedly compatible product, in fact, is not, the buyer will find out directly. Sellers will thus face a heavy market penalty for selling products that do not meet pertinent compatibility standards, and there is little reason to imagine that a private or public sector conformity assessment process is necessary. Quality is thus the focus of this section.

---

43. For studies favorable to competition among jurisdictions, or at least agnostic, see Revesz (1992) (environment) and Romano (1993) (corporation law). For studies critical of the outcome of federalism, see Shaviro (1993) (taxation), Beales and Muris (1993) (regulation of advertising), and Viscusi (1993) (product risk labeling). It is noteworthy, however, that in the three studies in which federalism was found wanting, "mutual recognition" was either absent or infeasible.

Ex Ante versus Ex Post: Why Is Conformity Assessment Needed?

Conformity assessment entails the inspection, testing and certification of products before the time that they or similar units are sold. In this sense, it is an "ex ante" measure for quality assurance.

Various alternatives exist that operate "ex post." When a product does not meet a pertinent health or safety requirement, for example, and risk to life or limb materializes, the seller or manufacturer can be subjected to civil penalties. Criminal penalties are also an option, either fines or incarceration. These options are by no means restricted to instances in which a regulation (as opposed to a standard) has been violated. Even if criminal penalties are limited to violations of mandatory quality requirements, civil penalties need not be and indeed are regularly applied for violations of quality standards.[44] Still further penalty options exist in international markets, as imports of goods from manufacturers whose products have proved substandard might be banned or might become subject to intensive ex ante conformity assessment only *after* some problem has been detected in units previously sold.

The obvious virtue of such ex post devices is that they place the burden of conformity assessment on sellers in the first instance (sometimes termed self-certification). Because only a subset of all products subject to standards or regulations needs to be evaluated under this system—those that manifest quality problems after sale—the costs of assessing conformity under an ex post system are often lower, possibly by a great deal, than under any ex ante system. Regarding the ex ante incentives for conformity in such a system, common sense suggests that they depend on the probability of a penalty being imposed for nonconformity and on the magnitude of the penalty. If ex post devices reduce the probability of a penalty, therefore, the effect on incentives can, as a first approximation, be eliminated by an increase in the magnitude. Assuming that the administrative costs of the system do not rise proportionally when the magnitude of the penalty rises, it follows that ex post devices may achieve incentives for quality comparable to ex ante conformity assessment with lower overall enforcement costs. This idea is directly analogous to the well-known proposition in the literature on optimal

44. Recall the examples in chapter 2.

criminal sanctions that a low probability of detection and a high penalty may comprise the most economical method for generating a given level of deterrence.[45]

Thus ex post approaches to policing compliance with quality requirements may have much to commend them, and it is instructive to inquire why ex ante measures are needed at all.[46] The answer is that for several practical reasons, ex post penalties may fail to generate sufficient incentives ex ante. If the ex post system entails civil litigation, conventionally measured monetary damages awards may understate the social loss from harm that occurs. This problem is often said to arise in the United States in cases involving fatal accidents.[47] In other instances, the harm suffered may be too small in relation to transaction costs for the injured party to have any incentive to pursue a remedy. Further, monetary penalties may prove inadequate because the manufacturer/seller lacks the financial resources to pay them. And manufacturers/sellers may reside outside the jurisdiction in which the harm occurs, with the result that their financial assets cannot be reached and incarceration penalties are not viable (a problem of particular importance in many cases in which the defective good is imported from abroad).

Yet it is important not to exaggerate these concerns. If civil damages understate social costs, it may be possible simply to adjust the damages award. If the harm is too small to provide an incentive to pursue a remedy, private action can be subsidized or those who "blow the whistle" to the appropriate public authorities can be rewarded. Solvency concerns can perhaps be addressed through requirements of bonds or through mandatory insurance requirements. Difficulties associated with offshore entities can be addressed similarly, so that overseas sellers can be forced to place sufficient assets at risk.

---

45. See Becker (1968); Polinsky and Shavell (1979); Posner (1992).

46. Related discussions may be found in Polinsky (1979); Ellickson (1973); Calabresi and Melamed (1972); White and Wittman (1983); Wittman (1977); Shavell (1984a); Shavell (1984b). To be clear, I am not addressing the wisdom of ex post quality assessments as a substitute for substantive quality standards and regulations. Vague standards for the imposition of civil liability, for example, such as an inquiry into the "reasonableness" of the design of a product after an accident occurs, have many deficiencies that need not be addressed here. See Shapo (1987, pp. 9–1) for a discussion of such matters. Rather I take as a point of departure that substantive standards and regulations have been promulgated ex ante, and the question is whether ex ante conformity assessment is dominated by a system that imposes penalties ex post for detected nonconformities.

47. See Viscusi (1984); Sykes (1989).

But there are other possible objections. Some quality problems, such as nutritional deficiencies in foodstuffs or the presence of carcinogens, will never be detected by the consumer. Even if harm materializes, its source will be unknown. Further, the claim that ex post measures are cheaper to administer is not correct in all cases. Even though fewer products must be evaluated, the resources devoted to their evaluation may soar because the stakes are high. Much may be spent on the factual issues relating to whether a product did or did not comply with quality requirements, whether any noncompliance was the cause of the harm that materialized, and what the proper valuation of the harm is. Measures to correct for the distortions associated with solvency problems and difficulties in reaching assets outside the jurisdiction will also be costly.

Nevertheless, in many instances, ex post measures may be adequate to achieve sufficient incentive for compliance with quality requirements and may do so far more cheaply than a system of ex ante inspection, testing, and certification. It is too strong to say that economic considerations counsel in favor of ex post measures in general, but it is not too strong to say that ex post options should be rejected only after careful attention to their possible deficiencies on a case-by-case basis.

Efficient Ex Ante Enforcement

Once a decision to proceed with ex ante conformity assessment has been made, many further issues must be confronted in designing the conformity assessment procedures. Among other things, the rate of inspection or testing must be determined; the penalty for nonconformity must be established; and testing facilities must be designated.

The insights of the optimal deterrence literature also have bearing here. In many instances, it is plausible to assume that all units of a product are alike, so that testing and certification with respect to one or a few units will suffice. In other instances, however, such as food contamination or cosmetic impurities, only a few units will be deficient, and a larger sample is necessary to achieve a high degree of confidence that products manufactured under unsafe conditions are being detected and excluded from the marketplace. But ultimately, the objective is to provide sellers with an appropriate incentive to ensure that their products meet applicable quality requirements. As always, there is an inverse relationship between the probability of detection and the magnitude of penalty necessary to a given level of such incentives. If the costs of conformity assessment rise with the size of the sample, therefore, while the costs of imposing a penalty are largely fixed, there is virtue to a smaller sample and a larger penalty. It is not necessary that monetary penalties be used here—the penalty may simply be a length of time that the manufacturer will be denied the certification necessary for market access and an opportunity to reapply for it.

The designation of testing facilities, and the related issue of whether foreign-generated test data are acceptable, have proven thorny in practice and a source of many disputes. Importing nations are understandably concerned that foreign data may prove unreliable or may indeed be fabricated by producers with an interest in obtaining certification. Likewise, it is often difficult and costly for private or public entities in importing nations to monitor the quality of testing performed abroad. If the response is to exclude the use of foreign test data, however, and to require submission of foreign products to domestic laboratories with all the attendant transaction costs and duplication of effort from country to country, the costs of conformity assessment can rise enormously. Once again, a solution may lie in a willingness to accept foreign test data, coupled with occasional spot checks to verify its accuracy and sizable penalties when inaccuracy is detected.

This approach will be facilitated by the development of laboratories in exporting nations that test a variety of products. Such entities have a strong self-interest in the accuracy of their work when inaccuracy is penalized by importing nations. The development of such facilities can allow exporters to supply necessary testing information to pertinent authorities around the globe on the basis of a single test or series of tests, greatly economizing on the duplication of effort that can arise when tests must be performed in each country of importation and also economizing on the transaction costs of shipment, language translations, and the like associated with multiple international testing sites. Testing in the country of exportation also avoids the dangers associated with capture of testing facilities in the country of importation by import-competing interests.

Generally acceptable international quality control standards can also economize on the costs of creating systems that rely on testing in the country of exportation. Compliance with such standards can be made the basis for acceptance of foreign testing and can be policed through periodic spot checks and audits coupled with appropriate penalties for violations.

To be sure, circumstances may arise in which testing in the country of exportation is unacceptable. The feasible penalties for fabricated test results may appear inadequate to deter them when long-term repeat dealing with the exporters in question is not anticipated. Alternatively, especially in the case of developing countries, reliable testing facilities may simply not exist in the country of exportation. Nations cannot be expected to accept all foreign testing efforts uncritically, therefore, but in many cases there may be no reason to doubt their adequacy. In those cases, economic considerations counsel reliance on them coupled with appropriate ex post penalties for fraud and inaccuracy.

Chapter 4

Models for Avoiding and Policing Technical Barriers

PREVIOUS CHAPTERS explored the scope and significance of technical barriers to trade and developed some positive and normative economic considerations bearing on the genesis of technical barriers and their economic consequences. This chapter discusses the legal/ institutional treatment of technical barrier problems, identifying the approaches that have been developed to discipline them and indicating, when possible, their strengths or weaknesses in practice.

Market Mechanisms and Multilaterally Subsidized Standardization

Given the staggering variety of standards and regulations in the international economy, it is perhaps surprising that technical barriers are not more of a problem in international markets and that much trade occurs without serious attention to them. This was true even before important international initiatives such as those of the General Agreement on Tariffs and Trade (GATT). Market activity alone suffices to avoid many technical barrier problems. When decentralized markets alone are not enough, firms move toward cooperative efforts undertaken by international organizations that resemble, in many respects, the private and public-private standardization entities that operate domestically in most trading nations. It would be misleading to characterize these organizations as affording a strictly "market" solution to technical barriers, for they are typically supported by a mixture of public and private funding, and their members include

57

both governmental and private sector entities. But they operate without benefit of much legal formality, drawing recommendations from technical expert groups and thereafter striving for "consensus" defined in one way or another. In this respect, their functioning is difficult to distinguish from many entirely private entities.

The international organizations develop standards addressing the entire range of issues discussed in this book—compatibility, health and safety, product quality, labeling, testing, and certification. The mere existence of such standards sometimes ensures (or reflects) their widespread adoption. Equally clearly, however, the international standards organizations cannot alone provide a complete solution to the technical barrier problem.

Overview of International Standardization Organizations

Of the important international standardization organizations still operating, the first was the International Electrotechnical Commission (IEC), established in 1908. It resulted from the rapid technical progress in electrical technology at the time and the perception that standards were necessary to maintain a reasonable level of compatibility among electrical products.[1] It remains the most important international standardization body for electrical and electronic goods.

The IEC is now affiliated with the International Organization for Standardization (ISO), formed in 1947, the same year as GATT. The impetus for its establishment came from the United Nations, following a breakdown of certain earlier standards organizations during World War II.[2] The "jurisdiction" of the ISO is unlimited, and in principle, the ISO may undertake standardization initiatives relating to any product or service market. In practice, the ISO tends to defer to the more specialized entities such as the IEC when they exist.

The members of both the ISO and the IEC are country representatives. Each nation may designate its own representative, with the result that some members are government agencies and others are private sector entities (the American National Standards Institute is a

---

1. See Verman (1973, pp. 150–54).
2. Verman (1973, pp. 154–59).

private entity that represents the United States). They are funded by dues collected from their members.

In the years after the creation of the ISO, particular concern over the trade effects of food standards led to initiatives before the United Nations Food and Agriculture Organization (FAO) and the World Health Organization (WHO) to reform them. The result was the creation of the Codex Alimentarius Commission, founded in 1962. The Codex develops standards for all manner of food safety and labeling issues. Its members are also country representatives, and its funding has been largely through the FAO and WHO. Interestingly, when the budgets of those agencies proved inadequate for a time, private sector organizations with an interest in the activities of the Codex stepped forward to contribute.[3]

This listing of organizations is hardly exhaustive. A few of the many other international bodies with significant interest in standardization activities include the International Telecommunications Union (ITU), the International Conference on Weights and Measures, the International Labor Organization, the International Bureau for the Standardization of Man-Made Fibres, the International Commission on Illumination, the International Air Transport Association, the International Institute of Refrigeration, and the International Institute of Welding.[4]

The detailed operation of each organization is slightly different, but the essence of what goes on is similar for most of them. The organization usually draws on interested members to form a working group or committee to consider the possibility of standards in a particular area. If this group can come to a reasonable "consensus" (the precise meaning of that term is variable), it will make a proposal for a standard. In one way or another, the member nations will then vote on whether to make the proposal into a "standard."[5] In the ISO, for example, committees of technical experts develop "recommendations," which are sent to member bodies for approval. A recommendation becomes a standard after a sufficient number of member bodies accept it—in the 1970s, the ISO moved from a unanimity rule

3. See Kay (1976a, pp. 18–19).
4. See Verman (1973, pp. 161–63).
5. See Kay (1976a, pp. 22–24), for a general discussion of Codex procedures. Discussion of the analogous procedures for standards adoption in various U.S. organizations may be found in Hamilton (1983) and in Hamilton (1978).

to a 75 percent rule for determining when to convert a recommendation into a standard.[6]

To be sure, member nations are not obligated to follow or adopt these standards in their national markets, even if they vote in favor of adopting them in the international body. The decision to create a standard, however, typically suggests that widespread (although not necessarily universal) adherence will follow.

Effectiveness of the International Organizations

I cannot hope to survey here the full scope of activity by these international bodies or to provide a catalogue of their successes and failures. But even a cursory review of their operations suggests that many potential technical barrier issues can and will be addressed reasonably well by them without benefit of any international legal discipline other than that implicit in the voting rules of the international organizations themselves. A glance at most any recent issue of the ISO bulletin, for example, reveals a wide range of new standards for compatibility, safety, and testing, all of which by definition have been accepted by 75 percent or more of the member bodies.[7]

This observation suggests that the trading community can avoid many technical barrier problems simply by ensuring that the existing international standards organizations are adequately funded, that new matters are brought promptly into their processes, and that their recommendations are evaluated quickly by national authorities and implemented when unobjectionable. Likewise, nations can protect

---

6. See ISO (1975, pp. 4–6).

7. The *ISO Bulletin* is published monthly. By way of illustration, the August 1989 issue (chosen because it was at the top of my stack) contains two new standards for "information processing" relating to "open systems interconnection," four new ship-building standards relating to "fire-resistant constructions" and "topology of ship hull structure," one standard for "technical drawings," three standards for steel products including two for spring wire and one for listing the results of chemical analysis of steel; three standards for road vehicles involving piston rings, quick-connect terminations, and high-pressure fuel injectors; two standards for the blades on agricultural harvesting equipment; a standard for calibration of petroleum tanks in ships; some definitions of terms for the tire industry; various terminological, safety, and testing standards for foodstuffs including fats and oils, coffee, condensed milk, and wheat; test methods for evaluating the quality of nonwoven fibers and yarns; standards for pulleys, welding, rubber products, metal containers, manganese ores, testing of refrigerant compressors, chemical analysis of cigarettes, and *many* others.

themselves against the emergence of many technical barriers to their exports simply by ensuring that their domestic industries participate effectively in these organizations, perhaps subsidizing participation when necessary.

It is also clear, however, that international organizations will not be able to solve all the problems regardless of the amount of effort they devote to them, for much the same reason that nongovernmental standardization activities do not resolve all problems in national markets. Most important, the emphasis on consensus, however defined, ensures that some matters will not be addressed at all through international standards and that others will be addressed only after many years. The difficulty lies mainly in situations in which national governments or industries have strong differences of opinion or vested economic interests that result in a divergence of preferences. The hormone-treated beef dispute between the United States and the European Union is again a case point, in which European interests and others blocked an action by the Codex favoring the U.S. position despite support for that position from the committee of technical experts.[8] Another example is the ongoing debate over high-definition television standards. Many issues with this technology have been settled, but a most vexing issue has proved to be the choice of a basic broadcast format. Japanese producers developed technology that meets one standard, and European producers another. U.S. producers vacillated, fought among themselves for a time, and finally formed a consortium to develop a jointly sponsored American standard. Although the collaborative effort in the United States may soon result in a U.S. standard promulgated by the Federal Communications Commission, the prospects for a single world standard are at this writing rather dim.[9] International wrangling has so far resulted in impasse before the International Radio Consultative Committee, an

8. The United States was able to persuade the technical expert committee at the Codex that a zero tolerance level for growth hormones was inappropriate based on the available scientific evidence, but the Europeans and others blocked the subsequent effort to establish an international standard that U.S. beef could satisfy. See "Hormone Residues in Animal Products Safe, International Committee on Food Safety Says," *BNA International Trade Reporter,* November 9, 1988, p. 1484;"Codex Commission Supports European Ban on Hormones in Meat," *Food Chemical News,* July 8, 1991, p. 8.

9. A nice survey of developments to date in the United States is that of Richard E. Wiley, "HDTV: The Shape of Things to Come," *Legal Times,* July 11, 1994, p. S24.

arm of the ITU, and the distinct possibility remains that national or regional markets will embrace incompatible broadcast formats as they did years ago with the introduction of color television.[10] Such problems are evidently common in telecommunications generally and before the ITU in particular.

Moreover, even when the requisite degree of consensus exists for the formal adoption of an international standard, individual nations or industries within them may decline to adhere to them. Sometimes the reason will be strategic. A domestic industry may have a cost advantage in meeting some standard other than the one embraced internationally or may simply prefer to maintain incompatibility to exclude competition in the home market. Likewise, national regulatory authorities may elect to deviate from the international standard for protectionist reasons. The Japanese ski standards dispute discussed in chapter 2, involving a domestic standard incompatible with one promulgated by the ISO, is perhaps illustrative of this class of problems.

The sheer volume of standardization activity around the world also makes it unlikely that all matters with significant trade implications will be addressed in timely fashion by international bodies. Inevitably, national bodies will act first at times, and many extant national standards were formulated before international standards became available.

High-minded objections to international standards are also possible. It is frequently argued, for example, that the Codex is dominated by producer interest groups and that the resulting food safety standards often err on the side of exposing consumers to undue hazards.[11] National food safety standards are thus more stringent than existing standards of the Codex in many cases, and it is likely that some of the differences have a principled basis.

Government and private sector support for international standards organizations, therefore, though it may accomplish much, will not put

10. Michael Binyon, "Japanese Fail to Secure Adoption of Television System," *Times*, May 26, 1990; Catherine Arnst, "Conference Assures Incompatible HDTV Systems," *Reuter Business Report*, May 28, 1990.

11. Rosman (1993); "Codex Process Should Be Opened, Public Citizen Says," *Food Chemical News*, July 6, 1992; "Groups Make Last Pitch to Halt Challenges to Food Safety Rules under Uruguay Round," *BNA International Trade Daily*, April 14, 1994, p. 20. A useful collection of papers on national and international regulation of hazards in foodstuffs is Middlekauf and Shubik (1989).

an end to international heterogeneities in standards and regulations, nor should it. Technical barrier disputes will continue to arise because international standards are lacking, because nations see fit to depart from them, or because national standardizers act or have acted before the existence of an international standard. The question then arises as to whether further discipline can be introduced to police technical barriers that arise despite the best efforts of international standardizing bodies. Existing and proposed efforts in this regard are the subject of the sections to follow.

Technical Barriers and the GATT System

GATT began as an effort among Western nations to reduce the high trade barriers that had been erected in the 1930s.[12] GATT negotiators focused their efforts on the lowering of tariffs, which were the primary method of protection in most nations. But they realized that negotiated tariff reductions would amount to little if nations could then substitute alternative trade restrictions. Hence much of the original GATT agreement is devoted to constraints on the ability of signatories to erect nontariff barriers.

Technical barriers were not addressed separately in the original agreement but were treated in conjunction with other nontariff barriers and subjected to the same restrictions and exceptions. As the perceived importance of the technical barrier problem increased with time, initiatives to introduce further discipline resulted in an Agreement on Technical Barriers to Trade during the Tokyo Round of GATT negotiations, commonly known as the GATT "Standards Code," to which at least thirty-eight nations have acceded.[13] Perceived deficiencies and omissions in the code led to further negotiations regarding technical barriers during the Uruguay Round, resulting in a new agreement on technical barriers as well as an agreement on sanitary and phytosanitary measures (SPMs) (relating mainly to trade in food). These new agreements broaden GATT discipline considerably and are part of the Uruguay Round package to which all GATT members accede. When

12. On the history of GATT generally, see Jackson (1969); Dam (1970).
13. GATT, "Committee on Technical Barriers to Trade," Basic Instruments and Selected Documents (BISD), 38S (July 1992, p. 102).

coupled with improvements in GATT dispute resolution, they have the *potential* to contribute substantially to a reduction of technical barriers. It remains to be seen how diligently nations comply with the new agreements, however, and even with a high degree of compliance, we may anticipate that many technical barrier problems will remain.

The inability of the GATT system to cope with all manner of undesirable technical barriers comes as no surprise. Despite the nearly fifty-year history of GATT, many tariffs and nontariff barriers survive in the trading system, and only some of them came under attack during the Uruguay Round. The reason, put simply, is that GATT does not exist to maximize global economic welfare but to promote the political interests, variously defined, of the officials that induce their nations to accede and to remain a party.[14] This general perspective on the GATT system suggests an interesting perspective on the technical barrier problem in particular. When the GATT system fails to address or solve a particular class of technical barrier problems, at least a weak inference arises that such technical barriers are "politically efficient." In other words, a weak inference arises that there are no political "gains from trade" to an agreement to eliminate such barriers, even with the possibility of side payments in the form of reciprocal concessions on other matters. It is interesting to inquire why this might be so and to inquire further whether there is any systematic relationship between the technical barriers that are politically expedient to retain and those that are economically valuable to retain.

The legal obligations of GATT in this area are many and complex, and this section will not undertake to provide a complete discussion of them. It instead focuses on those that seem most important and further indicates when GATT obligations seem weak or incomplete, both historically and at present.

Technical Barriers under the Original GATT Agreement

The Uruguay Round, which created "GATT 1994," incorporates the original GATT agreement of 1947.[15] The proper starting point for

---

14. This view is developed in many places including Baldwin (1988); Sykes (1991); Yarbrough and Yarbrough (1992).

15. See GATT 1994, para. 1(a).

an analysis of GATT obligations today, therefore, is an examination of the 1947 accord.

Consider first the question of who is bound by GATT obligations. One of the recurring concerns in the GATT system has been the ability of GATT to address technical barriers created by private standardizers or by subsidiary governments—states, municipalities, provinces, and so on. Because the signatories to GATT are national governments, GATT does not directly restrict private sector activities and does not apply directly to the activities of subsidiary governments within each country. Yet in many nations, the central government has the power to force both private actors and subsidiary governments to comply with GATT rules. A much debated issue over the history of GATT is the extent to which central governments must exercise that power.[16]

In the United States, for example, the Congress has the ability under article I, section 8 of the Constitution to regulate interstate and foreign commerce, and the supremacy clause of article VI, paragraph 2, ensures that federal legislation shall displace inconsistent state legislation. It is thus clear that the U.S. federal government can, if it wishes, eliminate state and local laws and regulations in tension with GATT, as well as enact laws to restrain the behavior of private entities engaged in interstate commerce. But the original GATT accord said nothing about forcing private entities to obey GATT principles, and as to subsidiary governments, it merely required "reasonable measures" to promote compliance.[17] The extent of this obligation proved controversial, and the United States generally took the position that this clause did not compel the elimination of inconsistent state laws by the federal government.[18] Thus, the original GATT generally had no impact on private entities, and the degree to which it could reach

---

16. See Jackson (1969, pp. 110–17).

17. GATT, article XXIV(12) in "The General Agreement on Tariffs and Trade," BISD, 4 (March 1969, pp. 1–78).

18. Interestingly, even if central governments do not force subsidiary governments into compliance with GATT, private lawsuits in some countries may invoke GATT to strike down inconsistent laws and regulations by subsidiary governments. In the United States, the legal argument is that GATT has the force of a treaty and that a treaty has the same status as a federal statute—the "supreme law of the land" under article VI of the Constitution. Thus, invoking the supremacy clause, GATT has been used on occasion to invalidate inconsistent state laws. See *Hawaii* v. *Ho*, 41 Hawaii 565 (1957); *Baldwin-Lima-Hamilton Corp.* v. *Superior Court*, 208 Cal. App. 2d 803, 25 Cal. Rptr. 798 (1st Dist. Ct. App. 1962).

technical barriers erected by subsidiary governments was always unclear. More is said about these matters below.

Consider now the substantive obligations of the original accord on national governments. Government *regulations* that prohibit or restrict the importation of foreign products that do not meet a compatibility or quality requirement, and that do not apply to like domestic products, can be characterized as a "quantitative restriction" in GATT parlance.[19] A law that prohibits the importation of "low-quality widgets," for example, is equivalent to a zero quota on low-quality widgets. Article XI introduces a general prohibition on such quantitative restrictions, subject to exceptions discussed below. Thus any mandatory compatibility or quality measure applicable only to imports is inconsistent with GATT unless an exception applies.

Usually, however, government standards and regulations apply to domestic as well as imported products. Such measures would ordinarily not be regarded as quantitative restrictions on imports, but as "internal regulations" that are governed by a different set of obligations.[20] Article III, the "national treatment" article, provides in paragraph 4 that "the products . . . of any contracting party . . . shall be accorded treatment no less favourable than that accorded to like products of national origin in respect of all laws, regulations and requirements affecting their internal sale, offering for sale, purchase, transportation, distribution or use." Product regulations are plainly within this language, and governmentally promulgated standards might be argued to fall within it as well (as a "requirement affecting internal sale"). Thus the national treatment obligation is applicable at least to regulations and precludes the application of more stringent requirements to imported goods than to domestic goods. A law requiring imports to meet more burdensome labeling requirements than domestic products, for example, or requiring imports to undergo a greater number of safety tests would run afoul of the national treatment principle. Article I, the "most favored nation" article, cross-

---

19. The text of the original GATT agreement is widely reprinted and may be found in "The General Agreement on Tariffs and Trade," BISD, 4 (March 1969, pp. 1–78).

20. The recent "tuna-dolphin" dispute suggests, however, that a regulation of the process by which a good is produced or manufactured, as distinguished from a regulation of end-product characteristics, is not within article III and may instead be treated as a quantitative restriction under article XI. See "United States—Restrictions on Imports of Tuna from Mexico," BISD, 39S (1993, p. 155).

references paragraph 4 of article III and makes clear that internal regulations must be applied on a most favored nation basis as well.[21]

Certain exceptions exist that somewhat weaken these obligations. The article XI prohibition on quantitative restrictions does not apply to "import . . . prohibitions or restrictions necessary to the application of standards or regulations for the classification, grading or marketing of commodities in international trade."[22] Little is available on the precise meaning of this clause, and it has not received much attention through the years. Likewise, the national treatment obligation of article III does not apply to government procurement (though the plurilateral Government Procurement Agreement has changed matters somewhat).

Some extremely important exceptions are contained in article XX. Article XX(b) exempts from the article XI ban on quantitative restrictions and from the article III national treatment obligation measures "necessary to protect human, animal or plant life or health." Article XX(d) similarly exempts measures "necessary to . . . the prevention of deceptive practices." At first blush, therefore, article XX opens the door to all manner of quantitative restrictions and discriminatory internal regulations in the name of public health and safety, animal or plant life protection, and the protection of consumers against misleading labeling or other sources of confusion over product characteristics.[23]

But, in fact, the scope of the article XX exceptions is more restricted. Its preamble states that measures under article XX shall not constitute a means of "arbitrary or unjustifiable discrimination between countries" or "a disguised restriction on international trade." Thus article XX introduces what might be characterized as a "sham principle," barring the use of its exceptions disingenuously. The difficulty with the sham principle is that it requires a complaining party to demonstrate that the true intention of the other party was to restrict trade rather than to promote a legitimate domestic objective, a showing that will not be easy. Further, even when a dispute resolution

---

21. This requirement is logically redundant in the sense that if all imports receive national treatment, they will also be receiving most favored nation treatment.

22. GATT, article XI(2)(b).

23. The tuna-dolphin case, however, suggests that the article XX(b) exception does not apply when the importing government claims to be protecting human, animal, or plant life outside its jurisdiction.

panel suspects sham, it will be reluctant to reach such a finding because of its diplomatic awkwardness. Not surprisingly, therefore, I have not been able to locate a GATT panel decision in which the sham principle was invoked as the basis for a ruling in favor of the complaining party.

A more important constraint on the use of article XX exceptions has evolved through narrow construction of the word *necessary* when it appears in that article. In the course of a recent dispute between Thailand and the United States concerning restrictions on imports of cigarettes, for example, Thailand sought to invoke article XX(b) to argue that an effective ban on the importation of cigarettes was permissible as a public health measure. Noting that Thailand had done nothing to restrict the production and marketing of domestically produced cigarettes, a GATT panel concluded that the import restrictions were not "necessary" to the protection of public health. Instead, the panel concluded, Thailand could achieve the same public health benefits through measures consistent with article XI and article III, such as a ban on cigarette advertising by all manufacturers or a hefty excise tax on all cigarettes.[24] In effect, the panel construed *necessary* to preclude recourse to Article XX if "less-restrictive means" exist to achieve the stated public policy objective. Hence the original GATT agreement goes far toward imposing legal restrictions on the most obvious methods through which product regulations can be used by national governments to create trade barriers. Regulations applicable only to imports or facially more burdensome for imports than for domestic goods must be justified by genuine health and safety or consumer protection objectives, and there must exist no alternative regulatory policy more consistent with GATT that would achieve the same objectives.

Still, important gaps exist in these obligations. The absence of clear reference to standards and conformity assessment measures means that nations have an argument to the effect that only substantive regulations are affected. Nothing is said as well about the process by which standards and regulations are promulgated, so that the original accord does not require nations to give advance notice of them or to

---

24. GATT, "Thailand: Restrictions on Importation of and Internal Taxes on Cigarettes: Report of the Panel Adopted on November 7, 1990," BISD, 37S (July 1991, pp. 222–26).

allow interested foreign parties any opportunity to express their views. Exporters may thus be taken by surprise when new regulations are promulgated. Finally, there are virtually no constraints whatsoever on standards, regulations, and conformity assessment procedures that accord with the national treatment obligation. When such measures are promulgated unabashedly for the purpose of disadvantaging imports, they fall under another "sham principle" contained in article III, paragraph 1. But that paragraph standing alone may be merely hortatory and, in any case, the difficulty with efforts to enforce sham principles has already been noted—in most cases, governments can offer a colorable public policy justification that will be difficult for a dispute resolution panel to reject. As a practical matter, therefore, the original GATT agreement has little to say about measures that arguably promote some legitimate public policy objective and do not discriminate against imports on their face, yet are highly burdensome to foreign suppliers.

A further concern with the original GATT accord before the Uruguay Round was the absence of a fully effective dispute resolution mechanism. Although GATT provides under article XXIII for a complaint procedure whenever a signatory has been denied the benefits of the agreement and further provides that the signatories acting collectively may authorize sanctions for recalcitrance, GATT practice before the Uruguay Round effectively required "consensus" before any violation of the agreement could be found. It even required consensus before a formal investigation of a complaint could be undertaken. The disputant "in the wrong" could block consensus and effectively preclude any investigation or sanctions. Hence the incentives for signatories to comply with their GATT obligations depended far more on the explicit or implicit threat of unilateral retaliation by parties aggrieved by a violation and on the existence of reputational penalties to flaunting the rules than on the prospect of any formal sanction.[25] Although the combination of concern for reputation and fear of retaliation has sufficed to induce signatories to comply with perhaps the bulk of their GATT obligations, some slippage was observed when the political stakes were high enough.

---

25. See Sykes (1992); Jackson (1990, pp. 56–80).

Tokyo Round Standards Code: Legal Structure

The weaknesses and limitations in the original GATT accord led to an initiative during the Tokyo Round of the 1970s to develop new obligations regarding technical barriers, culminating in an agreement known as the Standards Code. The Standards Code, like the other Tokyo Round codes, was a "side agreement" to which only a subset of GATT members subscribed. But its signatories did include most of the major trading nations (Canada, the European Community, Japan, the United States, Hong Kong, Korea, Singapore—Australia was a notable exception), and hence much of world trade was subject to its provisions.[26] It represented a significant advance over the obligations in GATT itself.[27]

First, the code applied to standards as well as regulations (using those terms as I have used them). It defined a *standard* as a technical specification with which compliance is voluntary and a *regulation* as a technical specification with which compliance is mandatory. A "technical specification," in turn, "lays down characteristics of a product such as levels of quality, performance, safety or dimensions."[28] Note the reference to *product characteristics* and the absence of reference to production methods—thus production and process standards were generally exempted. With respect to the standards and regulations within the code, it reiterated the most favored nation obligation and the national treatment obligations for central governments and further provided that central governments should not adopt standards or regulations "with a view to creating obstacles to international trade" or with "the effect of creating unnecessary obstacles to international trade."[29] These statements tracked the sham principle and the least-restrictive means principle of articles III and XX. They went beyond the original GATT, however, because they extended the least-restrictive means concept to measures that were consistent with the national treatment obligation. Likewise, there was no exception in the code to the national treatment obligation for measures to protect health and

26. A list of signatories may be found in "Committee on Technical Barriers to Trade," BISD, 37S (July 1991, pp. 317–18).

27. Like GATT, the Tokyo Round Standards Code is widely reprinted. It may be found in "Agreement to Technical Barriers to Trade," BISD, 26S (March 1980, pp. 8–32).

28. Tokyo Round Standards Code, Annex I contains the definitions.

29. Tokyo Round Standards Code, article 2.1.

safety or to prevent deceptive practices—it was thus unnecessary to invoke the least-restrictive means principle to argue that departures from national treatment were not "necessary."

The code further embodied a requirement that signatories use performance requirements rather than design requirements in the promulgation of both standards and regulations "wherever appropriate."[30] This principle is obviously a corollary of the least-restrictive means principle, but the drafters of the code viewed the matter as sufficiently important to warrant separate inclusion.

Another important initiative in the code, related again to the least-restrictive means concept, was an effort at international harmonization through appeal to international standards. It provided that signatories "shall" incorporate pertinent international standards into national standards and regulations "except where, as duly explained upon request, such international standards or relevant parts are inappropriate." A nonexhaustive list of reasons why international standards might be inappropriate included "the prevention of deceptive practices," "protection for human health or safety, animal or plant life or health," and "fundamental technological problems."[31] In short, the code encouraged but did not require resorting to pertinent international standards when they exist but did require nations to justify their decision to depart from them on request. There was thus some potential cost to a decision to disregard international standards, albeit perhaps a modest one. Another important limitation on this obligation is that while it clearly applied prospectively, it did not clearly require that existing standards and regulations be modified.

Other provisions of the code aimed at reducing the disruptive effects of changes in standards and regulations through advance notice. When new standards or regulations departed from extant international standards or when international standards did not exist *and* when the new measure "may have a significant effect on trade of other Parties," signatories were required to go through a notice-and-comment period before the standard or regulation takes effect. Advance notice of the proposed measure was to be given to the GATT secretariat, and interested parties were to be given a reasonable time

---

30. Tokyo Round Standards Code, article 2.4.
31. Tokyo Round Standards Code, article 2.2.

to comment.[32] The enactment of new measures was to be published "promptly," and for regulations there was to be a reasonable period of time between publication and entry into force to allow producers abroad "to adapt their products or methods of production."[33] Exceptions existed for measures that were urgent because of health, safety, national security, and environmental concerns.

Later sections of the code addressed the conformity assessment process. They distinguished "determinations of conformity" from "certifications," the latter apparently understood as a process through which a formal certificate or seal of approval was obtained for a product and the former encompassing all other testing requirements. Both conformity determination and certification when carried out by central governments were to be in accordance with national treatment and most favored nation principles.[34] Testing of imported products was to be "no more complex and no less expeditious" than for domestic goods.[35] The sham and least-restrictive means principles were extended to certification systems.[36] Fees for any conformity assessment of imports were to be "equitable" in relation to those charged for assessments of domestically produced goods.[37] The evident intention here was to allow higher fees if justified by higher costs, but not otherwise. Finally, "whenever possible," central government bodies were to "accept test results, certificates or marks of conformity issued by relevant bodies in the territories of other Parties; or rely upon self-certification by producers in the territories of other Parties . . . provided they are satisfied that the methods employed in the territory of the exporting Party provide a sufficient means for determining conformity."[38] The code thus encouraged the acceptance of foreign test data and self-certifications but did not, in any meaningful sense, require them.

Other provisions of the code required signatories to maintain information clearinghouses for standards-related inquiries, which have the effect of reducing the transaction costs of obtaining information

32. Tokyo Round Standards Code, article 2.5.
33. Tokyo Round Standards Code, articles 2.7–2.8.
34. Tokyo Round Standards Code, articles 5.1.1 and 7.2.
35. Tokyo Round Standards Code, article 5.1.2.
36. Tokyo Round Standards Code, article 7.1.
37. Tokyo Round Standards Code, article 5.1.3.
38. Tokyo Round Standards Code, article 5.2.

about standards in export markets.[39] It also contained an acknowledgment of special difficulties that developing countries might have in complying with the code and encouraged assistance to developing countries for the establishment of standards.[40]

Lastly, the code contained special provisions for dispute settlement. It provided for initial consultations between disputants, for the establishment of technical expert groups to advise on matters of scientific or engineering controversy, and for legal panels to assess the merits of complaints when consultations prove unsuccessful.[41] The Technical Barriers Committee oversaw the operation of the code and had the power to authorize sanctions in the form of a suspension of the obligations under the agreement owed by one party to another.[42] The voting rule for the committee was unspecified, however, and in practice the consensus principle applied. Thus the code reflected the same difficulties with dispute resolution as the original GATT agreement.

Contrasting the obligations under the code to those in place before it, the code made important advances in solidifying the national treatment obligation against erosion by "exceptions," it extended the reach of the least-restrictive means principle, it contained new obligations regarding notice and comment before the promulgation of standards and regulations, and it made clear that the national treatment requirement applied to standards and conformity assessment procedures as well as to substantive regulations. Other provisions addressed important matters such as the use of existing international standards, the choice between performance and design regulations, and the acceptance of foreign test data but limited obligations on these matters to "appropriate" circumstances.

It is also important to note what the code did *not* attempt to do. Like the original GATT, it did not require signatories to force private standardization to conform to the principles of the code. Also like the original GATT, its language did not clearly require central governments to force subsidiary governments to comply. Rather it too required signatories to take "such reasonable measures as may be available to them" to bring these other entities into compliance. Not

39. Tokyo Round Standards Code, article 10.
40. Tokyo Round Standards Code, articles 11–12.
41. Tokyo Round Standards Code, article 14.
42. Tokyo Round Standards Code, article 14.21.

surprisingly, this language was again interpreted as requiring no affirmative measures to force subsidiary governments into compliance.[43]

Recall as well the definition of *technical specification* given at the outset of this section, which referred to specifications regarding the "characteristics of a product." As noted, if a standard or regulation was drafted with reference to the method of production rather than with reference to properties of the end product, it fell outside the scope of this language and, thus at first blush, outside the scope of the code. This "loophole" to code obligations potentially vitiated much of what the code might accomplish, as nations can, in many cases, create a technical barrier with a production or process standard just as easily as with a product standard (indeed, the line between the two is often hazy).[44] The loophole may not have been as large as it seems, however, because article 14 provides that rights under the code would be impaired when "obligations under this Agreement are being circumvented by the drafting of requirements in terms of processes and production methods rather than in terms of characteristics of products."[45] But the proper construction of this proviso was unclear at best. If production standards were deliberately exempted from the coverage of the code, who was to say when their use was "circumvention" rather than a legitimate decision to use a less-constrained policy instrument?

Finally, the code did not eliminate problems with dispute resolution. The opportunity to impanel technical expert groups was potentially useful for improving the soundness of decisions, but the consensus rule still ensured that obstinate disputants could block the process from going forward at any point. The strategy of the European Community to block dispute resolution in the growth-hormone dis-

---

43. Thus the U.S. implementing legislation pursuant to the code provided that "it is the sense of the Congress" that state agencies and private persons should not engage in standards-related activity that creates unnecessary barriers to trade, and the President is directed to take "reasonable measures" to promote adherence to the requirements imposed on the federal government by the code. 19 U.S.C. § 2533. No action of any sort was required by the statute, therefore, and indeed the President's power to bring private entities and state governments into compliance was limited in the absence of specific legislation granting specific powers in this area.

44. Consider a law that prohibits the marketing of beef from any nation in which foot-and-mouth disease is present in cattle. Is that a product regulation or a production regulation?

45. Tokyo Round Standards Code, article 14.25.

pute with the United States illustrates how the consensus principle could cause the process to grind to a halt.[46]

Experience under the Tokyo Round Code

Little systematic information is available to aid in an evaluation of how well the code operated. Annual reports of the Committee on Technical Barriers, the only regular report on this point that is publicly available from GATT, were often only a couple of pages long and gave little detail. The facts of disputes that progressed to the point of formal dispute resolution are sketchy (even the identities of disputants are typically not reported), and there is no indication of the number of disputes that may have arisen and been resolved informally through consultations.[47]

The hard information that is available in the report tends to be of little use. As noted, for example, signatories must notify the secretariat when new standards and regulations may not incorporate existing international standards, and the report does indicate the number of new notifications each year. For the first several years of the code's operation, such notifications were received at an average rate of about 200 a year and seemed to be rising over time—they exceeded 350 in 1991.[48] Yet these data alone give little indication of how seriously the notification process has been taken, as there may well have been many standards that should have been notified but were not. Further, the data provide no indication of the number of instances in which international standards were used in national standards and regulations, as notification was unnecessary in such cases, and they provide no evidence of the extent to which pre-existing standards and regulations incorporated international standards.

Bits of anecdotal evidence do indicate, however, that the code had some important positive consequences. For example, nations clearly made some efforts to comply with the notice and transparency re-

46. See Hammonds (1990).
47. For a few illustrative examples of the Annual Report, see "Report (1981) of the Committee on Technical Barriers to Trade," BISD, 28S (March 1982, pp. 34–36); "Bodies Established under the 1979 MTN Agreements and Arrangements," BISD, 33S (June 1987, pp. 186–88); and "Committee on Technical Barriers to Trade," BISD, 38S (July 1992, pp. 102–03).
48. See the discussion in Nusbaumer (1984). Overman (1992, p. 2).

quirements of the code and to provide central clearinghouses for standards information.[49] The code also resulted in improved access by foreign interests to national and regional standardization bodies. The International Commission for Conformity Assessment of Electrical Equipment, for example, previously open only to European members, is now open to all nations as a result of the code.[50]

Also a few disputes have received considerable publicity, and press accounts afford some insight into the successes and failures of the code. The Japanese ski standards dispute, for example, first described in chapter 2, involved a new safety standard for downhill skis that departed from an existing ISO standard. The essence of the case involved a failure to use international standards as encouraged by article 2.2, and after extensive pressure from the European Community during the "consultations" phase of dispute resolution under the code, the Japanese retracted the standard.[51] Similarly positive results were obtained in the dispute between the United States and Japan over standards for metal baseball bats that closed the Japanese markets to U.S. exports. In this instance, the difficulty was with access to the certification process, raising questions of national treatment under article 7.2.[52]

A notable failure under the code, although progress has been made toward a final settlement as noted in chapter 2, is the dispute between the United States and Europe over the ban on imports of meat from nations that permit the use of growth hormones. It is not terribly surprising that the code should fail to resolve the dispute satisfactorily in a case such as this one, as the essence of the dispute goes to matters on which the code is weak. The directive could be characterized as a production regulation outside the coverage of the code, for example, and in any case, there was no denial of national treatment. The United States was thus placed in the position of arguing that the directive violated the sham principle (not terribly plausible in view of the public health history with hormone-treated beef in the Community) or that it was an "unnecessary obstacle to trade" on the grounds that

---

49. U.S. efforts in this regard are documented in Overman (1992).

50. Nusbaumer (1984, p. 546).

51. "Japan and EC Settle Ski Safe Goods Standard Issue," *Japan Economic Newswire,* December 11, 1986.

52. The history of this dispute and its settlement is nicely laid out in Coccodrilli (1984, pp. 148–56).

scientific support for the health threat was lacking.[53] The United States opted for the latter strategy and sought the appointment of a technical expert group, but the Community blocked the action, apparently unwilling to take the risk that its regulators might be told that they cannot appreciate and weigh scientific evidence properly.

From such limited information about the operation of the code, one must be cautious in drawing inferences about its strengths and weaknesses. Tentatively, however, it seems that the code was capable of addressing certain kinds of technical barrier problems effectively *if a nation determined to pursue formal dispute resolution.* Even weakly worded obligations, such as the obligation to use international standards except when "inappropriate," seemed to have some bite, at least when nations lacked a persuasive argument as to why circumstances were inappropriate for following them (in justification of their ill-fated safety standards for downhill skis, for example, the Japanese claimed that the snow in Japan was different).[54] But when there was no departure from international standards (or they did not exist) and no denial of national treatment, it seems that efforts to condemn standards or regulations as "unnecessary" on grounds of scientific or other doubts about the expert judgment under scrutiny were met with considerable resistance as an affront to sovereignty or integrity (the beef hormone case). Likewise, it is difficult to say how well or poorly the code performed in encouraging nations to avoid the creation of technical barriers in cases that lacked political visibility. What we know of its history is consistent with the hypothesis that code obligations are important only when a technical barrier is sufficiently troublesome that governments are induced to threaten formal GATT action—the day-to-day process of adopting new standards and regulations, in most cases, may not have been affected much.

Uruguay Round Agreements

Because agricultural issues were so contentious during the Uruguay Round and the subject of separate negotiations, technical barrier

---

53. See Meng (1990); Hammonds (1990); Froman (1989).

54. See Carla Rappoport, "Japanese Ski Makers Freeze Out the Competition," *Financial Times,* September 4, 1986, Section 1, p. 1.

issues relating closely to agriculture were also negotiated separately. The result was a freestanding agreement on the application of SPMs in the agricultural sector, with the remaining technical barrier issues covered by the new Agreement on Technical Barriers to Trade (TBT), which supersedes the Tokyo Round Standards Code. These agreements are referred to as the SPM and TBT agreements, respectively. Both are included in an appendix to this volume.

The TBT Agreement retains the Standards Code obligations described above but refines or adds to them in several important respects. It now defines both standards and regulations to include "processes and production methods," thus extending the reach of the obligations under the agreement to matters excluded from the Standards Code and closing one of the most important loopholes left by the Tokyo Round.

With particular regard to regulations, the agreement reiterates the familiar most favored nation, national treatment, and sham principles, as well as the requirement to use performance standards "wherever appropriate."[55] It also retains the notice-and-comment system applicable when international standards do not exist or a proposed regulation or standard would depart from international standards. Regarding the use of international standards by national governments, the obligation is reworded slightly to require their use except when they would be an "ineffective or inappropriate means for the fulfillment of the legitimate objectives pursued."[56] Further, the text makes clear that the obligation to use international standards extends to pre-existing regulations, not just new ones—a signatory may ask another signatory to justify any regulation that it is "preparing, adopting *or applying*" (emphasis added), and such justification must include an explanation for a decision not to use international standards.[57]

The least-restrictive means principle is expressly included as before, but an effort is made for the first time to articulate principles for assessing whether a regulation has become an unnecessary barrier to trade. The proposal here amounts to a limited kind of balancing test,

55. All these obligations for central governments are found in the GATT TBT Agreement, article 2.

56. GATT TBT Agreement, article 2.4.

57. GATT TBT Agreement, article 2.5.

whereby "technical regulations shall not be more trade-restrictive than necessary to fulfill a legitimate objective, taking account of the risks non-fulfillment would create."[58] There is also an obligation to discard outdated or unnecessary regulations.[59] A failure to use international standards might also be found to constitute an "unnecessary obstacle" to trade.

Another interesting addition is the provision requiring signatories to "give positive consideration to accepting as equivalent technical regulations of other Members, even if those regulations differ from their own, provided they are satisfied that these regulations adequately fulfill the objectives of their own regulations."[60] In other words, parties are encouraged to afford "mutual recognition," although they remain the arbiters of whether mutual recognition will serve their domestic regulatory purpose adequately. As with other weakly stated obligations in the existing code, the likely effect of this provision would be to require signatories to justify a refusal of mutual recognition and thus to make arbitrary or anticompetitive refusals of mutual recognition more visible.

Unfortunately, the applicability of the obligations to subsidiary governments remains somewhat muddled. The "reasonable measures" language has been retained, and we may anticipate continued insistence by national governments that they need not do everything in their power to force subsidiary governments to adhere. For its part, the United States has taken the position that the Uruguay Round agreements do not displace inconsistent state or local laws except in an action brought by the federal government.[61]

An interesting change that may affect both private entities and subsidiary governments, however, is the Code of Good Practice for the Preparation, Adoption and Application of Standards. All standardizing bodies—international, regional, national, and local, whether public or private—are invited to accede to it, and central government standardization efforts are required to obey its principles.[62] Substantively, it embodies much the same obligations as

58. GATT TBT Agreement, article 2.2.

59. GATT TBT Agreement, article 2.3.

60. GATT TBT Agreement, article 2.7.

61. Uruguay Round Agreements Act, section 102(b), reprinted in *Congressional Record*, September 27, 1994, p. S13454.

62. GATT TBT Agreement, article 4.

those applicable to technical regulations—the most favored nation, national treatment, sham, and least-restrictive means principles, and the preferences for international standards and performance standards.[63] It also contains notice-and-comment provisions, requiring attention to comments from parties abroad, an explanation for any deviation from international standards, and a reply to any comment received if requested by the author of the comment. Finally, the code encourages members to avoid duplicative standardization measures and to harmonize standards within nations.

If the Code of Good Practice gains widespread adherence, it has the potential to affect standardization activities by private and local government entities significantly. Its provisions would, at a minimum, improve the transparency of standardization and allow interested firms to obtain systematic advance notice of new standards. Further, it can make deviations from international standards more evident and more costly politically and likewise increase the political visibility and costs of decisions that disadvantage foreign suppliers. Especially when technical barriers result not from calculated efforts to create them but from arbitrary or ill-considered decisions taken in the absence of any attention to their international consequences, the opportunities for broader input into the standardization process could reduce the incidence of such decisions. But there is no intimation that accession to the Code of Good Practice will create any legal rights of action against a standardizing body that does not live up to its obligations (other than a central government). Hence a question arises as to whether organizations that accede to the code will really take its obligations seriously. Also little will be accomplished unless foreign entities potentially affected by new standards take advantage of the notice system to review draft standards with some care and comment on them before they become final. Much of what the Code of Good Practice is designed to accomplish requires not only the opening of national standardization processes to foreign scrutiny, therefore, but a willingness of foreign interests to incur the costs of participating in them. Given the volume of standardization activity around the world, these costs can be considerable.

With regard to conformity assessment procedures, the TBT Agreement abolishes the Tokyo Round distinction between conformity

---

63. "Code of Good Practice for the Preparation, Adoption, and Application of Standards," contained in annex 3 of the GATT TBT Agreement.

determination and certification in favor of a single set of obligations applicable to both. These obligations track closely those applicable to technical regulations. Again, the most favored nation, national treatment, sham, and least-restrictive means principles are included, as is the requirement that fees be "equitable" in relation to those imposed on domestic producers.[64] The agreement adds an obligation to use conformity assessment procedures developed by international standardizing bodies, if they exist, unless such procedures are "inappropriate," with an explanation for any deviation to be provided on request.[65] The agreement also adds some obligations regarding publication of conformity assessment procedures and a notice-and-comment period for the adoption of new conformity assessment procedures that may have "a significant effect on trade."[66] The provisions in the Standards Code encouraging mutual recognition of conformity assessment procedures are elaborated somewhat, although still qualified by the proviso that each party may determine whether the procedures used by other signatories are adequate. Further, signatories are "encouraged" to pursue negotiations toward agreements "for the mutual recognition of [test] results."[67] These provisions do not appear to include any striking innovations, but the extension to conformity assessment of obligations previously applicable only to the creation of standards and regulations could prove important, as might the increased encouragement of mutual recognition.

A final change in the TBT Agreement is the exclusion of SPMs.[68] As before, the TBT Agreement would apply both to agricultural and industrial products, but standards and regulations falling within the agreement on SPMs are to be governed exclusively by that agreement.

The SPM Agreement defines SPMs as "laws, decrees, regulations, requirements and procedures" to protect against the entry of pests, to protect human, plant or animal health against disease or the spread of disease, and to protect human or animal health against risks from additives, toxins, and contaminants in foodstuffs. They include all relevant "laws, decrees, regulations, requirements and procedures including, *inter alia*, end product criteria; processes and production

64. See generally, GATT TBT Agreement, article 5.
65. GATT TBT Agreement, article 5.4.
66. GATT TBT Agreement, articles 5.2.2 and 5.6.
67. GATT TBT Agreement, article 6.3.
68. GATT TBT Agreement, article 1.5.

methods; testing, inspection certification and approval procedures; quarantine treatments; . . . and packaging and labeling requirements directly related to food safety."[69] As in the TBT Agreement, therefore, processing and production regulations are covered. The definition is somewhat unclear as to whether voluntary "standards" are covered, although the focus is plainly on mandatory measures.

The substantive obligations in the SPM Agreement relate closely to those in the TBT Agreement, but differ in some significant respects. The sham principle is included, whereas the most favored nation and national treatment obligations are expressed as an obligation not to discriminate "arbitrarily or unjustifiably" between territories where "identical or similar conditions prevail."[70] The reference to "similar conditions" suggests the possibility that nominally nondiscriminatory measures might, in fact, be impermissible—a measure banning meat imports from a nation that has had an outbreak of foot-and-mouth disease within the past five years, for example, might be attacked on the grounds that nations free of the disease for four years are "similar" to those free of it for five. The least-restrictive means principle appears more than once, with the provision that measures be applied only to the extent "necessary" to achieve their goal, and in the requirement that measures be "not more trade-restrictive than required."[71] An additional and potentially quite important requirement is that measures not be maintained "without sufficient scientific evidence" except when scientific evidence is lacking and a party wishes to apply a provisional measure while undertaking scientific investigation.[72] These principles are elaborated at considerable length in a series of paragraphs that require signatories to look carefully at the available scientific evidence, to take into account the negative trade effects of proposed measures and the "cost-effectiveness" of alternatives, and so on.[73]

The agreement also encourages harmonization of SPMs by urging the use of international standards when they exist, by encouraging signatories to participate in the work of international standards organizations, and by establishing formal liaison between the SPM Com-

69. See GATT SPM Agreement, annex A, para. 1.
70. GATT SPM Agreement, article 2(3).
71. GATT SPM Agreement, articles 2(2) and 5(6).
72. GATT SPM Agreement, articles 2(2) and 5(7).
73. GATT SPM Agreement, article 5(3).

mittee of GATT and the Codex Alimentarius, the International Office of Epizootics, and the Secretariat of the International Plant Protection Convention.[74] Like the TBT Agreement, however, the SPM Agreement leaves considerable latitude to signatories to set more stringent standards than those established internationally "if there is a scientific justification" or if a careful balancing of all the effects of more stringent measures results in the conclusion that they are advisable.[75] Also like the TBT Agreement, the SPM Agreement makes clear that the obligation to use international standards applies to existing as well as prospective measures.[76]

The agreement also includes strong encouragement for mutual recognition. Importing signatories "shall" accept the measures of an exporting signatory as equivalent, "if the exporting Member objectively demonstrates to the importing Member that its measures achieve the importing contracting Member's appropriate level of . . . protection."[77]

Later sections of the agreement import most of the procedural requirements of the TBT Agreement, requiring prompt publication of new regulations, a central clearinghouse for information, and a notice-and-comment period for new regulations that may have a "significant" effect on trade and that are not substantially the same as an existing international standard.[78] Regarding the actions of subsidiary governments, the draft perhaps goes beyond the old code in requiring "positive measures" to promote the observance of the agreement by subsidiary governments, although as to private bodies, the requirement remains "reasonable measures."[79] Finally, as to conformity assessment procedures, the familiar TBT Agreement principles are incorporated—most favored nation and national treatment, equitable fees, and so forth.[80]

In summary, the SPM Agreement has the first-order effect of extending the central principles of the TBT Agreement to SPMs. Its

---

74. GATT SPM Agreement, articles 3, 3(4), and 12(3).

75. GATT SPM Agreement, article 3(3).

76. GATT SPM Agreement, article 3(3), establishes conditions under which members may "introduce or maintain" measures more strict than the relevant international standards.

77. GATT SPM Agreement, article 4(1).

78. See GATT SPM Agreement, annex B.

79. GATT SPM Agreement, article 13.

80. GATT SPM Agreement, annex C.

substantive obligations do not go much beyond those of the TBT Agreement and in some respects fall short of it, but the draft does make an interesting effort to articulate at some length the importance of looking carefully at scientific evidence, of balancing negative trade effects against the putative benefits of regulation, and of affording other signatories the chance to "objectively demonstrate" the equivalence of their own SPMs.[81] It will be interesting to see to what extent these last provisions have impact. At a minimum, they open the door to complaints about the soundness of the regulatory processes of signatories, which would presumably be defended by an explication of the evidence and reasoning processes that go into them. Even if dispute resolution panels remain reluctant to denounce national regulatory decisions as sham or scientifically insupportable, this prospect of having the national regulatory process go "on trial" before a GATT panel can raise significantly the political costs of regulations that have little scientific support or minimal health benefit.

One other result of the Uruguay Round warrants mention. The signatories concluded a new Understanding on Rules and Procedures Governing the Settlement of Disputes (Dispute Agreement) within GATT generally, which applies to all matters that arise under the TBT and SPM agreements in particular. Without going into great detail, the Dispute Agreement allows complainants to obtain a dispute resolution panel essentially as a matter of right, as well as appellate review.[82] It provides that panel reports will be adopted as definitive by the signatories unless they decide not to do so by consensus or the report is appealed, provides that appellate reports will be adopted as definitive by the signatories unless they decide not to do so by consensus, and provides for sanctions if a signatory does not abide by dispute resolution findings.[83] The authority for sanctions can no longer be blocked by the losing disputant.[84]

Because of these provisions, the prospects for definitive legal interpretations of controversial or ambiguously worded GATT obligations are greatly enhanced. Of particular relevance here is the possibility

81. For some discussion of the genesis of the various provisions and the initial negotiating position taken by various subgroups within GATT, see Bredahl and Forsythe (1989).

82. GATT Dispute Agreement, articles 6.1 and 17, published in GATT Secretariat (1994).

83. GATT Dispute Agreement, articles 16 and 17.14.

84. See GATT Dispute Agreement, article 22.6.

that panels may begin to second guess national authorities on the question whether the use of international standards is "appropriate," for example, or whether an SPM is against the weight of scientific evidence. Likewise, the political costs of recalcitrance will be increased, and perhaps the economic costs as well as the prospect of GATT-authorized trade sanctions becomes a reality. The long-term significance of GATT obligations in the technical barrier area, therefore, may well be enhanced considerably by these innovations in the dispute resolution system.

Summary and Recapitulation for the GATT System

The historical evolution of the GATT system reflects steady movement toward increasing the discipline on technical barriers to trade. The progression began in the original agreement with a most favored nation obligation and a national treatment obligation qualified by exceptions and limited in scope. The Tokyo Round Standards Code moved to more unqualified most favored nation and national treatment requirements, coupled with broadened sham and least-restrictive means principles applicable even when national treatment is accorded. Standards and conformity assessment procedures were brought under discipline expressly, and much was done to encourage notice, comment, and transparency in the standardization and regulatory activities of central governments. Much was done also to encourage reliance on international standards. The Uruguay Round agreements do still more to encourage harmonization when possible under international standards and mutual recognition when it is not. They also reflect serious effort to bring private entities into the process through the Code of Good Practice on standardization, to bring many important process and production standards under discipline, and perhaps to place somewhat greater responsibility on central governments to induce compliance by their subsidiary governments.

But the GATT system can hardly be expected to eliminate technical barrier problems. The obligations of signatories to police the practices of subsidiary governments are at most limited, and it remains to be seen how effectively the Code of Good Practice will solve difficulties with private entities. The obligations respecting harmonization and mutual recognition remain, on the whole, weakly worded and thus qualified by considerable deference to national regulators who may not wish to accept them in given instances. The likely degree of movement toward mutual recognition and harmonization will thus be uncertain.

As before, measures that afford national treatment to imports will remain the hardest to attack, especially when a domestic political constituency favors an existing standard or regulation. When technical barriers result from capture or interest group manipulation of the standardization, regulatory or conformity assessment processes or when deeply held differences of opinion over appropriate risk levels or scientific controversies arise, importing nations will have ample basis in the text of GATT to resist change in their policies. In the main, GATT strategy for dealing with such cases has been and will continue to be simply to expose them to the light of day, on the premise that transparency and the attendant publicity will increase the costs of self-serving or scientifically dubious decisionmaking and thus discourage it.

Finally, it must be emphasized that the GATT system is oriented toward the creation of rules to govern intergovernmental disputes over technical barriers. Its impact on day-to-day standards and regulatory activities, which only infrequently become a source of high-level disputes, is much more unclear. This will depend on the commitment of governments and private entities to participate actively in the notification-and-comment system and to support and rely on the work of international standardization bodies, a policy that can prove costly both economically and politically.

Technical Barriers and the European Union

Efforts to reduce technical barriers to intra-European trade predate the Tokyo Round Standards Code by several years and have proceeded through several stages. Early efforts relied on policing through the Court of Justice and on sporadic harmonization directives for specific products. A "new approach" to technical barriers, designed to accelerate harmonization, was announced by the European Commission in 1985 in conjunction with the EC 92 initiatives. A "global approach" to conformity assessment was introduced a few years later.

Legislative Approach in Europe

The member states of the European Union have ceded to the European level of government a considerable measure of sovereignty, over commercial affairs especially, that enables more to be accomplished through centralized action in Europe than can possibly be accomplished in the world at large. Consequently, attention is omitted here to many features of the legislative program in Europe. Nevertheless, it is interesting to observe the limitations that remain on the powers of the central authority in Europe, as well as the manner in which the member states have agreed on mutual recognition, as some basis for inferences about what might be accomplished on a broader scale. A brief discussion of the legislative approach in Europe, particularly the "new" and "global" approaches and the mutual information directive, is thus in order.

The "New" Approach

The Treaty Establishing the European Economic Community (Treaty of Rome) authorized the European Council of Ministers, on a proposal from the European Commission, to issue directives to "approximate" (that is, harmonize) the measures of member states that "directly affect the establishment or functioning of the common market."[85] The authority for harmonization under article 100 required unanimous action by the council, a requirement subsequently amended but only after a decision had been made to adopt the "new approach" discussed below.

The "old approach" to harmonization through council initiatives involved the promulgation of detailed technical regulations,

---

85. Treaty of Rome, article 100. The Council is the primary legislative body in Europe, from which most Community legislation emanates. It consists of country representatives (ministers) that act in accordance with various voting rules, dependent on the subject matter of the action. The Commission is a group of distinguished citizens, acting in their individual capacity rather than under the direction of their home countries, charged with undertaking many of the initiatives required by the Treaty of Rome. Typically, as here, the Commission makes proposals to the Council, which then acts on them, subject at times to the requirement that it seek advice from other entities such as the European Parliament. The Parliament has relatively little power. For a general description of the governmental structure of the Community, see Steiner (1992).

product by product. Products that met the specifications could circulate freely within the Community, although member states were sometimes free to require their own producers to meet a different set of technical specifications. Many harmonization initiatives grew out of this process, affecting motor vehicles, pressure vessels, measurement instruments, and a host of other products. But the process proved cumbersome and slow. The unanimity rule no doubt played a role in this regard, as did the level of detail that was required in each directive.[86]

In the mid-1980s, the Commission and the Council embraced a "new approach" that delegated the detail work to others. The effort was facilitated by the Single European Act, which amended the Treaty of Rome to allow directives on matters of technical harmonization to be promulgated through "qualified majority" voting.[87] Under the new approach, the Council continues detailed harmonization efforts when sensible in the light of the degree of harmonization already in place or when the new approach encounters political obstacles. But otherwise, the Council limits itself to setting out the "essential requirements" that products must meet. These essential requirements are understood to encompass primarily (although not necessarily exclusively) health, safety, environmental protection, and consumer protection. The amended treaty stipulates that the level of protection for such interests should be "high."[88]

The 1989 Machinery Directive affords a nice illustration.[89] It includes some general principles of safe construction for machinery, such as to "eliminate or reduce risks as far as possible" and to "take the necessary protection measures in relation to risks

86. For discussions of harmonization by the Council under the "old" approach, see van de Walle de Ghelcke, van Gerven, and Platteau (1990, pp. 1550–52); Costello (1990).

87. See article 100a of the Treaty of Rome, added by the Single European Act. Qualified majority voting is a procedure by which the votes of member states are weighted by size, and a majority of the weighted votes is required for passage of an initiative before the Council. In effect, two large states can be outvoted by everyone else, and up to six small states can be outvoted when the large states band together. See van de Walle de Ghelcke, van Gerven, and Platteau (1990, p. 1549).

88. Treaty establishing the European Economic Community signed in Rome on March 25, 1957, article 100a.

89. "Council Directive of June 14, 1989, on the approximation of the laws of the member states relating to machinery," *Official Journal of the European Communities* L 183/9 (June 29, 1989).

that cannot be eliminated."[90] It then proceeds to a higher level of detail, discussing the need for integral lighting for certain types of machinery, the importance of readily accessible devices to stop all moving parts, the need for controls to avoid accidents due to power supply interruptions, the need for measures to ensure stability against vibration and other disturbances, the importance of eliminating sharp edges, and so on. The directive thus addresses virtually every conceivable type of product hazard and lays down general principles for avoiding it. Yet the directive applies to a vast array of machinery products. Indeed its application extends to virtually every product that, in common parlance, might be called a "machine," with a few enumerated exceptions such as "mobile equipment," "medical equipment," "steam vessels," and "firearms."

When the Council issues an essential requirements directive, member states must conform their national laws and regulations to it, subject to an "escape clause" provision to be described below. The European Court of Justice is empowered to assess whether national conformity has been achieved, and the Commission is also empowered to determine that the national measures are "equivalent" to the essential requirements. The Council has the option and frequently elects to refer the task of formulating detailed standards that meet the essential requirements to Europe-wide organizations such as Comité Européen de Normalisation (CEN), Comité Européen de Normalisation Electrotechnique (CENELEC), and European Telecommunications Standards Institute. A product that conforms to the resulting standards or that conforms to national measures deemed "equivalent" by the Commission is presumed to meet the essential requirements and is entitled to be marketed freely within the Community, again subject to an escape clause.[91] The system is thus designed to eliminate technical barriers attributable to national regulations that do not relate to the "essential requirements." And when national differences persist as to the manner of achieving the agreed-on regulatory objectives, the new approach can force mutual recognition.

90. *Official Journal of the European Communities* L 183/15 (1989).
91. See van de Walle de Ghelcke, van Gerven, and Platteau (1990, pp. 1551–60).

An escape clause is found both in the treaty itself and in the new essential requirements directives as they are issued.[92] Roughly, the former permits nations to deviate from the requirements of a directive, whereas the latter permits nations to determine also that the objectives of the directive have not been achieved by the applicable international standards or standards of other nations. The treaty escape clause permits nations to deviate on grounds such as public morality; protection of human, animal, and plant life and health; protection of intellectual property; and protection of the environment. The directive escape clause is typically narrower, focusing on dangers to human or animal health and property.[93] Any state invoking either escape clause must notify the Commission, however, which is to determine whether the action is justified or is instead an unacceptable restriction of trade. Complaints may also be filed before the European Court of Justice. Neither type of escape clause has been invoked much in practice.

Despite the absence of central authorities in the world at large with powers comparable to the Council of Ministers, several features of the new approach might have limited transferability to global problems. In particular, an effort to agree on essential requirements for regulation, coupled with mutual recognition covenants, could be undertaken by larger groups of nations. As in Europe, nations could work toward agreement on the essential objectives of regulatory policy with respect to categories of products and covenant not to apply regulations more stringent or regulations concerning "inessential" matters. The ISO/IEC, the Codex, and other international organizations could then undertake the task of drafting standards to meet the essential objectives, and they or some other authority might be given the ability to declare national regulations sufficient to meet the essential objectives. A covenant to allow free importation of goods that met the international standards, or the national standards deemed equivalent, would then do much to alleviate the technical barriers associated with disparate regulatory policies.

92. Treaty of Rome, article 100a (4), which cross-references the grounds for derogation in article 36 and adds protection of the environment and working environment. See, for example, Council Directive 89/392 on the approximation of the laws of the member states relating to machinery, *Official Journal of the European Communities* L 183/12 (June 29, 1989), article 7.

93. *Official Journal of the European Communities* L 183/9 (June 29, 1989), article 7.

The procedural structure of the escape clauses is also intriguing. These clauses require notice to the central authorities in the event of a decision to invoke them and require any state that relies on them to defend its actions. In this respect, they are analogous to the provisions in GATT that apply when a signatory deviates from international standards or enacts, in the absence of international standards, new standards that may significantly affect trade. They go beyond GATT obligations, however, by requiring a statement of justification *whether or not another party has complained.* This procedural requirement could prove useful elsewhere (although, to be sure, it creates administrative burdens). A requirement of notice and explanation raises the costs of decisions that depart from international standards or mutual recognition principles and may be expected to dissuade departures at the margin when the interests at stake are not very important or when the explanation would appear questionable or disingenuous.

The substance of the escape clause provisions is interesting for another reason, as it reflects the priorities and political sensitivities associated with different kinds of regulation. The protection of human, animal, and plant life and health appears as the most prominent basis for opting out of a directive or for declining to recognize the standards developed elsewhere. Environmental protection also receives careful mention.[94] A striking omission is any generalized concept of "consumer protection" beyond that relating to health and safety. Likewise, there is no reference to "deceptive practices" and the like. Hence the European system treats the broad notion of consumer protection as a possibly "essential requirement" but limits it as a basis for opting out of harmonization directives or mutual recognition requirements. The weak inference to be drawn from this structure is that consumer protection measures unrelated to health and safety may be easier to compromise at the national level than matters of health and safety or environmental concern. If this proved to be the case more broadly in the trading community, it might be possible to achieve tight mutual recognition pacts on consumer protection matters not relating to health and safety (by *tight* I mean a pact without an opt-out provision), at least among developed countries, and subject to the use of labeling requirements to inform consumers of product differences. Likewise, a weak inference arises that tight mu-

94. Treaty of Rome, article 100a(4).

tual recognition pacts relating to health and safety matters are not likely to be attainable at any time in the near future—if they are unattainable in Europe, they are even less likely to prove feasible in a more heterogeneous trading community.

Mutual Information Directive

Like GATT, the European Union has made considerable effort to avoid the creation of new technical barriers by requiring advance notice to a central authority of new standards and regulations at the national level. The most important initiative here is the 1983 Mutual Information Directive.[95]

The directive requires national standard setting organizations and regulators to notify the Commission and certain European standards-setting organizations of proposed standards or regulations before their adoption. With respect to standards, a standing committee may determine that a proposed national standard may interfere with trade and can then refer the task of standard-setting to a Europe-wide organization such as CEN or CENELEC or direct that interested member states collaborate on a standard. If the first option is chosen, member states must then prevent their national standard-setting organizations from enacting a standard pending the completion (or noncompletion within a set period) of efforts by the Europe-wide entity.[96]

With respect to regulations, member states must notify the Commission of proposed new regulations, which then disseminates that information to other member states. Complete drafts of the proposal must be provided unless the regulation simply adopts in full an existing international standard. Either the Commission or another member state may object to a proposed regulation and request that it be modified to avoid adverse trade effects. The Commission may also opt to prepare a harmonization directive on the subject. In either case, final adoption of the proposed regulation must be delayed and may be prevented altogether by an incompatible harmonization directive.

95. "Council Directive of March 28, 1983, laying down a procedure for the provision of information in the field of technical standards and regulations," *Official Journal of the European Communities* L 109/8 (April 26, 1983).

96. *Official Journal of the European Communities* L 109/8 (April 26, 1983), articles 5–7.

The only exceptions are in cases of "urgent reasons relating to the protection of public health or safety."[97]

Experience with the directive suggests that the standards notification process tends to generate an enormous volume of material, so much that without a very sizable bureaucracy to process it, much is overlooked or ignored. But in the regulatory area, the directive is said to be far more successful and to have contributed importantly to the avoidance of new barriers.[98]

It is instructive to contrast the European notification system with that of GATT. One difference relates to the criteria for what must be notified—in Europe, every new standard or regulation is covered by the directive. Under GATT, by contrast, only those that in the judgment of the notifying nation are likely to have a "significant effect" on trade must be notified. A second difference lies in the power of member states and the Commission to delay the implementation of new regulations if they object to them. Another obvious difference lies in the power of the Commission to issue harmonization directives when adverse effects on trade seem likely.

This last difference between the two systems is surely inevitable, given the absence in the global community of an entity with powers comparable to those of the Commission. But one can imagine GATT signatories agreeing to notify a central entity of *all* new product regulations and covenanting to delay their implementation briefly while other nations have an opportunity to review and comment on them. Such a system would have the advantage that noncompliance would be more obvious and thus more costly politically than under than the current system of notification only when the regulator anticipates a "significant" trade effect. It could also reduce the trade impact of new regulations by giving foreign suppliers somewhat more time to adapt. Such a system would also be more costly, and the net balance of costs and benefits is not obvious.

Global Approach to Conformity Assessment

The "new approach" to harmonization outlined above addressed differences in substantive standards and regulations but

---

97. *Official Journal of the European Communities* L 109/11 (April 26, 1983), articles 8–9.
98. See Center for European Policy Studies (1992).

did little to solve technical barrier problems associated with conformity assessment. Even when the underlying product requirements were the same, it proved quite difficult to develop confidence in testing and certification abroad. To ameliorate these problems, the Commission introduced its "global approach" to conformity assessment.[99]

The starting point for the global approach is to encourage all parties involved in certification and testing—both product manufacturers and third-party testing laboratories—to embrace European quality control standards to govern their activities. The general quality assurance standards for manufacturers, promulgated by the Europe-wide standards organizations as the EN 29000 standards, are generally adapted from the "ISO 9000" quality control standards of the ISO.[100] These elaborate and extensive standards are differentiated by generic product categories and sectors and provide general quality control principles for all manner of products and services. The European standards organizations supplemented them with elaborate standards for the operation of various kinds of testing laboratories and certification bodies, promulgated as the EN 45000 standards.

Having settled on a common set of quality control standards for all such activity, the next step in the global approach is to promulgate guidelines for when and where the necessary testing and certification for each product will occur. These guidelines, in the form of "modules," are designed to minimize the cost and intrusiveness of testing and certification while still meeting essential regulatory objectives. For some products, self-certification by the manufacturer will be deemed sufficient; for others, spot checks by third-party laboratories will be required; and in the limit, testing of each unit of output might be required. Whatever "module" is adopted for a particular product, however, those engaged in the requisite testing and certification are encouraged follow the pertinent Europe-wide standards at all times and would be subject to some degree of auditing to ensure that they comply with them. The requisite degree of auditing, like the under-

99. "Commission: A Global Approach to Certification and Testing," *Official Journal of the European Communities* C 267/3 (October 19, 1989).

100. See ISO (1994). The ISO is not the only source of such standards. Standards for quality control in pharmaceutical manufacture, for example, were approved by the World Health Assembly in the 1970s. See Kay (1976b).

lying testing and certification procedures themselves, will be attentive to the risks of noncompliance.[101]

With this system in place, coupled with new approach legislation to harmonize national regulation pursuant to "essential requirements" directives, goods manufactured pursuant to the requirements of the global approach will be permitted to display a generic mark of conformity—the "CE" mark. All goods displaying that mark will be entitled to circulate freely within Europe and will be exempted from further conformity assessment by an importing nation. The implementation of this system has been slow because of the backlog of standardization work at the European standards organizations, but over the long run, it is expected to reduce considerably the extent of technical barriers associated with conformity assessment.[102]

The global approach and the new approach are closely linked, in that much of the global approach presumes the existence of new approach "essential requirements" directives to harmonize the underlying regulatory requirements. Absent a substantial move toward regulatory harmonization internationally, therefore, much of the global approach is not transferable to the trading community at large.

Certain features of the global approach, however, do not require convergence of the underlying regulatory requirements. In particular, a commitment to ISO 9000 standards for quality control by manufacturers and the development of analogous standards for the operation of testing laboratories, coupled with audits by mutually acceptable third-party auditors, could be implemented at a much broader level. Under such a system, national regulators could continue to maintain different requirements and even specify in detail the particular conformity checks that are necessary, yet could rely to a much greater extent on self-certification and third-party testing abroad.

Although movement toward such a system might be initiated by international agreement, it need not be. An importing nation could well announce unilaterally that it will accept conformity assessment undertaken abroad if certain procedures are followed, if those procedures are conducted in accordance with pertinent international quality control standards, and if the entities involved in implementing

---

101. See generally, "Commission: A Global Approach to Certification and Testing," *Official Journal of the European Communities* C 267/15–24 (October 19,1989).

102. See Center for European Policy Studies (1992).

them will open themselves to periodic audit. In some instances, this policy could reduce significantly the costs of conformity assessment. Experiments along these lines seem worth encouraging.

Role of the Judiciary in Europe

Article 30 of the Treaty of Rome provides that "quantitative restrictions on imports and all measures having equivalent effect shall, without prejudice to the following provisions, be prohibited between the Member States." Among the provisions that follow, the one pertinent to technical barriers is article 36:

> The provisions of Articles 30 to 34 shall not preclude prohibitions or restrictions on imports . . . justified on grounds of public morality, public policy or public security; the protection of health and life of humans, animals or plants; the protection of national treasures . . . ; or the protection of industrial and commercial property. Such prohibitions or restrictions shall not, however, constitute a means of arbitrary discrimination or a disguised restriction on international trade.

These articles raise a number of interpretive issues, implicitly left to the Commission and to the Court of Justice. It was settled quickly that article 30 would have broad applicability and, in particular, that it would encompass all manner of technical barriers. A 1969 directive from the Commission stated that product regulations can have "equivalent effect" to quantitative restrictions.[103] In the view of the Commission, product regulations applicable to imports exclusively ("distinctly applicable measures") were automatically covered by article 30, and regulations applicable to domestic and imported goods alike ("indistinctly applicable measures") would be covered or not in accordance with a balancing test—it was necessary to inquire whether "the restrictive effects on the free movement of goods are out of proportion to their purpose" and whether "the same objective can be attained by other means which are less of a hindrance to trade."[104]

103. See "Commission Directive of December 22, 1969," *Official Journal of the European Communities* L 13/29 (January 19, 1970).
104. "Commission Directive of December 22, 1969," *Official Journal of the European Communities* L 13/31 (January 19, 1970), article 3.

In 1974 the Court of Justice took an even more expansive view of the measures that might run afoul of article 30 in the well-known case of *Procureur du Roi* v. *Dassonville:* "All trading rules enacted by Member States which are capable of hindering, directly or indirectly, actually or potentially, intra-Community trade are to be considered as measures having an effect equivalent to quantitative restrictions."[105] The *Dassonville* formulation makes no distinction between distinctly and indistinctly applicable measures and requires no balancing test as under the 1969 directive. It does require actual or potential "hindrance" to trade, a concept that has proved elusive to define. Because any regulation or conformity assessment measure that prohibits the importation of a good or substantially increases the cost of importation would surely qualify, however, the details of the hindrance concept need not detain us.

The Court backed away somewhat from the broad sweep of its *Dassonville* test in a case known popularly as *Cassis de Dijon,* which involved a German prohibition on the importation of certain spirits, including Cassis de Dijon, with an alcohol content less than 25 percent.[106] The Court held that "disparities between the national laws" must be "accepted in so far as those provisions may be recognized as being necessary in order to satisfy mandatory requirements relating in particular to the effectiveness of fiscal supervision, the protection of public health, the fairness of commercial transactions and the defence of the consumer." Although the language is unclear, *Cassis* is generally interpreted as establishing a kind of "rule of reason" test to determine whether indistinctly applicable measures violate article 30. Further, the list of "mandatory requirements" to which the Court refers was subsequently held not to be exhaustive.[107] After *Cassis,* therefore, the Court applies a "two-tier" test: For distinctly applicable measures, the member state must justify them on the basis of the article 36 criteria noted above. For measures that are indistinctly applicable, a rule-of-reason test applies that allows regulations to be justified on the basis of mandatory requirements not

---

105. [1974] E.C.R. 837.

106. *Rewe-Zentral AG* v. *Bundesmonopolverwaltung für Branntwein,* [1979] E.C.R. 649 (hereafter *Cassis de Dijon*).

107. The encouragement of cultural activities, for example, or the interest in maintaining "socio-cultural characteristics" can qualify as mandatory requirements. See Steiner (1992, pp. 86–87).

enumerated in article 36. Those that fail this test cannot be applied against imports. Hence *Cassis* provides a tool by which the judiciary can compel a form of "mutual recognition."

Article 36 also requires some interpretation. With reference to technical barriers, the two provisions of greatest relevance are the exception for measures to protect human, animal, and plant health and the "public policy" exception. The latter has been construed very narrowly, however, and has proved to afford essentially no protection to the member states outside of a few areas of little pertinence here.[108] Thus as a practical matter, the only article 36 exception likely to be of any use to the importing nation in a technical barrier dispute is the health exception. Given the breadth of the *Dassonville* test for measures within the scope of article 30, therefore, technical barriers that result from distinctly applicable measures will almost certainly be struck down unless a health justification can be shown.

As to indistinctly applicable measures, *Cassis* seems to afford national governments considerable latitude to assert that some "mandatory" requirement justifies their actions. But the *Cassis* decision itself indicates that the Court will scrutinize these justifications closely. The German government claimed in that case that the minimum alcohol requirement served two purposes: (1) the protection of public health, and (2) the protection of the consumer against unfair practices. Regarding public health, the German government argued that the availability of low-alcohol beverages was dangerous because such beverages may more easily promote a tolerance toward alcohol. Rather than challenge this argument as disingenuous, the Court responded that there were many low-alcohol beverages available other than Cassis de Dijon, so that restricting its importation would not do any good in meeting the government's health objective.[109] Regarding consumer protection, the German government argued that low-alcohol liqueur was cheaper to produce (due to taxes on alcohol content) and that consumers could not distinguish it from higher-alcohol liqueur. Thus the lower-alcohol product had an unfair competitive advantage, the argument ran, and consumers would not realize that they were getting something less. To this the Court replied that it was enough for the alcohol content to be included on the label. Thus the

---

108. See Steiner (1992, p. 95).
109. *Cassis de Dijon*, para. 11.

prohibition was not "necessary" to the fulfillment of any mandatory requirement and was held to violate article 30.[110]

After *Cassis de Dijon* was decided, the Commission seized the initiative with a letter to the member states interpreting it.[111] In that letter, the Commission stated:

> Any product imported from another Member State must in principle be admitted into the territory of the importing Member State if it has been lawfully produced, that is, conforms to rules and processes of manufacture that are customarily and traditionally accepted in the exporting country, and is marketed in the territory of the latter.
>
> Only under very strict conditions does the Court accept exceptions to this principle; barriers to trade resulting from differences between commercial and technical rules are only admissible:
>
> if the rules are necessary, that is appropriate and not excessive, in order to satisfy mandatory requirements (public health, protection of consumers or the environment, the fairness of commercial transactions, etc.);
>
> if the rules serve a purpose in the general interest which is compelling enough . . . ;
>
> if the rules are essential for such a purpose to be attained, i.e., are the means which are the most appropriate and at the same time least hinder trade.
>
> [A] Member State may not in principle prohibit the sale in its territory of a product lawfully produced and marketed in another Member State even if the product is produced according to technical or quality requirements which differ from those imposed on domestic products. Where a product "suitably and satisfactorily" fulfills the legitimate objective of a Member State's own rules . . . the Member State cannot justify prohibiting its sale in its territory by claiming that the way it fulfills the objective is different from that imposed on domestic products.

The case law since the directive has proved broadly consistent with these principles.

110. *Cassis de Dijon*, paras. 12–14.
111. "Communication from the Commission Concerning the Consequences of the Judgment Given by the Court of Justice on 20 February 1979 in Case 120/78" (*Cassis de Dijon*), *Official Journal of the European Communities* C 256/2 (March 10, 1980).

Thus after *Cassis,* measures that discriminate against imports can only be justified on health grounds, and such justifications will be scrutinized closely by the Court for their reasonableness. Measures that accord national treatment to imports can be justified on other grounds, but only if those measures serve a sufficiently important objective in the view of the Court and only if they represent the "least-restrictive means" of meeting the regulatory objective. Further, a presumption exists that products lawful in one state ought be allowed into another, and the Court can force a kind of "mutual recognition" when the regulations in force in the exporting nation achieve the legitimate objectives of the importing nation, even if they do so in a manner that differs from the importing nation's own approach.

These principles have led the Court to find against the importing nation in a wide variety of cases.[112] Greek and German prohibitions on beer imports with certain additives were held to violate article 30 in substantial part because no scientific evidence could be adduced of any health hazard.[113] Various import restrictions on food products have also been held to violate article 30 when the Court was unpersuaded that the health justifications were bona fide or that least-restrictive means had been used.[114]

The application of the least-restrictive means principle, in particular, has resulted in almost routine condemnation of indistinctly applicable product regulations justified by a purported need to protect consumers against confusion about product attributes or to protect the producers of close substitutes against unfair competition. In case after case, the Court has responded that such objectives can be attained less restrictively through appropriate labeling requirements.[115]

---

112. A more thorough survey may be found in Steiner (1992, pp. 87–91, 96–97).

113. *Commission* v. *Greece* (Re Beer Purity Standards), [1988] 1 C.M.L.R. 813; *Commission* v. *Germany* (Re Beer Purity Standards), [1988] 1 C.M.L.R. 780.

114. *Commission* v. *United Kingdom* (Re UHT Milk), [1983] 2 C.M.L.R. 1; *Commission* v. *United Kingdom* (Re Imports of Poultry Meat), [1982] 3 C.M.L.R. 487.

115. See, for example, *EC Commission* v. *Germany* (Re The Use of Champagne-Type Bottles), [1988] 1 C.M.L.R. 135; *Criminal Proceedings against Karl Prantl,* [1985] 2 C.M.L.R. 238; *EC Commission* v. *Germany* (Re German Sausages), [1989] 2 C.M.L.R. 733; *EC Commission* v. *Italy* (Re Low-Fat Cheese), [1992] 2 C.M.L.R. 1; *Miro BV,* [1986] 3 C.M.L.R. 545. A critical view of these developments, skeptical of the ability of consumers to appreciate labels fully, may be found in von Heydebrand (1991). A survey of consumer protection policies in Europe, both judicial and legislative, is that of Lewis (1993).

Summary and Recapitulation for Europe

Unlike the trading community at large, Europe has a central authority with considerable power to force harmonization of disparate standards, regulations, and conformity assessment measures. Many initiatives at harmonization have been undertaken, and other initiatives have been undertaken to promote mutual recognition. Despite their commitment to the free movement of goods, however, the European nations have carefully preserved some latitude to opt out of harmonization or mutual recognition requirements, particularly on grounds of health concerns. But they have also shown considerable willingness to narrow the range of public policy objectives that may be invoked as a basis for national regulations. They have appeared particularly willing to reject purported "consumer protection" objectives, unrelated to health and safety, as a basis for restricting imports other than by appropriate labeling requirements.

The "new approach" of the European Council is also of interest. The "essential requirements" directives amount to international accords, product category by product category, on the basic objectives that regulation should meet. They illustrate how prior agreement on the basic objectives of regulation can facilitate tighter accords regarding deference to international standards and mutual recognition of national standards. Another interesting feature of the system concerns the procedure for opting out of a harmonization or mutual recognition initiative. A nation seeking to do so must disclose the fact and come forward with an explanation even absent complaint by another party.

The mutual information directive creates an important procedure that precludes the adoption of *any* new product regulation before both the Commission and other member states have had an opportunity to consider its trade impact and to urge modification when appropriate. The directive also serves to provide producers in other member states with more advance notice and thus more lead time to adapt to new regulations and gives the Commission advance indication of when harmonization efforts may prove important.

The "global approach" to conformity assessment represents an innovative effort to develop mutual confidence in certification and testing conducted abroad, through a combination of reliance on international quality control standards and a mutually acceptable auditing procedure to ensure that they are followed. Certification and testing under the global approach holds the promise of eliminating much of the conformity assessment now undertaken by importing nations.

Judicial enforcement of the Treaty of Rome, as modified through the years, effectively prohibits measures that deny national treatment absent a convincing health justification. Measures that afford national treatment are more tolerated, but their justification must appear to the Court to be persuasive. The least-restrictive means principle is applied ruthlessly by the Court of Justice, which has proved willing to question the scientific foundation for regulation as well. One consequence has been the development of a strong presumption that labeling is adequate to meet all consumer protection objectives that are not convincingly health-related. Interestingly, the legal standards that the Court applies are not terribly different from those embodied in the GATT Standards Code and the Uruguay Round initiatives. Hence the European experience with article 30 may have much to say about how the GATT system will function with a more effective system of dispute resolution, in particular, a system without the consensus rule.

Finally, in keeping with the idea that regional trading arrangements may become "building blocks" toward mutilateral trade liberalization, recent European initiatives may over the long term facilitate greater reliance globally on international standards.[116] The increased emphasis on the development of CEN and CENELEC standards within the Community will eliminate many disparities in standards and regulations among this important group of trading nations. At least when the resulting European standards are not adopted with any strategic purpose, subsequent negotiations over worldwide standards may be facilitated by the reduction in the number of competing options.

Note on the U.S. Federal System

The inefficiencies of noncooperative trade policies under the Articles of Confederation are said to have provided much of the impetus

---

116. Lawrence (forthcoming).

for the Constitution of the United States.[117] The Constitution imposes a number of explicit restrictions on state commercial policies, such as a prohibition on export or import duties without the consent of Congress.[118] It also grants to the Congress the "power . . . to regulate commerce with foreign nations, and among the several States" (the commerce clause), thus affording Congress the power to constrain state action expressly through statutory enactments.[119] But not all restrictions on state activities in the commercial sphere are express. State policies that are in tension with federal regulatory policy may be deemed implicitly "pre-empted" by the federal regime.[120] And even when the Congress has taken no action on a subject pursuant to the commerce clause, state action may be found to violate the Constitution because of the "negative implications" of that clause—the so-called dormant or negative commerce clause.[121]

This allocation of powers has much to say about technical barriers within the United States. The Congress has eliminated trade impediments in many areas (although sometimes as an incidental consequence of federal regulation). The Food, Drug and Cosmetic Act, for example, establishes a federal mechanism for the approval of prescription drugs that pre-empts state drug regulation.[122] The Federal Communications Act affords the Federal Communications Commission authority to standardize such matters as television broadcast formats. The Ports and Waterways Safety Act, by promulgating safety standards for the design of tanker vessels, pre-empts more stringent state standards.[123] Innumerable other examples might be offered.

Yet many technical barriers remain outside the scope of federal legislation, even under the implied pre-emption doctrine. States and localities maintain their own building codes, health regulations, pollution control regulations, and a wealth of other product-related mea-

117. See, for example, Tribe (1988, p. 404); Kurland and Lerner (1987, pp. 477–528).
118. U.S. Const., art. I, § 10(2).
119. U.S. Const., art. I, § 8(3).
120. See, for example, Tribe (1988, pp. 479–501).
121. This listing of constitutional restrictions on state actions that affect commerce is not intended to be exhaustive. Other and sometimes similar constraints emanate from the privileges and immunities clause, the equal protection clause, and a range of other provisions.
122. In general, the act delegates the authority to promulgate regulations to an agency—the Food and Drug Administration—and allows the agency to decide whether to give its regulations pre-emptive effect. See Tribe (1988, p. 501).
123. *Ray v. Atlantic Richfield Co.*, 435 U.S. 151 (1979).

sures. These regulations are a source of impediments to commerce domestically and have been a matter of considerable interest internationally. The lack of much prior GATT discipline over these state and local measures, owing to the "reasonable measures" requirement of the GATT system, was discussed earlier.

A potentially greater source of constraints on state and local regulation is the dormant commerce clause. The jurisprudence of the dormant commerce clause is thus of interest for much the same reasons that the decisions of the European Court of Justice are of interest—the principles that American courts have developed to give force to the dormant commerce clause might also be applied to disputes among nations. As shall be seen, however, these "principles" are, in fact, exceptionally vague and do not generate an entirely coherent body of decisions.

One impediment to the development of coherent doctrine has been the absence of clear guidelines in the Constitution to limit state and local powers in the regulatory arena. The Constitution contains nothing to compare with article 30 of the Treaty of Rome, for example. Indeed the absence of clear constitutional limitations on state power led some early judges to conclude that none existed and that the states were free to regulate subject only to congressional preemption.[124] But other judges maintained that the grant to Congress of power over interstate and foreign commerce restricted state powers by implication, and this view ultimately prevailed in the Supreme Court.[125]

The leading case from the early era was *Cooley* v. *Board of Wardens of Port of Philadelphia,* which upheld the power of the state of Pennsylvania to require ships entering the port of Philadelphia to employ local pilots.[126] *Cooley* drew a distinction between aspects of interstate and foreign commerce so "local" in character as to demand diverse treatment and aspects so "national" in character as to demand a uniform rule. The great difficulty with that rule is that it contains no basis for operationalizing the distinction, and efforts to classify the subject of regulation as local or national were eventually abandoned.[127]

124. See *License Cases*, 46 U.S. 504, 573 (1847) (opinion of Chief Justice Taney).
125. The leading judicial exponent of this view was Chief Justice Marshall. See *Gibbons* v. *Ogden*, 22 U.S. 1, 209 (1824).
126. *Cooley* v. *Board of Wardens of Port of Philadelphia*, 53 U.S. 299 (1851).
127. For a brief discussion, see Tribe (1988, pp. 403–13).

Beginning in the 1930s and extending into the modern era, the Supreme Court moved toward a balancing test in its commerce clause decisions. The modern analysis begins with the question of whether the challenged practice effectuates a "legitimate local public interest," a necessary condition for the regulation to be sustained.[128] If any discrimination against interstate commerce is to be tolerated in pursuit of a legitimate interest, it must be because of the absence of adequate "nondiscriminatory alternatives."[129] Finally, whenever a demonstrable burden on interstate commerce exists, with or without discrimination against out-of-state producers, the Court will weigh the interests of the state against the burden. Discriminatory policies are far more likely to be struck down under this balancing analysis, whereas nondiscriminatory policies are upheld unless "the burden imposed on [interstate] commerce is clearly excessive in relation to the putative local benefits."[130] Thus the modern U.S. approach reflects several principles that are by now familiar. Overtly discriminatory measures are subject to tighter scrutiny than measures that afford national treatment and are much more likely to be invalid. A least-restrictive means principle can also be found in many of the cases. The balancing test resembles certain aspects of European case law under article 30.

The dormant commerce clause has been used to invalidate many state measures that create technical barriers. Examples of measures struck down by the courts include a prohibition by one state on imports displaying a quality grade applied by another state, justified by purported concerns over consumer confusion;[131] prohibitions on the sale of dairy products containing milk substitutes justified on the same grounds;[132] prohibitions on the use of trucks over a certain length when safety benefits could not be proved;[133] and prohibitions on the import of food products from outside the radius in which state inspectors can reasonably operate.[134] The cases also exhibit a high

128. For example, *Pike v. Bruce Church*, 397 U.S. 137, 142 (1970).
129. For example, *Hunt v. Washington State Apple Advertising Commission*, 432 U.S. 333, 353 (1977).
130. *Pike v. Bruce Church*, 397 U.S. 137, 142 (1970).
131. *Hunt v. Washington State Apple Advertising Commission*, 432 U.S. 333 (1977).
132. *Dean Milk v. City of Madison*, 340 U.S. 349 (1951); *Dean Foods v. Wisconsin*, 478 F. Supp. 224 (1979).
133. *Kassel v. Consolidated Freightways*, 450 U.S. 662 (1981).
134. *Miller v. Williams*, 12 F. Supp. 236 (1935).

degree of deference to bona fide health and safety and environmental concerns. State laws requiring beverages to be sold in reusable containers have been upheld with regularity,[135] for example, as have state measures that require imported live animals to come from an area certified free of disease[136] or that ban imports altogether due to health concerns that cannot be met through inspections or certifications.[137] Recalling the discussion of the European experience in the last section, the reader will no doubt note many similarities.

The operation of the dormant commerce clause has proved unsatisfactory in some respects, however, particularly as to the application of the "balancing" test. The questions whether the local public interest is "legitimate," whether nondiscriminatory alternatives are "adequate," and whether the local benefit "outweighs" the burden on commerce often require difficult value judgments that judges have no special capacity to make and that are ordinarily entrusted to the political branches of government. Further, if the balancing of interstate burden against local benefit is to be taken seriously, it likely requires a wealth of empirical information that will often be unavailable in U.S. courts. The result has been considerable unpredictability of outcomes, including instances in which laws have been upheld despite considerable suspicion that protectionism may have been involved in their passage.[138]

For these and other reasons, the commentators are, in the main, critical of dormant commerce clause doctrine, as are several prominent jurists. Lawrence Tribe suggested that "the Supreme Court's approach to commerce clause issues . . . often appears to turn more on ad hoc reactions to particular cases than on any consistent application of coherent principles."[139] Chief Justice Rehnquist wrote in a 1981 dissent:

---

135. See *Minnesota* v. *Clover Leaf Creamery Co.*, 449 U.S. 456 (1981); *American Can Co.* v. *Oregon Liquor Control Commission*, Or. App. 517 P.2d 691, 697 (1973).

136. See *Mintz* v. *Baldwin*, 289 U.S. 346 (1933).

137. *Maine* v. *Taylor*, 106 S. Ct. 2440 (1986).

138. See the comments on *Mintz* v. *Baldwin* in Tribe (1988, p. 415); and on *Florida Lime and Avocado Growers* v. *Paul* in Tribe (1988, p. 495). In the latter case, 373 U.S. 132 (1963), the Supreme Court sustained a California law restricting the marketing of avocados on the basis of their oil content, justified by a purported need to protect the consumer from less tasty products. The burden of the regulation fell mainly on exports from Florida, and the record disclosed a history of "avocado warfare" between the two states. Tribe (1988, pp. 495–96).

139. Tribe (1988, p. 439).

The true problem with today's decision is that it gives no guidance whatsoever to these States as to whether their laws are valid or how to defend them. . . . We know only that [the challenged state] law is invalid and that the jurisprudence of the 'negative side' of the Commerce Clause remains hopelessly confused.[140]

Among the law and economics scholars, Frank Easterbrook and Edmund Kitch have argued that the dormant commerce clause strays beyond the limits of judicial competence and may even be unnecessary given the realities of competition and the incentives for cooperation among the states.[141]

These criticisms cast doubt on the wisdom of an open-ended balancing approach to such cases, even in wholly domestic disputes. Such an approach is even less likely to be politically acceptable internationally and is thus perhaps of rather little interest for present purposes. Nevertheless, the U.S. experience is instructive in several respects. Regularities in the case law tend to confirm the usefulness of distinctions between discriminatory and nondiscriminatory measures and the usefulness of least-restrictive means principles. As elsewhere, it is difficult to find decisions in which the courts declare the stated objectives of state governments to be sham. The cases also reflect the pattern evident in GATT and in Europe of according greater deference to particular public policy objectives, especially health and envi-

---

140. *Kassel* v. *Consolidated Freightways,* 450 U.S. 662, 706 (Rehnquist, J., dissenting).

141. See Easterbrook (1988, pp. 53, 55–62); Kitch (1981). Justice Scalia evidently agrees with these views. See *CTS Corp.* v. *Dynamics Corp. of America,* 481 U.S. 69, 95. Richard Posner, however, takes a more charitable view of the doctrine. Posner (1987, pp. 4, 17). For the argument that a proper constitutional interpretation does not support the creation of a dormant commerce clause by the judiciary, see Redish and Nugent (1987). Proposals for reform of dormant commerce clause doctrine thus abound. Easterbrook and Kitch impliedly argued that the dormant commerce clause ought be largely abandoned, leaving the Congress to police any state malfeasance under the "positive" commerce clause. Donald Regan urged the Court to reject its "balancing" exercise in favor of an inquiry as to whether the challenged practice has a "protectionist motive," an approach that he contended is followed already to a considerable degree in the guise of balancing language. Regan (1986). Saul Levmore favored greater attention to the question of whether a challenged practice imposes substantial costs on citizens of other states by exploiting state market power or whether instead the economic costs of the practice are borne mainly within the jurisdiction. Levmore (1983). A similar proposal, although directed to the proper application of the "state action" doctrine under the antitrust laws, is that of Frank Easterbrook (1983). For the argument that the aggregate efficiency consequences of state legislation will not depend systematically on whether the state is able to exploit nonresidents, see Fischel (1987, pp. 75–78).

ronmental protection, as well as the pattern of skepticism toward other "consumer protection" objectives. Finally, the widespread dissatisfaction with the balancing that goes on under current law suggests the importance of clear guidelines for technical barrier disputes with a high degree of predictability in their application. Both the GATT system and the European system, notwithstanding their ambiguities and imperfections, appear considerably superior in this regard.

Note on the North American Free Trade Agreement

To a great extent, the provisions of the North American Free Trade Agreement (NAFTA) on technical barriers resemble the Uruguay Round accords. As in the GATT system, NAFTA contains separate accords on technical barriers and SPMs, with parallel or identical language in many places. The discussion here is thus brief.

With respect to the NAFTA accord on technical barriers, it too encompasses all standards and regulations, including those applicable to "processes and production methods."[142] The familiar principles of GATT are made applicable to all such measures at the national government level, including the most favored nation, national treatment, sham, and least-restrictive means principles. The obligation to use international standards unless "ineffective or inappropriate" applies as well. As under GATT, the obligation with respect to subsidiary governments and private entities is apparently a weak one—here the phrase is *appropriate measures* rather than *reasonable measures,* but the intended effect is evidently to allow the parties discretion whether to force compliance.[143]

NAFTA's technical barriers provisions go somewhat beyond the GATT draft in committing the parties to "make compatible" their standards-related measures "to the greatest extent practicable," provided that this shall not reduce "the level of safety or protection of human, animal or plant life or health, the environment or consumers."[144] When harmonization is absent, NAFTA's technical barrier accord reiterates the basic principles of the GATT SPM Agreement, requiring mutual recognition when a party demonstrates the equiva-

142. North American Free Trade Agreement, pt. 3, ch. 9 (hereafter "NAFTA Technical Barriers Accord"). NAFTA Technical Barriers Accord, article 915.
143. NAFTA Technical Barriers Accord, article 902(2).
144. NAFTA Technical Barriers Accord, article 906(2).

lence of its regulations and requiring mutual recognition of conformity assessment procedures when parties are "satisfied" as to their
adequacy.[145] A decision not to afford mutual recognition is to be
explained in writing on request.[146] The remaining provisions differ
from the GATT TBT Agreement only incidentally and include a
section on the proper assessment of product risks and a requirement
of prior notice and publication of new standards.

The NAFTA accord on SPMs is also quite similar to the GATT SPM
Agreement.[147] Analogous to the NAFTA technical barrier accord, it
commits the parties to pursue "equivalence" of measures to the greatest
extent practicable and without "reducing the level of protection" and
thus goes somewhat beyond GATT.[148] It does even less than the GATT
Agreement, however, to create obligations with respect to subsidiary
governments and private entities, omitting almost any reference to them.
Otherwise, it is roughly comparable in most respects—requiring a risk
assessment and attention to scientific evidence in the formulation of
SPMs, encouraging the use of international standards, encouraging
advance notice of new measures, and so on.

To be sure, there are several modest differences in wording. For
example, the NAFTA SPM accord requires that no measure be maintained "where there is no longer a scientific basis for it."[149] In the GATT
SPM Agreement, by contrast, the obligation is not to be maintained
"without *sufficient* scientific evidence" (emphasis added).[150] The NAFTA
requirement can be read as less stringent (the difference between "some
scientific basis" and "sufficient scientific evidence"), and if so, the
NAFTA provision prevails in a dispute between the parties to
NAFTA.[151] On the whole, however, there is not a great deal of interest in
NAFTA beyond what is familiar from the GATT negotiations. Both use
similar strategies for addressing technical barriers to a roughly comparable extent.

145. NAFTA Technical Barriers Accord, article 906(4),(6).
146. NAFTA Technical Barriers Accord, article 906(5).
147. NAFTA, pt. 2, ch. 7, sec. B (hereafter "NAFTA SPM Accord").
148. NAFTA SPM Accord, article 714.
149. NAFTA SPM Accord, article 712(3)(b).
150. GATT SPM Agreement, article 2(2). This obligation is qualified by reference to a
later provision that authorizes provisional measures when scientific data are incomplete.
151. See NAFTA, article 103.

Chapter 5

Implications: Adequacy of the Existing Approach and Prospects for the Future

A S CHAPTER 4 indicated, present international efforts to address technical barriers have several dimensions. When decentralized markets forces alone do not function adequately, standards-related problems are entrusted in the main to subsidized international standardization organizations. National standardizing and conformity assessment entities participate in these international organizations but are free to depart from the resulting international standards or procedures if they wish. The international community relies on these same entities to a limited degree in the formulation of regulatory policy and relies further on intergovernmental compacts that place constraints on the regulatory policies of individual nations, primarily those of the national government. Broader efforts at harmonization of national policy exist within Europe but not much elsewhere.

This concluding chapter explores the adequacy of the existing and proposed treatment of technical barriers in the international community and indicates where further progress might be made. It is convenient to separate the bulk of the discussion into three segments—(1) compatibility issues, (2) quality and labeling issues, and (3) additional issues relating to conformity assessment measures. The chapter concludes with a note on the developing countries.

Compatibility Issues

Compatibility issues are special because many of the legal principles that can apply elsewhere are of little relevance here. It makes no sense to worry about most favored nation or national treatment for incompatible products, for example, if the problem lies in consumer rejection of them. Likewise, "mutual recognition" typically borders on the absurd. The main questions here are few and straightforward— Should products be made compatible or not? and Who should make the determination?

Many compatibility issues, whether national or international, resolve entirely in the marketplace without the need for any cooperative activity. Often firms create incompatibilities through deliberate product differentiation. Consumers then decide whether the differentiation is desirable, and if not, the market drives out competitors until only a set of compatible products remains. There can be no assurance that the market will function perfectly in performing this function given network externalities, imperfect competition, and so on. But when incompatibilities are associated with *potentially* valuable product differentiation, the possibility of market imperfection does not provide much of a case for intervention, for neither the government nor a private standardizing body will have the information to know how to intervene. Perhaps the buyers of Beta system videocassette recorders now lament their purchase, for example, as may the owners of Next computer systems, but few observers would argue for any effort to suppress competition between such products through the harmonization of their features. Likewise it is rare to observe standardization efforts by the private sector or by government that would destroy potentially valuable product differentiation, and that is probably as it should be.

Many incompatibilities do not create valuable differentiation, however, and it is here that their emergence is presumptively undesirable. In many cases, the sellers of incompatible products bear some or all costs of these incompatibilities. When incompatibility does not facilitate any cost reduction or accretion of market power, firms generally suffer from it because they lose profits on the sales that might have been made in a broader market. The result is a private incentive to solve the problem, either through direct firm-to-firm cooperation when the number of players is small enough or through the formation of private standardizing bodies when the number of players is larger. The private sector may also prevail on government to subsidize such activities, and indeed government assistance can be important in overcoming collective action problems at times. Governments have historically proved fairly responsive to these concerns. The result is a wide array of private and private-public standardization entities at the national and international level. These organizations generate untold numbers of compatibility standards that are widely followed by their members and have done a good deal to reduce technical barriers.

Historical experience suggests at least two important classes of cases in which the network of standard-setting organizations has not averted international compatibility problems, however, and perhaps a third that is potentially important in principle although examples are difficult to provide. It is instructive to inquire what, if anything, should be done.

The first group of cases involves standards that develop before trade opens or becomes important, a problem that reflects not a lack of standards but the existence of different standards in different isolated markets. Sometimes the differences in national standards are associated with international cost differences, but the focus here is on those that are arbitrary and arise largely by chance. Some of the differences between the imperial and metric systems, between the voltage standards in different nations, and between plugs and sockets around the globe appear to fall into this category.

In the developed world, the emergence of such arbitrary incompatibilities may be largely a thing of the past. The examples above, for the most part, date from decades ago, when the volume of trade was immensely smaller, and before the formation of the International Organization for Standardization (ISO), the International Telecommunications Union (ITU), and most of the other important international standardizing bodies. Because trade barriers in general are so much lower presently and because commerce has expanded so greatly, it seems unlikely that many important incompatibilities will arise in the developed world in the future when there are no significant international cost differentials to encourage them. Exporting interests have every interest in avoiding incompatibilities when joint gains will be realized, and organizations such as the ISO and the International Electrotechnical Commission can ensure those joint gains. To be sure, these organizations are sometimes criticized for acting too slowly, and more resources might productively be devoted to funding them, but their ability to resolve this class of problems can hardly be doubted.

Furthermore, as to standard setting by national governments, much has been done under the General Agreement on Tariffs and Trade

(GATT) system to encourage notice-and-comment periods before
the adoption of new standards, so that foreign suppliers will have the
opportunity to bring to the attention of national standard-setters any
pointless incompatibilities that they might create. The Code of Good
Practice that emerged from the Uruguay Round Code urges private
and subsidiary government entities to do the same.

Thus perhaps the most important future initiatives toward the avoidance of these kinds of incompatibilities will be at the national level. In
particular, national governments need to ensure that their industries
participate in international standardization efforts to avoid situations in
which domestic standards develop without attention to their international implications. Sometimes subsidization may be required.

The danger that arbitrary incompatibilities may arise is no doubt
greater with developing nations, where standards may develop in the
local market before the development of export capability or involvement in international standardization efforts. Such problems are discussed briefly in the concluding section of this chapter.

The second important class of cases in which international
standardizing bodies have failed to avert incompatibilities involves
strong divergence of preferences internationally as to the appropriate standard. The problem is usually associated with differences in
producer rather than consumer preferences, often because of incompatibilities among proprietary technologies that are developed
more or less simultaneously. The choice of standard (often enacted
subsequently into regulation) can then confer large quasi rents on
the chosen technology, and perhaps monopoly rents as well. Some
obvious examples have arisen in the television industry—years ago
with the divergence of preferences over color television broadcast
formats and more recently with respect to high definition television
standards.

Divergent preferences among producer groups need not be fatal
to pure market solutions, as the Coase Theorem teaches us. Explicit side payments among the interested producer groups may be
difficult, but mergers, joint ventures, appropriate licensing arrangements, and the like may provide a mechanism for those who
gain from a particular compatibility standard to compensate those
who lose. When producer interests diverge initially, therefore, they
may converge eventually—the recently formed HDTV consortium
among U.S. producers is perhaps an example. Equally clearly,

however, producer accords do not always resolve the problem, especially at the international level, and persistent disputes over the appropriate standard are all too common. The task of resolving the matter then befalls one or more of the international standards organizations discussed earlier.

Experience suggests, however, that the international standard-setting process frequently breaks down. The principal reason is that international standardization organizations generally seek some form of "consensus" before acting, and a divergence of preferences among important players can then preclude the adoption of any standard. And even if the international organization can overcome some dissent under its voting rules and settle on an international standard, it lacks the power to force member nations to adopt it in their national markets. Thus when producer interest groups in a dissenting nation are unified in their opposition to the international standard, they are likely to prevail on their national standardizing bodies or national governments to eschew it.

If the international standards organizations have difficulty addressing this set of cases, what of the international compacts such as those in the GATT system? Unfortunately, none of the international legal arrangements discussed in chapter 4 are likely to provide a satisfactory solution either (although the European Commission has the power to solve these problems within Europe). Under the GATT system, if no international standard exists, signatories need only observe a notice-and-comment procedure before adopting their preferred standard or regulation. This requirement is not likely to prevent a determined national coalition from achieving its objectives. When international standards do exist, nations can opt out on grounds of "fundamental technological differences." The sham principle applies here, to be sure, and other nations might assert that the choice of an incompatible standard is a "disguised restriction on international trade." Given the difficulties with motive review under the sham principle generally, however, and the fact that arguments for the technical superiority of a standard can usually be mustered, this prospect seems unlikely to pose much of an obstacle either. Finally, if the national standard is set by a nongovernmental body, there is even less GATT restraint. The Code of Good Practice contains a sham principle, too, but otherwise the private entity can act as it wishes after affording appropriate opportunities for international comment, and the Code of Good Practice may or may not achieve widespread acceptance.[1]

Realistically, when a strong divergence among producer interest groups pushes national standardizers or regulators toward incompatibilities, the problem can only be solved by an international institution with the power to override the national decisions of its constituent members. Perhaps the global community will one day find it politically expedient to create such an institution in the standards arena, but it is well short of creating it presently. Moreover, it is by no means obvious that such an institution is desirable. Nothing can ensure that producer coalitions would not capture it to their own advantage or that it would operate free of serious error. The inefficiencies that arise presently because of incompatibilities could well be exceeded by the inefficiencies of forced compatibility using the "wrong" standard or suppressing valuable product diversity. It is possible, therefore, that existing institutions handle the problem of divergent preferences about as well as it can be handled notwithstanding their undeniable failings.

A third way in which the current system may fail with some regularity relates to the transparency and timing of standardization efforts, especially by subsidiary governments and private entities. Even when standardization decisions can do nothing to exclude rivals in the long run, rivals may need time to retool to meet a new standard. A strategic advantage attaches to inside information about new standards that, if exploited, may produce transitory monopoly problems or transitory periods in which lowest cost producers are excluded from the market while they retool. The GATT system imposes potentially useful restrictions in this regard on standard setting at the national level, involving a requirement of notice and comment (although it is not clear how well nations have adhered to these obligations). But these principles do not yet extend generally to subsidiary governments or to private entities except when national governments have done so voluntarily. The new Code of Good Practice in the

---

1. It is worth noting that because GATT is less effective at constraining private entities than national governments, nations that entrust much of their standardization efforts to the private sector may be at a strategic advantage in some instances (when the private entity is likely to act to promote the national advantage, perhaps at the expense of other nations) and a disadvantage in some instances (when the private entity will promote domestic monopoly, for example).

Uruguay Round TBT Agreement creates for the first time a requirement of notice and comment for private entities, although it remains
to be seen how widely it is accepted. Should adherence prove widespread, however, much will have been done to improve the transparency of the process in local government and private standardizing
entities.

However, we cannot be entirely certain that the gains from transparency always exceed the transaction costs of transparent procedures and thus cannot conclude that the procedures in the Code of
Good Practice should necessarily be followed by all standardization
entities. In this regard, recall the limitation on the notice-and-
comment obligations of the national governments under the Technical Barriers Agreement—the measures at issue must "significantly
affect trade." This proviso saves administrative costs when the benefits of notice and comment are likely to be small or negligible but, as
noted, may excuse neglect or invite abuse. The proper accommoda-
tion between administrative costs and precaution against neglect and
abuse remains unclear.

The discussion above suggests that relatively little can be done in
the short run by way of different approaches for addressing compatibility problems in international markets. Nevertheless, it is important
that financial support for existing international standardization efforts
continue, and perhaps be expanded. National governments should
take steps to ensure that their interests are adequately represented in
international standards organizations and subsidize participation in
one manner or another when needed to overcome free rider problems. Governments should also take seriously the existing notice-and-
comment requirements of the GATT system. But situations may
continue to arise in which national interest groups push their own
preferred standards and produce international gridlock, perhaps with
inefficient incompatibilities in the end. Yet there is no easy solution to
the problem in principle, much less a solution that would prove
politically feasible in the foreseeable future. Over a longer time hori-
zon, an international organization with the power to override dissent
by individual nations over the standard to be chosen might emerge,
and further restrictions may be observed on the activities of private
and subsidiary government standard-setters. It is not self evident that
such measures would be desirable, however, given their administrative costs and the risk of errors when fiat is used to resolve incompat-

ibilities. Thus it is not unreasonable to suppose that the current international response to incompatibility problems is on the whole satisfactory in view of the feasible alternatives.

Quality, Labeling, and Conformity Issues

By far the bulk of government-to-government disputes over technical barriers relate to international heterogeneities in quality or labeling requirements and in the procedures used to assess conformity with those requirements. Divergent health and safety regulations are of particular importance, as are divergent regulations to promote other "consumer protection" objectives.

The array of remedial options here is far broader than with compatibility issues. At one end of the continuum lies complete deference to national sovereigns (including the activities of national standardizing entities, public or private), perhaps coupled with cooperative voluntary standardization efforts at the international level through organizations such as the ISO and the Codex. Although such a regime exists to an extent in some international services markets, the trading community long ago abandoned this option in goods markets with the formation of GATT.

At the other end of the continuum lies total harmonization, when nations covenant to pursue policies that are identical in every respect. This too is rare on a global level, although it has emerged in Europe to a degree.

In between the extremes lie many alternatives that impose greater or lesser constraint on national sovereigns while still affording some opportunity for variations across nations. Many of these alternatives involve "policed decentralization," whereby national authorities are largely free to pursue their own policy objectives but must do so subject to a set of broadly applicable legal constraints. The options here include non-discrimination principles, the sham principle, transparency requirements, generality requirements, presumptive deference to international standards with specified procedures for deviation, mutual recognition, and benefit/burden balancing tests. They also include rules that qualify the extent of the international obligation in accordance with the subject matter of the regulation—for example, a rule that requires mutual recognition except on matters relating to human, animal, or plant health and safety. A set of alternatives to policed decentralization, still short of total harmonization, involves "partial harmonization." An important option for partial harmonization is "regulatory objective harmonization," when nations agree on the essential objectives of regulation but permit those objectives to be satisfied in a variety of ways. This section discusses all these options, noting their advantages and disadvantages and considering whether they should be used more or less extensively.

Decentralized Policing of Policy Implementation: Least-Restrictive Means and Related Principles

The GATT system, whether in its original inception, in the Tokyo Round Standards Code, or in the Uruguay Round accords, is a system of policed decentralization. The North American Free Trade Agreement (NAFTA) takes the same approach for the most part, and the principles developed by the European Court of Justice under article 30 and by U.S. courts in dormant commerce clause litigation also represent guidelines for policed decentralization. Thus this strategy in one form or another already predominates in international and, to a lesser extent, national goods markets.

One principle that appears in all these systems is the least-restrictive means principle—the requirement that policy objectives be achieved in the manner that is least restrictive of free trade and open markets. The justification for a least-restrictive means principle is self-evident. If a given objective can be achieved in a variety of ways, the trading community benefits in the aggregate when the least-cost way is selected.

This principle is arguably more important than any other. In fact, one might argue that most of the important principles of policed decentralization are corollaries of the least-restrictive means principle. Discriminatory measures achieve policy objectives, if at all, only in a manner that usually distorts trade unnecessarily, and thus are not least-restrictive. A "disguised restriction" on trade is, by definition, not the least-restrictive way to achieve a legitimate policy objective. Performance regulations allow the desired level of performance to be achieved in the cheapest fashion possible by each producer, whereas design regulations typically do not. Notice-and-comment procedures, deference to international standards, and mutual recognition are also at times the least-restrictive means to a given end.

Because the least-restrictive means concept animates so many of these more specific principles to be discussed below, its application will not be discussed in any detail here. Instead, I simply note its fundamental limitation: The least-restrictive means inquiry accepts the underlying objective of national policy uncritically and asks how best to meet that objective; it plainly cannot address many of the technical barriers that arise because of disparate national policy objectives. Thus a distinction is drawn at the outset between efforts to ensure that policy objectives are achieved in the best fashion and efforts to ensure that the policy objectives themselves are reasonable. This section focuses on principles of policed decentralization that fall into the first category.

Nondiscrimination Principles

Each of the legal systems discussed in chapter 4 pays close attention to whether the challenged measures are discriminatory. Discriminatory measures invariably invoke closer scrutiny and are at times impermissible per se.

Because so many troublesome measures escape condemnation under nondiscrimination principles, particularly the measures at issue in certain recent and highly publicized disputes, it may be tempting to dismiss nondiscrimination norms as unimportant or peripheral. Quite the contrary, nondiscrimination requirements foreclose the most obvious methods by which standards and regulations can be manipulated by domestic producer interests to create technical barriers to trade, as chapter 3 indicates. Nondiscrimination requirements are thus a potent weapon against unjustifiable technical barriers that result from capture of the standard-setting or regulatory process. Further, because discrimination in trade distorts the pattern of production and investment by preventing lower-cost producers from outcompeting higher-cost producers, discriminatory measures are costly even in the absence of any capture. A further virtue of nondiscrimination principles lies in their relative ease of administration in most cases (the foot-and-mouth disease illustration below suggests some exceptions). It is usually easy to ascertain in principle whether standards and regulations are applied evenhandedly.

A difficult and intriguing question concerns the extent to which exceptions should be permitted to nondiscrimination principles. Starting with the most favored nation requirement, it is difficult to imagine *any* justification for an exception (but note the clarification discussed below). Whatever the perceived threat to health, safety, or other consumer interests, there can be no basis for knowingly disregarding the threat from some countries but not others. To be sure, the *effect* of a nondiscriminatory policy may vary across trading partners, but the criteria for excluding imports or otherwise interfering with trade should not.

The question whether exceptions should exist to the national treatment obligation is more subtle. Suppose, for example, that France bans the importation of live animals from any nation in which foot-and-mouth disease is present, and that occasional outbreaks of foot-and-mouth disease occur in France anyway. Is there any denial of national treatment? If France makes no effort to quarantine diseased herds domestically, the answer seems to be yes, and indeed such a policy would appear highly suspicious. Hence national treatment, at least to this extent, should probably be required. But even if France quarantines diseased herds, a ban on the importation of animals from an entire country, even from herds with no evidence of disease, seems considerably more restrictive than the hypothesized domestic quarantine policy and thus might still be argued to deny national treatment. Should the ban on imports nevertheless be permitted?

The answer may turn on additional facts, facts that are possibly unknowable. Suppose that France instead were to ban the importation of animals from herds that cannot be certified free of disease for some period of time before importation, seemingly a less-restrictive alternative. How well will that accomplish the regulatory objective— for example, what is the probability that diseased animals will enter from herds not known to be diseased? And how serious are the consequences of an occasional animal entering the country carrying the disease in relation to the economic costs of an import ban? Given the obvious empirical difficulties here, as well as the conceptual difficulty in defining what national treatment means in this context, it is not unreasonable to conclude that exceptions to the national treatment obligation may occasionally be justified, although least-restrictive alternatives must, at least, be considered and a plausible argument against them offered. Likewise, if exceptions are not permitted, the battle will simply shift to the conceptual problem of whether national treatment has been afforded, and the answer may well turn as a practical matter on the reasonableness of the measures at issue. Thus I tend to doubt that the existence of limited exceptions to the national treatment obligation will make much difference, as long as they are, in turn, policed by the least-restrictive means principle.[2]

Similarly, it is easy to imagine cases in which national treatment *is* afforded, yet the least-restrictive means have not been used—suppose that France bans imports from nations where, unlike France, vaccinations are not required for all animals, yet the risk of foot-and-mouth disease is demonstrably no greater in nations with an effective quarantine policy. Here again, the least-restrictive means principle may be far more useful than the national treatment principle in ferreting out unnecessary barriers.

The integration of least-restrictive means and nondiscrimination principles may be useful in yet another set of cases. Take the example of a ban on imports from nations with foot-and-mouth disease once again, and suppose that a few cases of foot-and-mouth disease have been reported in New Jersey. Suppose further that no other cases of the disease have been reported in the United States for many years. Here a ban on imports that extends to all fifty states seems excessive, even though it is facially nondiscriminatory. The solution may be to require that such measures be limited to *regions* where the disease is present, defined in some sensible way in relation to the epidemiology of the disease and the locations in which it has been reported. So modified, the import ban might result in the complete exclusion of imports from some nations with the disease and only a partial exclusion of imports from other nations with the disease. The modified ban would be less restrictive of trade and should be permissible despite its facial affront to the most favored nation principle. The provisions on "adaptation to regional conditions" in the GATT Sanitary and Phytosanitary Measures (SPM) Agreement are evidently motivated by this concern and represent a valuable clarification of the most favored nation obligation.[3]

2. I conjecture that persuasive arguments for an exception will likely be confined to cases involving regulations to prevent the spread of pests or disease.

3. GATT SPM Agreement, article 6.

In sum, although the application of nondiscrimination principles may occasionally raise subtle issues, it is both understandable and desirable that they should play a central role in any system of policed decentralization. As chapter 4 indicates, they already apply broadly to the policies of national governments, and the Uruguay Round Code of Good Practice would extend them to the activities of private entities and subsidiary governments. Such a development should be welcomed, and indeed I suspect that the trading community would benefit from universal mandatory application of these principles in all standardization and regulatory activity.

Sham Principle

Another principle common to most of the existing systems of policed decentralization is the "sham principle," typically phrased as an obligation to ensure that standards or regulations not be used to create "disguised barriers" to trade. As suggested previously, the difficulty with this principle lies not in its conception but in its administration. It requires the arbiter of a dispute to determine whether the stated justification for the measure under investigation is disingenuous, a determination that is diplomatically and politically awkward, to say the least. Therefore the sham principle is rarely invoked and, to my knowledge, has never been invoked in the GATT system.

It does not follow that the sham principle is altogether useless. Its existence places national authorities on notice that they may be asked to explain their policies, and it may then discourage occasional measures for which no colorable, high-minded justification can be concocted. On the whole, however, its significance is probably minimal, and efforts to police "disguised restrictions" are better concentrated elsewhere.

Notice, Comment, and Publication Requirements

Notice, comment, and publication requirements serve three functions, all important. First, they reduce the costs to foreign producers of obtaining information about quality and labeling requirements and thereby reduce the costs of serving foreign markets. Second, they provide foreign suppliers with time to retool before new requirements take effect and thus avert temporary monopoly problems and the temporary exclusion of low-cost foreign suppliers. Third, they can help avert the enactment of requirements that differ arbitrarily from those elsewhere and that are not essential to regulatory objectives. Of course, they cannot by themselves preclude the enactment of requirements that are calculated to disadvantage foreign rivals and thus do not respond effectively to certain problems that can result from capture. Finally, as noted earlier, the danger that notice, comment, and publication requirements will create unnecessary administrative cost must be thoughtfully considered and balanced against the danger that qualified obligations will lead to neglect and abuse.

Chapter 4 demonstrates how the GATT system, the European Union, and NAFTA all rely significantly on notice, comment, and publication requirements. It is much too early to tell how well NAFTA or the post-Uruguay round WTO/GATT system will function here. The European system has apparently been fairly effective at avoiding new technical barriers, especially in the regulatory area, but the extent to which GATT obligations have been taken seriously in the past is in doubt.

For the future, it seems that the legal requirements for notice and comment are largely in place and sufficient on their face. The task is to ensure that they are taken to heart by national governments. The extension of such requirements to private entities and subsidiary governments through the Code of Good Practice is also an important and valuable Uruguay Round initiative.

Generality Requirements

An obvious corollary of the least-restrictive means principle is that quality and labeling requirements should be formulated at the highest possible level of generality consistent with regulatory objectives. Such formulations allow objectives to be achieved in a variety of ways, and each producer can select the least-cost alternative. The provision in the GATT Technical Barriers to Trade (TBT) Agreement that encourages the use of performance standards over design standards is a particular application of this principle, but its applications are much more extensive.

For example, chapters 2 and 4 touch on a class of recurring cases in which certain consumer protection objectives are pursued through the regulation of product characteristics rather than through labeling requirements. In general, the question as to when informative labeling is adequate for consumer protection is controversial and turns more on empirics than on any matter of theory. It is tempting to argue that labeling requirements should always be preferred to regulation of other product characteristics whenever the danger to consumers is small if they do not read or appreciate the label. To draw the line constructively, one might distinguish regulatory objectives relating to a "significant" threat to human, plant, or animal health from other regulatory objectives and urge that labeling regulations be the only permissible ones for the latter class of cases. Such a principle could be added to both the GATT TBT Agreement and the SPM Agreement. When a serious threat to health or safety exists, exclusive resort to labeling is more problematic, although the importance of preserving consumer choice should not be easily dismissed.

Reliance on International Standards

International standards do not exist for many quality and labeling requirements, and thus reliance on international standards is only feasible in some instances. Further, regulatory authorities may find international standards insufficient to meet their objectives. If international standards are adequate in this respect, however, reliance on those that exist can eliminate many different technical barriers and will do so at no cost to the efficacy of regulation.

Thus the question arises whether nations should *ever* be allowed to deviate from international standards when they suffice to achieve their objectives. As noted in chapter 4, the Tokyo Round Standards Code allowed signatories to deviate from international standards when formulating technical regulations whenever the international standards are "inappropriate." The Uruguay Round accords require signatories to use international standards except when they would be an "ineffective or inappropriate means for the fulfillment of the legitimate objectives pursued." This change in language is potentially significant, as it forces parties to articulate why international standards are inadequate in relation to domestic objectives. But the new language stops short of requiring reliance on international standards whenever they suffice to achieve the domestic objective—even if they are not "ineffective," they may still be "inappropriate."

How can international standards be inappropriate even though adherence to them will achieve the regulatory objectives effectively? A possible response is that when international standards differ from established domestic standards, domestic producers may have to incur substantial additional costs to change over to the international standard. The added costs to domestic producers of adopting the international standard might then exceed the cost savings to foreign producers. This argument is unpersuasive, however, for it implies a regulatory regime that violates the generality requirement. From the hypothesized facts, the least-restrictive means of regulation is to allow the sale of goods that meet *either* the international standard or the established domestic standard. Perhaps a response to this objection is that the costs of conformity assessment would rise unduly if the conformity assessment process had to test goods against two or more standards, but it is by no means obvious that this would occur, especially with appropriate recognition of foreign testing and certification.

Hence I question whether there is any persuasive argument why goods that conform to an international standard should be excluded if that standard "effectively" meets the domestic regulatory objective. GATT members should consider strengthening the TBT and SPM agreements by requiring signatories to determine that international standards are insufficient for the attainment of the domestic regulatory goal before discarding them.

Mutual Recognition

Much the same points might be made about mutual recognition. Sometimes the quality and labeling requirements of trading partners are insufficient to meet bona fide domestic regulatory objectives, but in other instances, they will achieve those objectives adequately, albeit in a different way. In such cases, the case for mutual recognition is compelling. To be sure, importing nations may worry about the adequacy of conformity assessment on exports from other nations and may wish to adopt some mechanism for testing and certification to ensure that "cheating" does not occur. But this is no objection to mutual recognition of substantive standards and regulations.

The Uruguay Round accords address mutual recognition expressly for the first time in the GATT system. As noted in chapter 4, the TBT

Agreement requires parties to give "positive consideration" to mutual recognition, except when technical regulations abroad do not "adequately fulfill the objectives" of the importing country. The SPM Agreement is similar, adding that parties must be allowed to "objectively demonstrate" the equivalence of their regulations. These obligations go far toward embracing the principle suggested here—that parties should be required to base a refusal of mutual recognition on a determination that the policies of the exporting country are inadequate to meet the objectives of the importing country. Again, therefore, much of the necessary legal apparatus is in place as to national governments. The task is to ensure that it is taken seriously and to extend it to the activities of other entities.

Obligation to Give Reasons and the "Standard of Review"

It was argued above that nations should justify a refusal to rely on pertinent international standards or to afford mutual recognition on the grounds that to do so would undermine the attainment of legitimate regulatory objectives. Plainly, if nothing but a conclusory assertion to that effect is needed, this requirement may be limited in its effectiveness to cases in which domestic regulators or their constituencies have no interest in disadvantaging imports. But the international community as a whole would also benefit from reliance on international standards and mutual recognition when resistance to them is based on anticompetitive or other economically counterproductive objectives unrelated to the legitimate ends of regulation.

The sham principle might serve this function in the abstract, but its difficulties have already been noted. Probably the best alternative is to require national regulators to detail reasons why their legitimate objectives would be undermined by international standards or mutual recognition and to require as well that they lay bare the factual evidence that supports their claims. Even if the arbiter of disputes is deferential to this showing, as might perhaps be expected from an international dispute panel, the concern of signatories for their reputations and for the possibility of retaliation when their explanations are transparently weak may discourage many abuses. The GATT system embraces this strategy to a considerable degree.

It is also important to consider the appropriate "standard of review" for dispute resolution under the GATT accords, a matter that the technical barrier agreements do not address expressly. To be politically acceptable within the international community, dispute resolution probably must remain reasonably deferential to the honest judgments of national regulators. But excessive deference makes dispute resolution ineffectual, and some "intermediate" level of deference thus seems appropriate. The U.S. system of administrative law may provide a useful model. Appellate review of administrative agency actions in the United States typically entails an effort to ascertain that the agency has given legally sufficient reasons for its action and that the record of the administrative proceeding contains some factual evidence that a reasonable person could take to support the agency's determination, even if the appellate court disagrees with it. Such determinations are far more comfortable politically than findings of "sham" or, more or less equivalently, findings of a "disguised restriction on trade." They can thus be issued with some level of comfort when sham or stupidity is suspected and have considerable potential to discourage abuse and to police capture. At the same time, this standard of review is still deferential, requiring only a proper application of the rules and a plausible factual basis for the challenged action. To encourage dispute resolution panels to apply such a standard, it might be worth articulating it clearly in the technical barrier agreements.

Conclusion

Many of the existing international legal obligations respecting quality and labeling requirements may be understood as encouraging national regulators to pursue their objectives in the manner least restrictive of trade. Other obligations may be understood as part of a strategy to expose national decisions to international scrutiny and thus to make it somewhat more costly politically to use the regulatory process for protectionist ends or to capriciously ignore the international ramifications of national policy.

Stringent application of the least-restrictive means principle and its corollaries can discourage and eliminate many technical barriers, although not all. Because its logic is so compelling, there can be little objection other than perhaps administrative cost to extending it to matters not yet covered—most important, to the activities of private standards and certification entities and to the activities of subsidiary governments.

Decentralized Policing of Policy Goals and Objectives

The preceding discussion suggests that "policed decentralization" can in principle do much to ensure that nations pursue their legitimate regulatory objectives in a manner that is least restrictive to international commerce. Many technical barrier problems result not from a failure to use least-restrictive means, however, but from a divergence of views over what constitutes a sensible regulatory policy. The growth-hormone dispute between the United States and the European Community, for example, is at least arguably a dispute over whether a zero-risk policy is sensible despite the absence of evidence of any health hazard from some of the growth hormones (the other view is that the zero-risk policy is pretense). The new stringent nutritional labeling requirements of the U.S. Food and Drug Administration likewise reflect a judgment about the importance of such information to consumers, a judgment that regulators in other nations may not share. The decisions by national regulators to adopt food safety standards more stringent than those of the Codex afford many other illustrations.

The legal principles and strategies discussed in the last section are largely ineffectual for resolving disputes that fall into this class of problems. Nondiscrimination principles are of no value either because national treatment is afforded or because a reasonable argument can be made for denying it (recall the foot-and-mouth disease illustration). The sham principle has the familiar difficulties. Notice, comment, and publication requirements may help somewhat by flagging potential disputes before they arise and occasionally avoiding them but can do nothing to resolve disputes once regulators decide to pursue a more stringent policy than others. Generality requirements typically accomplish little as well, because the problem lies in the stringency of the policy objective rather than the means to achieve it. International standards will be rejected because they are inadequate to achieve the policy objective, and mutual recognition will be rejected for the same reason.

One strategy that may retain limited vitality here is the obligation to give reasons and disclose evidence, even if the standard of review is highly deferential. For example, in the growth-hormone dispute, European regulators might be required to demonstrate that *some* evidence exists to support the existence of a health hazard from the prohibited hormones before a zero-risk policy can be deemed acceptable, however strong the evidence on the other side. But even this sort of requirement can prove controversial or even ineffectual. Why, it might be argued, is it impermissible for national authorities to require that food additives and chemical residues be "proved" safe before they are allowed, rather than proved unsafe before they are banned? Why is it impermissible to pursue a zero-risk policy when there is any suspicion of possible hazard? Is not evidence of a health hazard from one growth hormone (DES) sufficient to constitute "some evidence" of a health hazard from all growth hormones? As chapter 4 indicated, the GATT SPM Agreement is sensitive to such arguments, allowing "provisional measures" when scientific data are "insufficient." Its ability to resolve this particular dispute comfortably, therefore, may be doubted.

A more expansive legal inquiry, modeled along the approach of U.S. courts in dormant commerce clause cases and the rule of reason inquiry before the European Court of Justice, might undertake to balance the benefits of the regulatory policy against its costs on a global scale. But the practical and political difficulties here are obvious. Such a broad-based balancing test requires that nations be willing to sacrifice their national regulatory objectives, often touching on such matters as human health and safety, to the purely "economic" cause of international commerce. Experience suggests that they are not. A balancing inquiry also presupposes that the required "balancing" can be undertaken with some degree of legitimacy, reliability, and predictability by the arbiter of disputes, when, in fact, it almost certainly cannot. Not surprisingly, nothing in the GATT system empowers dispute resolution panels to conduct an open-ended inquiry into the reasonableness of regulatory objectives or to balance the benefits of regulation against its burdens.

For these reasons, I suspect that strategies for policed decentralization can (and do) accomplish little to achieve a satisfactory resolution of disputes that result from a bona fide divergence of views over the appropriate regulatory policy, particularly when sensitive issues of health and safety are involved. The same difficulty arises when disputes result from sincere disagreements about the weight of scientific evidence.

Perhaps this is as it should be. Nothing can ensure that a central authority with the power to second-guess national regulators will do so sensibly or correctly. Moreover, as discussed in chapter 3, heterogeneities in regulatory policy can yield data over time that allow disagreements to be resolved amicably rather than coercively. They may also be justified by differences in well-informed citizen preferences or by income differences across nations. In the end, it is not at all unreasonable to take the position that bona fide differences in regulatory objectives should simply be tolerated and do not require much policing.

The counterargument is that many differences in policy may result from differences in information, so that cooperative activity to develop a shared perception of hazards and other regulatory concerns can promote a mutually satisfactory convergence in policy. Likewise, national regulators may not appreciate the commercial burdens associated with disparate policies and may be persuaded that some of their goals are unduly costly once informed about them. To a limited extent, policed decentralization can and does encourage constructive cooperation to resolve disputes in this fashion—the GATT system, for example, requires government-to-government consultations before dispute resolution panels can be appointed. But more can be done to promote cooperation among national regulators before the emergence of a dispute. I thus turn to the options and prospects for harmonization.

Harmonization

Extensive efforts to facilitate harmonization of international quality and labeling policies have been under way for decades. The ISO and the Codex, among other entities, pursue such matters routinely. Some progress has been made, but on many matters, international standards do not yet exist; on others, national regulators continue to pursue their own policies.

The GATT system reflects considerable effort to increase the impact of international standards. The initiatives are essentially two: (1) to encourage nations to use international standards when they exist unless they have good reason not to; and (2) to encourage nations to participate more actively in international standardization organizations. Both initiatives are to be applauded.

The question here is whether more can and should be done to promote beneficial harmonization. I believe that the answer is yes.

Identify Opportunities

Recalling the discussion in chapter 2, it is difficult indeed to assess the significance of the technical barrier problem in international markets. Anecdotal evidence exists for some industries and nations; more systematic evidence exists for a few well-publicized disputes; and occasional case studies provide somewhat more in-depth information by sector. If the global community is to make more rapid progress toward eliminating the technical barriers that can and should be eliminated, it would be most helpful to know more about them.

The European Community recognized the importance of developing additional information some years ago, resulting in the Commission-sponsored studies surveyed in the Cecchini Report. Similar efforts might be made at the global level to identify the industries and sectors in which technical barriers prove most important and to identify the specific regulatory measures that are the greatest source of concern. A broad survey of business leaders in major trading nations, followed by careful case studies of the industries in which technical barriers are most widely cited as important, is a sensible way to proceed.

Such efforts might be undertaken by any number of existing institutions. The ISO and Codex are sensible possibilities, as is the Organization for Economic Cooperation and Development. Historically, GATT has undertaken relatively little in the way of basic economic research of this sort, but there is no reason in principle why it might not do more in the future. The key here is a high-level political commitment to funding the research.

Ensure that Regulators Participate

Regulators are more likely to deem international standards adequate to meet their objectives if they have participated closely in their development. Representatives of regulatory agencies do participate in international standardization efforts at times but only haphazardly—the U.S. representative to the ISO, for example, is a private body (American National Standards Institute). More systematic participation by regulators should be encouraged. It is equally important that national representatives to international bodies include high-level officials with close links to policy formulation and thus with the capacity to negotiate standards that their agencies will likely accept.

Consider Opportunities for Partial Harmonization

Experience in the international standardization organizations, as well as experience under the "old approach" to harmonization in Europe, suggests that global agreement on detailed standards, product-by-product, is time-consuming and difficult. The problem is compounded if high-level participation by national regulatory authorities is required, yet without it the danger arises that national regulators will refuse to accept international standards.

At least in some sectors, the European "new approach" model may have value. As indicated in chapter 4, the "essential requirements" directives reflect high-level agreement on regulatory objectives at a considerable level of detail for broad product categories, whereas the task of formulating product-by-product standards to meet the essential requirements is delegated to lower-level technical experts in the national and international standardizing agencies. Similar efforts could be undertaken at the global level. Under the auspices of the ISO or GATT, for example, high-level officials from interested nations might undertake to reach agreement on the essential safety requirements for, say, toys or children's sleepwear. Technical expert groups in the pertinent international standards organization (ISO, Codex, ITU, and so on) might then undertake to draft standards to meet the essential requirements and might also be authorized to issue an opinion on whether existing national standards in various countries meet the essential requirements already. National regulators might reserve the right to dispute the adequacy of the work performed by technical expert groups but otherwise covenant to allow free entry of products certified to meet either the international standards or the national standards found equivalent to them.

To be sure, international agreement on essential requirements may at times prove difficult or impossible, in which case harmonization will prove impossible as well. But the European model has the potential to expedite harmonization efforts considerably when harmonization is unobjectionable, both by reducing the number of issues that high-level officials must address and by increasing the likelihood that standards developed at the international level will be found adequate for domestic objectives.

Conformity Assessment

Put succinctly, the central objective of international conformity assessment should be to use the least-restrictive means available to provide adequate assurance of conformity. Thus much of what was said above about the usefulness of the least restrictive means principle and its corollaries applies here as well. Policed decentralization in accordance with these principles can accomplish a good deal if taken seriously, and as noted, the GATT accords do apply least-restrictive means concepts to conformity assessment.

The one issue that is "special" to conformity assessment, in my view, concerns the willingness of national authorities to rely on foreign test data and other aspects of conformity assessment undertaken in the country of exportation, including self-certification by the exporter. As chapter 3 indicated, the global costs of conformity assessment can be reduced considerably when confidence in overseas conformity assessment develops and national authorities can then accept it without further testing in the country of importation. But those authorities will naturally be reluctant to do so without reasonable assurances as to its accuracy, and in many settings, an incentive for fraud or carelessness may be present.

Perhaps the easiest cases are those in which the substantive standards and regulations in the country of exportation are the same as those in the country of importation or achieve the objectives of the country of importation adequately. Mutual recognition of the substantive standards and regulations should then be possible, as should mutual recognition of conformity assessment in most instances.

The harder cases arise when the country of importation imposes more stringent standards and regulations than the country of exportation. Authorities in the importing country cannot then expect that products circulating freely abroad will usually meet their standards, and the need arises for special conformity assessment measures applicable to exports. Once again, the least-restrictive means principle should govern the design of such measures, and optimal deterrence theory has something to say about the least-restrictive means.

Because self-certification is surely the cheapest form of conformity assessment, it is to be preferred except when it cannot be trusted. The self-certifier must have proper incentives to tell the truth and to use certification procedures that are reasonably free of error. For such incentives to exist, the self-certifier must anticipate an appropriate penalty for incorrect certifications.

Chapter 3 developed the considerations that bear on the appropriate penalty structure. Put simply, the self-certifier may, in many cases, be confronted with adequate "ex post" penalties in the event that a product fails and causes harm, either through civil litigation, through fines, or through customs sanctions. When it is difficult to penalize the exporter adequately ex post, it can suffice to penalize the importer, who will then have a proper incentive to ensure that the self-certification by the exporter is accurate. Devices such as bond posting can ensure the adequacy of ex post penalties when they might not work otherwise.

If ex post penalties will not provide proper incentives for self-certifiers, some sort of ex ante conformity assessment system will be needed. In general, the greater the number of units of a product that must be tested or inspected, the greater the costs. The penalty for nonconformity, however, can often be raised rather cheaply. Thus the costs of ex ante conformity assessment may, at times, be reduced by lowering the number of units to be tested or inspected and by increasing the penalty for nonconformity accordingly. In effect, it may be possible to rely heavily on self-certification, coupled with a limited number of "spot checks" accompanied by stiff sanctions.

Existing international standards can play an important role here. As under the "global approach" in Europe, manufacturers can promise to follow the pertinent quality control procedures of the ISO 9000 standards. Periodic audits, attended by sensibly calibrated penalties for violations, can ensure adherence to them. The ISO 9000 standards are also helpful in providing a well-researched benchmark for adequate quality control, thus reducing the costs to individual importing nations of devising rules for the acceptance of foreign testing and certification.

Foreign testing laboratories can also economize on the costs of ex ante conformity assessment by providing a single series of tests, in a single location, to meet the requirements of many different export markets. Much the same ideas can inform the guidelines for acceptance of their test data. Although it is unlikely that a testing laboratory will be subject to civil liability or fines if a product that it tests proves defective in some way, it is often possible to "spot check" the quality of testing abroad and impose stiff penalties when it proves deficient, such as the refusal to accept test data from the laboratory in the future. When such incentive mechanisms can be put in place, testing by foreign laboratories should be perfectly acceptable. One can readily imagine the evolution of a complete set of international standards to assist in this system, along the lines of the EN 45000 series.

In short, importing nations typically have many different incentive devices at their disposal for punishing false certifications and discouraging mistakes and can use them to ensure the reliability of information generated abroad. In some cases, these incentives are already in place, and in other cases proper incentives can be created through an additional system of spot checks and penalties administered by customs or other authorities. Importing nations should use such incentives when possible and rely on information generated abroad in preference to requiring extensive on-shore conformity assessment. The costs of doing so can be greatly reduced by reference to international standards for quality control as the basis for the requirements that foreign certifiers and testers must meet.

The GATT system already encourages nations to accept foreign test data and self-certification but does not address expressly any of the considerations that bear on the reliability of such information, leaving it to national authorities to determine when they are "satisfied" with it. There may well be considerable merit to elaborating the conditions under which foreign testing or self-certification might be presumed adequate, and to adding an obligation for national authorities to give reasons when they refuse to accept foreign test data or certifications.

Note on Developing Countries

Little has been said about developing countries to this point, largely because I see only a few issues in the technical barrier area that are special to them. In the main, the developing countries have fewer standards and regulations than developed countries and often less stringent standards and regulations when matters of quality are concerned. As a result, they may have greater difficulty meeting the requirements of importing nations, including conformity assessment requirements. Also some of the principles that make sense for trade among developed nations—the preference for performance standards in particular—have some drawbacks for developing nations that strengthen the case for certain forms of development assistance. A further concern is that developing nations are at times subject to exploitation by exporters who ship merchandise that is unsafe or unwholesome. This prospect is really the opposite of a technical barrier problem, but I will nonetheless touch on it briefly. Lastly, developing nations may wish exemption from some of the obligations of technical barrier agreements, on the grounds that strict adherence would be too costly or otherwise undermine "development."

As to the first issue, one would not expect developed nations to make much of an allowance in formulating their standards and regulations for compliance difficulties in developing nations. Importing nations are not likely to sacrifice public health and safety standards to promote development abroad, for example, and purchasers are unlikely to tolerate incompatible products out of sympathy for the plight of poorer nations. It is not surprising that the GATT accords simply urge developed nations to "consider" making allowance for the problems of developing countries in meeting standards abroad and do not require anything specific. Likewise, it is no surprise that NAFTA is silent on this issue. Perhaps the most sensible response to these problems is not to introduce inefficiencies into the standards and regulations of the developed world, but rather for the developed nations to subsidize the efforts of developing country exporters to learn about standards and regulations abroad and to conform their exports to them, as well as perhaps to provide broader technical assistance. Some commitments along these lines are contained in the technical cooperation and assistance articles of the GATT agreements and NAFTA and implicitly in the rules for setting the contribution of each nation to the international standardization organizations, a contribution that is typically a function of the gross national product and per capita income. Perhaps more might be done quantitatively in this regard, but it is difficult to imagine much else that should be done qualitatively.

Another problem for developing countries is the use of performance standards in developed countries, in preference to design standards, which may have the arguably perverse effect of inhibiting technology transfer. Design standards often contain detailed information about exactly how a product must be made. Access to such standards, therefore, can provide manufacturers in developing nations with a good deal of information about state-of-the-art technologies. Performance standards, by contrast, leave it to the manufacturer to find a way to meet them. Again the solution is probably not to introduce inefficient design standards into the developed countries but instead to provide technical assistance to developing nations that have difficulty meeting performance standards.

Regarding the danger that developed nations may knowingly export unsafe or unwholesome products to developing countries, it is interesting that existing international obligations place no burden on developed countries to prevent such problems. Several inferences are possible. One is that the problem has not arisen often enough to become a matter of serious concern, perhaps because the quality standards and regulations that are in place in the developed nations are enforced well enough to protect the developing nations as well. A second possible inference is that the developing nations do not wish the developed nations to undertake measures to protect them against these problems, on the theory that the costs would be passed along in the prices of the goods that they import and would not be worth the benefits. A third possible inference is that the developed nations are unjustifiably insensitive to the problem.

The empirical evidence is scant, although it is not difficult to find examples in which developed nations export goods to developing nations that would violate safety regulations in the country of exportation. One recent study mentions the export of children's sleepwear treated with a carcinogenic fire retardant chemical, the export of pesticides widely banned and thought to create a serious threat to human and animal health, and the over-the-counter sale of drugs dangerous to children without proper warnings.[4]

Whatever the magnitude of the problem, developed nations can help developing countries to protect themselves by informing them of the safety regulations in place elsewhere and by counseling them with

4. Agege (1985, pp. 403–04).

respect to their own regulatory apparatus. The commitment to provide technical assistance in existing GATT accords is thus helpful here as well. Developed nations might also undertake on their own to ban exports that did not meet domestic health and safety standards, but as noted, it is by no means clear that developing nations would benefit on balance.

Finally, as to the question whether developing nations should be exempted from certain technical barrier obligations, existing and proposed GATT accords do make allowances for developing countries that have difficulty meeting their commitments by affording them additional time to comply or even allowing them a waiver.[5] To some extent, these allowances are of no importance to trade—a decision by a developing nation not to adopt an international safety standard, for example, will often reflect a decision to adopt a *lower* standard and will not become a source of any trade impediment. But other provisions are more worrisome. The TBT Agreement provides, for example, that developing countries "should not be expected to use international standards . . . which are not appropriate to their development, financial and trade needs."[6] This provision opens the door for developing countries to construct their standards and regulations to protect the domestic industries that they deem important to development, much as article XVIII of GATT itself permits developing nations to take measures otherwise inconsistent with the agreement to promote their "infant industries."

I do not wish to replay the debate over the infant industry argument and related ideas here, although I confess to being a skeptic and having the view that an undue tolerance for protective measures by developing countries pervades the GATT system. In the technical barriers area as elsewhere, therefore, one might question the wisdom of provisions that allow developing countries to remain more protective of their markets than the developed nations.

5. See, for example, GATT TBT Agreement, article 12; GATT SPM Agreement, article 10.

6. GATT TBT Agreement, article 12.4.

Comments

Kalypso Nicolaïdis

Should countries surrender sovereignty in the name of freer trade? Be they politicians or citizens, few would argue in the affirmative. Indeed, the most vehement opposition to ratification of the Uruguay Round of the General Agreement on Tariffs and Trade (GATT) by the United States prior to December 1994 rested not on calculations of economic costs and benefits but on the "sovereignty argument." Under the new World Trade Organization (WTO), the likes of Ross Perot, Pat Choate, and Ralph Nader argued, an international panel of unelected experts would now be allowed to annul national laws and regulations duly passed by the U.S. Congress and reviewed by the courts. This made the WTO unacceptable in their eyes. Interestingly, defenders of the agreement followed the same logic by countering that the WTO did not involve any forfeiture of sovereignty.

In fact, Ralph Nader is right. Any country, including the United States, can theoretically be forced under GATT to withhold applying to foreign products and producers its national standards and regulations designed to protect consumers. This situation questions not only sovereignty *at the border* but also sovereignty *within borders*. But he is also wrong on three counts. This situation is neither new nor very bold. Moreover, there are ways to make such sharing of sovereignty ultimately beneficial to domestic and foreign consumers alike.

Kalypso Nicolaïdis is assistant professor at the Kennedy School of Government, Harvard University. She also teaches at the Ecole Nationale d'Administration in Paris.

As Alan O. Sykes's extensive and insightful overview recounts, the international policing of technical barriers to trade has been conducted under GATT since the Tokyo Round. As he further demonstrates with great clarity, such policing does not put into question the underlying objectives of national regulations but only the means through which these objectives are attained, and only as far as foreign products entering national territory are concerned. This minimal encroachment on sovereignty is embodied in the "least-restrictive means" requirement at the heart of GATT remedies. Sykes is most cautious in drawing recommendations that would call for further forfeiture of sovereign jurisdiction over standards and regulations. He rightly insists on the fact that heterogeneous national standards and regulations are often grounded in bona fide differences in national preferences and incomes and thus should generally be "simply tolerated" when stemming from different regulatory objectives.

Although I would contend that the author's diagnosis and analytical arguments are most persuasive, I will build further on the prescriptive dimension of the study and argue that the mutual recognition strategy that is only mentioned in passing deserves a much more central place—indeed the central place—in any assessment of future approaches dealing with technical barriers to trade. In this light, the European experience should be seen not only as a potential if unlikely model for the world, but more important as the starting point of an expanding dynamic under which dealing with technical barriers to trade involves *product-specific bargaining over acceptable regulatory differences* between countries. In closing, I will add a few remarks on areas left out of the study, namely, regulations applied to services imports and environmental and labor standards, to which this study is relevant (as the author suggests), although not applicable wholesale.

Decentralized Policing Is Not Just an Option

The policing of so-called technical barriers stems from the realization that differences in standards and regulations across countries generally impede trade even when not applied discriminatorily against foreigners. If we leave aside compatibility issues and concentrate on quality standards and quality regulations, Sykes's starting dichotomy is between cases in which such heterogeneity in standards is justified and cases in which it is not. The latter cases are those that call for centralized cooperation. Most often, however, a technical barrier becomes an issue precisely because heterogeneity is *justified* and yet facilitating trade is also *desirable*. As the author turns to the alternative existing and potential remedies for dealing with technical barriers (chapter 5) he distinguishes between two broad approaches that implicitly revolve around this diagnosis of heterogeneity. Under a system of "policed decentralization" national authorities, although largely free to pursue their own policy objectives, must do so subject to a set of broadly applicable legal constraints, above all the "least-restrictive means" principle. In other words, heterogeneous standards remain but are policed to make room for imported products. "Harmonization," on the other hand, may be total or may involve agreement among nations on the essential objectives to be achieved by regulations, leaving it up to each nation to satisfy these objectives in its own ways. In this case, heterogeneity is to a great extent sacrificed on the altar of free trade. This categorization, I would argue, needs to be amended, to correct marginal inconsistencies but above all also to offer a dynamic rather than a static picture of the trade liberalization process.

Sykes points out that policed decentralization, although the currently dominant approach, is limited by the fact that it accepts the underlying objectives of national policy uncritically and simply asks how best to meet these objectives. At the same time, however, he includes mutual recognition and reliance on international standards as part of policed decentralization, since policed decentralization calls for adoption of these approaches, or justification for their nonadoption, on the part of national regulators. But where would such international standards or "mutual" recognition agreements come from if not from processes of centralized negotiation? In such negotiations is it possible to separate clearly acceptance of international or foreign rules as concessions on alternative means to achieve unchanged objectives from concessions on these regulatory objectives themselves? Indeed, under "harmonization," Sykes calls for a limited approach or partial harmonization along the lines of Europe's "new approach." This approach is in fact widely referred to in Europe as the "mutual recognition" or *Cassis de Dijon* approach, whereby recognition of equivalence is combined with minimal harmonization. Sykes charac-

terizes partial harmonization as an *alternative* to decentralized policing when in fact such partial harmonization (the only type usually
possible in practice) has often constituted a precondition for replacing simple national treatment requirements with some of the more
demanding elements included by the author under policed decentralization. The two approaches go hand in hand and widely overlap as
the two faces of a single type of strategy that I will refer to as
"managed mutual recognition."

I would contend that a broader underlying distinction that retains
the spirit of that offered by Sykes without its apparent inconsistencies
is that between *unilateral assessments* and *plurilateral bargains* regarding
acceptable differences between national standards and regulations. In
both cases, and in the absence of world-level centralized regulatory
agencies, countries need to perfect a system of decentralized policing of
the behavior of both the host country and the home country. In the first
case, parties may be under a legal obligation to restrain their use of
regulations that may affect trade but are only constrained by the policing
of their action according to the least-restrictive means principle. Clearly,
by bringing into question even nondiscriminatory national standards,
the least-restrictive means principle goes beyond national treatment
requirements in outlawing unnecessary regulatory barriers. Thus it may
be akin to a unilateral recognition of the equivalence of another country's
laws and regulations. But it does not involve a process of mutual accom-
modation by the parties involved. In the second case, if countries want to
go further in the liberalization process, they need to engage in a political
exercise whereby national regulations are explicitly compared to each
other, their degree of convergence is assessed, and a level of "acceptable
differences" between them is commonly agreed upon. Such a process
may or may not lead to some degree of harmonization of regulations
through negotiations among national regulators or reliance on standardization bodies. It will in any case involve decentralized policing in the
implementation phase. What is policed here is host countries' adherence
to recognition commitments on market access, as well as what the
commitments themselves are premised on, that is, the home countries'
continued adherence either to their original "acceptable" and "recognized" standards and regulations or to agreed-upon minimal harmonization requirements.

The questions therefore become: What are the incentives for shifting
from the first to the second approach, and under what conditions do and

should national regulators engage in this process of mutual recognition?

The European Approach: Managed Mutual Recognition

Under the "new approach" followed in the European Community (EC) since 1985, member states negotiate over the essential requirements to which regulations must attend, declare international standards or national regulations as sufficient to meet these essential objectives, and enter covenants not to apply more stringent regulations or regulations concerning inessential matters to products originating from other member states. I call this approach one of "managed" mutual recognition in that mutual recognition is conditioned on both ex ante convergence of standards and regulations and their ex post mutual monitoring, and it is premised on the gradual development of trust among regulators across borders.[1] To what extent is such an approach transferable to the world level?

Sykes suggests in his concluding chapter that the European Union's approach to technical barriers could be implemented among developed countries in general on consumer protection matters not relating to health and safety provided that adequate labeling is enforced to inform consumers of differences among products. He does not indicate however, why and how such policy transfer might occur. One clue may lie in the interaction between the role of the judiciary and the political bargaining process in promoting trade liberalization in the EC. This is overlooked in Sykes's historical overview, despite his very thorough discussion of the *Cassis de Dijon* ruling of 1979 (chapter 4). This interaction, however, is key to understanding the success of the new European approach in bringing about the single European market. To start with, we must stress that the Court's criteria for deciding whether to enforce unilateral recognition constitute a remarkable deviation from international arbitration on trade matters since they lead to questioning the *internal* effectiveness of regulations independently of their *external* effect on trade. In order to make the case for recognition in *Cassis de Dijon*, the European Court of Justice (ECJ) convincingly showed that the regulation under consideration

1. See Nicolaïdis (1993).

was not necessary in order to safeguard the public interest since it did not achieve its stated objectives at the domestic level (causality) and could be replaced by alternative requirements on labeling (proportionality). If such reasoning were accepted it would become harder to argue why such regulations should apply at all to national and foreign producers alike. Whether or not mutual recognition would force a change in the host country's standards through the dynamics of competitive pressure, its very adoption would undermine their legitimacy.

Thus the significance of *Cassis de Dijon* went beyond its immediate outcome, which was to impose unilateral recognition by judicial fiat. It lay, if not in the introduction, at least in the legitimization of the *idea* of mutual recognition within the Community. In *Cassis de Dijon*, contrary to the *Dassonville* case also referred to by Sykes, the Court proceeded to reverse the way in which it had argued for liberalization until then and to shift the focus of its inquiry away from having to question the legitimacy of a given state's domestic regulatory measures to a comparison of regulatory measures *across* member states. Thus, through *Cassis de Dijon*, the Court turned the traditional negative framing of free trade obligations into a positive philosophy: a presumption that, when the product under consideration had been "lawfully produced and marketed" in one member state, it was fit for consumption in that member state and should therefore be considered as fit for consumption in all other member states. Generalizing to products with similar characteristics as the one covered by *Cassis de Dijon,* the baseline assumption would be that national standards across the Community were sufficiently equivalent to be mutually recognized. Recognition of equivalence, which would come to be referred to as the principle of "mutual recognition," was a message of unquestionably greater political appeal than eliminating nontariff barriers to trade.

Judicial review was important within the Community for promoting mutual recognition more in providing an idea and an incentive for trade negotiators to act than in achieving the outcome itself. In fact, subsequent ECJ decisions have been more cautious than Sykes makes them out to be, starting with the *Nisin Additive* case of 1981. They have found putative local policy purposes to be legitimate and have clearly left to the political realm decisions as to whether rules based on socioeconomic facts should be considered equivalent. Moreover, as Sykes points out, the Court both limited and expanded states' regulatory discretion in adding new grounds for "nonrecognition," such as protecting the environment or national culture. Ultimately, judicial review is in any case limited by its case-by-case nature, even if a consistent jurisprudence may constitute an incentive for governments to take the issue out of the Court's hands.

Recognition of foreign regulations constitutes a leap of faith on the part of national regulators, whether or not it involves prior partial harmonization. It means concluding that regulations that are prima facie different can be considered "comparable." The greater such difference, the less recognition can be a judicial option and the more it needs to be a political option. Indeed, the *Cassis de Dijon* decision was immediately seized upon by the European Commission in 1980 in an attempt to translate it into a broader political agenda. Yet it was not until five years later that the idea was translated into an operational work program through the white paper on "Europe 1992," when its message of speedy liberalization could be combined with a newly heightened political will and a commitment to complete the creation of an internal market in Europe. Thus the Court's jurisprudence forced a reappraisal of the traditional harmonization method in the Community and prepared the ground for Europe 1992, but it was up to national negotiators to work out the preconditions and the scope of broadly based mutual recognition among member states.

The straightforward "solution" that *Cassis de Dijon* suggested in the case at hand was not that generally adopted by the 1992 program. As already stated, what has been adopted in the Community instead is a form of managed mutual recognition, conditional upon the strengthening and setting up of extant institutional coordination and safeguard mechanisms that bear little resemblance to the "simple" solution provided by *Cassis de Dijon*. This is to be expected since acceptance by states of the logic of mutual recognition implies surrending what can be called "regulatory sovereignty" to a greater extent than was necessary through the harmonization approach followed in the 1970s. In the latter case, regulations relevant to foreign products were at least jointly determined with other countries; in the pure mutual recognition case, host countries would lose control entirely. Managed mutual recognition is a way to avoid the cumbersome harmonization prerequisite for free trade while at the same time avoiding giving a totally free hand to home countries that in the future may change their regulatory policies in unacceptable ways.

Although obviously unique, the European way of dealing with technical barriers offers lessons for the rest of the world. First, if even so strong a judiciary as the ECJ cannot impose broadly based recognition of standards and regulations, dispute resolution under the GATT codes cannot be relied upon to push the agenda of trade liberalization. Mutual recognition cannot be imposed as a generic legal obligation but must be the result of case-by-case political bargains. Second, the factors that led in Europe from the limited emergence of mutual recognition as a legal obligation to its broad-ranging adoption as a political option were, to a great extent, clearly exogenous to the technical debate over the merits and drawbacks of mutual recognition. Ultimately, mutual recognition as a systematic approach to economic integration must be an a priori choice made by governments, who can then leave the details up to their respective negotiators. Third, it would be hard in this process to distinguish between decentralized policing of policy implementation and that of policy goals and objectives along the lines suggested by Sykes. Balancing the benefits of the national regulatory policy against its cost in terms of trade is relevant at all levels.

Perhaps most important, the developments in Europe can indeed serve as an engine for the rest of the world. Having developed a pool of expertise to deal with the issue of recognition, the European Union can now reap "regulatory economies of scale" by negotiating similar deals with the outside. This was done before their accession negotiations with the European Free Trade Association (EFTA) countries, and such a process has also been initiated with the United States. By developing transparent criteria for determining when standards and regulations should be deemed comparable, such a regional process of implementing mutual recognition can be seen as contagious, expanding its reach progressively to the rest of the world.

From the Uruguay Round to Bilateral or Plurilateral Arrangements

Sykes's discussion makes clear that the two amended codes on technical barriers and sanitary and phytosanitary measures resulting from the Uruguay Round do not include firm constraints on standards and regulations that accord with the national treatment principle. They do, however, serve to make refusals to grant unilateral recognition more visible by requiring that parties, in Sykes's words, "give positive consideration to accepting as equivalent technical regulations of other parties, even if those regulations differ from their own provided they are satisfied that these regulations adequately fulfill the obligations of their own regulations." Moreover, signatories must have the chance to "objectively demonstrate" the equivalence of their own standards and regulations to those of the importing country. Sykes's overall diagnosis of the Uruguay Round agreements is that they encourage harmonization where it is possible and mutual recognition where it is not. I would contend that increasingly the logic runs the other way around. The codes encourage mutual recognition and point to the need to respect international standards when this is not possible. It is not surprising that a greater extent of recognition must be encouraged given the length of time it takes standards to be adopted (54 months for the International Standards Organization [ISO] in 1992 and 30 months for the International Electronical Commission [IEC] in 1994) and the ensuing obsolescence of those standards.

In short the GATT framework follows the EU lead by forcing some (if less) multilateral recognition and encouraging mutual recognition through a further political process, beyond code obligations themselves. As mentioned previously, recognizing the potential benefits of moving beyond the GATT framework at a faster pace than other signatories, the United States and the European Union started to negotiate Mutual Recognition Agreements (MRA) both of testing and of standards and regulations in 1993. Under these negotiations they must assess together in which cases mutual recognition can apply unconditionally and in which cases it must be conditioned on further regulatory convergence. In doing so, they must necessarily rethink the very concept of regulatory effectiveness at an international level.

Information Requirements versus Minimal Harmonization: The Specificity of International Market Failures

In chapter 3, Sykes provides a most useful analysis of the rationale for regulating quality domestically in lieu of leaving it up to market incentives to induce quality. But he does not analyze market incentives to induce quality for foreign consumers. It may be argued that the tension between paternalistic government policies and consumer sovereignty inherent in domestic standards setting is magnified by the features of cross-border consumption. If market imperfections are greater internationally, regulations are required all the more urgently when goods travel across borders. For one, consumers are generally less well informed about the quality of products from abroad. Their willingness to pay will adjust to changes in quality more slowly; at the same time, the provision of information by producers seeking to establish quality levels may be more costly across borders. At the same time, the development of market-wide reputation through word of mouth or investment in brand names is generally harder at the international level. The issuance of warranties, another device for signaling quality, yields less present value for the buyer given the greater difficulty in enforcing them across borders. Although they will still be comparatively cheaper for the high-quality seller from abroad relative to the low-quality producer from abroad, such warranties are likely to be more expensive for the foreign high-quality producer than for the domestic low-quality producer. Finally, consumers' cognitive capacities, in particular regarding risk assessment, may be most greatly hampered when they are faced with a "language" with which they are not familiar. Thus consumers' apparent tolerance of risk in an import may be even more easily attributable to market failure than to favorable market judgment. Sykes's remark that, in cases of cognitive rather than information failure, information remedies are inadequate and will be dominated by regulatory solutions seems to have an even greater bearing at the international level.

Clearly the significance of such differences between intra- and international regulation will vary with the products under consideration. It could even be the case that the relationship may be reversed. One could argue for instance that the signposting game that allows firms to "oversell" certain positive characteristics of their products through advertising and similar mechanisms is harder to play internationally. Producers can better manipulate the consumers they know. Moreover, the argument for the market's ability to satisfy different preferences regarding quality is all the more valid when the international dimension is taken into consideration. For the most part, national regulators will regulate products irrespective of whether they are for sale inside or outside their country. Market incentives operating "better" domestically will simply spill over internationally, in the same way as positive externalities are produced by a few well-informed consumers at the domestic level.

On balance, therefore, there might be only a weak case for a greater need to regulate products when they are sold across borders. But, as Sykes points out, diversity in regulation might have unquestioned democratic legitimacy if it arises from different experiences and genuine variations in the preferences of citizens across nations rather than simply poor information. This important argument leads one to reject high-harmonization solutions, but it should not necessarily preclude mutual recognition in that such "experience" is an evolutionary process. It is by being exposed to foreign goods—or rather foreign-regulated goods—that consumers might expand their preferred basket. In short, to the extent that some form of minimal harmonization addresses the existence of international market failures, consumer sovereignty is ultimately well served by mutual recognition of remaining regulatory differences.

Decentralized Enforcement: Recognition of Conformity Assessment

One of the great merits of this study is its highlighting of the significance of host country testing of conformity as a barrier to trade. Here again, however, some of its prescriptive conclusions can be slightly amended. Sykes describes how the "global approach" introduced in 1989 in Europe to promote recognition of testing and certification in the exporting country promulgated testing guidelines and allowed national "testers" to grant an EC mark of conformity. He argues that absent a substantial move toward regulatory harmonization internationally, this approach is not transferable to the trading community at large. One can take issue with this diagnosis, noting that although recognition of conformity assessment followed rather than preceded recognition of substantive standards in Europe, it was the focus of the first step of liberalization efforts both within EFTA and in the current EU-U.S. context. If the global approach as such is hardly transferable, parts of it are likely to be effectively emulated under GATT and international standardization bodies.

Although the willingness of national authorities to rely upon conformity assessment undertaken in the exporting country rests on mutual confidence to an even greater extent than substantive mutual recognition, it does not necessarily necessitate approximation of national regulations. Importing countries can rely on third-party testing abroad according to their own criteria without having to recognize widely different standards. The EC experience in what one may call "auditing the auditors" could be reproduced at the global level through a more customized approach, that is, without the granting of a "global mark of conformity." Given the cost of monitoring the quality of testing done abroad, the testing of laboratories could be centralized in part through a system of accreditation with the GATT, which would in turn allow for economies of scale in spot-checking the quality of testing in exporting countries as well as in imposing penalties when such results prove deficient. This would in effect constitute a system of *centralized auditing of decentralized policing*. Along these lines, the ISO and the IEC are currently developing a joint voluntary scheme known as Quality System Assessment Recognition for worldwide recognition of ISO 9000 quality management system registrations that would ensure that a certificate granted in one country would be recognized as valid worldwide. A complementary approach would be to rely on secondary reputation markets, whereby private bodies granting seals of approval would themselves develop reputations for adequate "testing of testers."

In order to yield tangible results, such opening of national enforcement of conformity to international scrutiny must be complemented by support and training for countries that do not have the means for adequate testing, including Eastern Europe and many developing countries. The new United Nations Conference on Trade and Development mechanism for facilitating trade (the so-called trade points) could be enlarged to include such facilities. Alternatively, this could become part of the technical support provided by multilateral financial institutions or action programs of the United Nations Development Program.

Finally, in discussing conformity assessment the author points out that the approach may be quasi-unenforcible (through penalties) if the producer's assets are located abroad. Such reasoning does not take into account the possibility of cooperation in enforcement or even ex-post enforcement between the home and host countries. Here again, it would seem that cooperation among testing entities in different countries is key.

Beyond Product Standards: From Production
Standards to the Social Contract

Beyond rules applying to the characteristics of products, Sykes mentions how standards or regulations drafted with reference to the method of production ("process standards") have long fallen outside the scope of the GATT code. This loophole is supposed to have been remedied in the new agreement on technical barriers. Yet the issue is bound to reemerge as part of the broader current debate over the desirability of linking labor and environmental standards with trade. In effect, production standards are part of the broader contract prevailing in the home country, which pertains to the working, social, political, and physical environment. In this sense we should not assume that the same notions discussed under production standards are simply applicable to this realm. To some extent many of the differences in production regulation have been the fuel of international trade, and eliminating them is likely to *decrease* rather than increase international trade—at least in the short run.

Production and process standards were long exempted from GATT simply because they were not so much of an issue. Implicit recognition of the setting of such standards by the home country was generally the rule. In effect, we are faced with an apparent paradox today: whereas *explicit* mutual recognition has progressively come to represent one of the dominant options for product standards, we are witnessing the exactly reverse trend in production standards, where *implicit* mutual recognition has come to be increasingly contested. In these cases importing countries seek to make access to their markets conditioned on the adoption of international standards or on extra territorial adoption of their own standards. Yet to the extent that free trade ultimately consists of accepting the dictate of comparative advantage, it always implies an implicit recognition of the advantages granted by the special characteristics of national policies and regulations that influence conditions of production in the exporting or "home" countries. Increasingly, differences in national standards are contested even if they do not constitute technical barriers to trade simply because they are considered to create "illegitimate" comparative advantage. To what extent should the leverage of market access and free trade be used by host states to obtain desired changes in other polities that cannot be justified by some direct effects on the citizens of their own countries, as were product standards or regulations? The answer to this question may require adapting our traditional trade paradigm to a world in which global economic integration leads consumers to want to be able to pick and choose among national regulations while at the same time demanding a greater say in those foreign social contracts that affect them indirectly.

Beyond Trade in Goods: Policing Barriers to Trade in Services

Finally, although some of the dimensions of this study might be generalizable, it is worth mentioning in closing that the policing of barriers to trade in services has brought and will bring about significantly different challenges than that discussed here for trade in goods. Clearly the General Agreement on Trade in Services (GATS), adopted as part of the Uruguay Round package, is only the beginning of a long process of liberalization.[2] Yet, given the highly regulated nature of most services—from professional to financial to communication services—the new regime has had to tackle up front the trade-impeding nature of nondiscriminatory services regulations. Yet, in spite of the claims of the architects of the Europe 1992 program, which was mainly aimed at liberalizing services, the goods paradigm is hardly directly transferable to trade in services. For one, services do not cross barriers per se but often do so in the form of a service provider, be that a person or a firm. The costs of adaptation to host country regulations (such as acquiring a new diploma to be allowed to practice one's profession across borders) are often prohibitive in the case of services. In cases in which a service is delivered across borders through the movement of information, imposing host country standards simply means that cross-border trade is outlawed and must be replaced by the local establishment of an office. Moreover, the provision of a service is more a process than a product, so that the recognition of foreign regulatory authority over services provided from abroad constitutes an ongoing granting of jurisdictional authority over transactions conducted on domestic territory. The equivalent of conformity assessment for services is not a one-shot deal, as with

2. For a more detailed overview, see Nicolaïdis (1995).

goods, but rather ongoing regulatory control that encompasses the accreditation, supervisory, and enforcement responsibilities of regulatory authorities. Mutual recognition of home country control cannot be easily disentangled from recognition of substantive home country services regulations.

In short, replacing national treatment with mutual recognition is both much more demanding and much more necessary for services than for goods. Given the ongoing nature of regulatory supervision for services, as well as the fact that services providers may operate simultaneously in several countries at once, cooperation among regulators across countries is key to the sustainability of the regime. In a global economy in which consumers increasingly buy packages of goods and services, such differences may ultimately provide important lessons for goods as well.

Jacques Pelkmans

Professor Sykes provides an elaborate analysis of how a system of international rules to reduce existing and prevent emerging technical barriers to trade (TBT) should look. His treatment is based on a wide-ranging and yet concise and accessible survey of economic aspects of compatibility issues for complementary products and of regulation possibly resulting in obstacles to trade. The system of rules and principles as proposed is compared to the pre- and post-Uruguay Round regimes and also draws from the unique experience to remove TBT in the European Community. A rich and inspiring chapter of conclusions and recommendations would seem to fit the purposes of the Brookings project. Sykes's book is a major accomplishment in an area scarcely supplied with analysis, whether economic or otherwise, at all.

The approach taken blends institutional and legal analysis with the economics of regulation and a bit of political economy. It is not based on empirical work. It is good to realize that, in this field, there is virtually no other way. Empirical economic work on TBT is scant and probably far from representative (as TBT are so extremely diversified in nature). There are no data sets as they exist for, for example, tariffs and trade flows. Empirical methodology has remained underdeveloped. This book is also hardly empirical on how the General Agreement on Tariffs and Trade (GATT) TBT Agreement is actually used. Again, only with extensive field work (which is time-consuming and, for this topic, very costly) would it be possible to overcome this gap.

Taking TBT seriously, including more effective ways to remove and prevent them, would be a welcome manifestation of the shift in trade policy toward regulatory issues. After the Uruguay Round, quotas will quickly reduce in number and importance, and their "gray-area" substitutes like voluntary export restraints will be outlawed by 1999. The economic significance of tariffs has steadily declined in the Organization for Economic Cooperation and Development area and has begun a remarkable downward trend among developing countries since the mid-1980s, further articulated by the concessions in the round. The round has already addressed several regulatory issues, and the proposals for the World Trade Organization's (WTO) initial agen-

Jacques Pelkmans is senior research fellow at the Centre for European Policy Studies, Brussels and Maastricht University.

da are heavily biased toward regulatory issues such as trade and environment and trade and competition policy. The amended GATT TBT Agreement (and the annexed Code of Good Practice) is a too-little noticed yet prime example of the regulatory approach to trade liberalization. The importance of the code has increased for at least three reasons. First, it has been strengthened. Sykes's book forms an excellent guide to the essentials of these amendments. Second, the link with international standards and standardization is bolstered, both in the text of the Code and by formulating the Code of Good Practice. Third, by virtue of the fact that the round was considered an integral undertaking, the application of conditional most favored nation (MFN) (inherited from the Tokyo Round) was replaced by unconditional MFN treatment for the entire Marrakesh package, except when explicitly provided for. This has the effect of tripling the number of countries adhering to the TBT Agreement to about 115.

Moreover as a corollary, an agreement on the application of sanitary and phytosanitary measures (SPM) was concluded (also discussed by Sykes) and again is to be complied with by all WTO members. Therefore the recent intensity of the efforts at the world level, the greater scope of already concluded GATT agreements, and the newly accomplished country coverage demonstrate the increasing awareness that the removal of TBT should be taken more seriously. Far better and more convincingly than ever before, at least to my knowledge, Sykes's book clarifies that these are essentially problems of economic regulation (except when noncooperative compatibility standardization is at stake). And their resolution will require the trade policy specialist to become more familiar with the core issues of proper economic regulation in a setting of globalizing product markets. These issues are far less clear-cut than, for example, those of tariffs and quotas. Even more difficult, if not impossible, is to apply the GATT tradition of liberalization through reciprocal concessions in negotiations. Instead, a framework for economic regulation principles and derived rules should be established, backed up by accepted institutional mechanisms to give them credibility and resolve conflicts about compliance with them. Tackling TBT effectively, therefore, implies a very different approach. It relies more on principles and is rules-based rather than driven by negotiations. It requires a different institution than the old GATT, thriving largely because of occasional rounds. Removing TBT demands much greater emphasis on permanent cooperation about the degree of regulatory convergence and on more judicial forms of dispute settlement.

This justifies the predominantly legal approach Alan Sykes has taken. The attention paid to economic regulation and the judicial aspects is also borne out by the learning-by-doing process of removing TBT in the internal market of the European Community.

Contrasting the EC and GATT Approaches

For policymakers, most economists, political scientists, and, not least, engineers involved in standard setting or conformity assessment, however, the combination of the economics of regulation and legal analysis is outside their specializations. Such an approach may well heighten the barriers to the understanding of obstacles already too often disregarded in the world trading community. The probability that the study may not easily find its way to many policymakers and scholars outside economic and trade law is further increased by the high level of abstraction befitting economic theories of regulation and the basic principles used in the TBT and SPM agreements as well as in judicial review in, for example, the internal markets in the EC and in the United States.

In the following, I attempt to stylize the overall approach to the removal and prevention of TBT. It is hoped that this simplifying approach—although losing many of the legal and other subtleties of Sykes's paper—facilitates the understanding for standardizers, public affairs executives in business and economics less familiar with regulatory issues and judicial review. To contrast this attempt with the book, I proceed in a somewhat different fashion by first stylizing the new regulatory approach of the EC aimed at the removal and prevention of TBT. Then the question is asked whether elements could be usefully adopted at the world level to liberalize world trade, and if so, what elements. Sykes deals with the latter question at considerable length, but his approach is largely based on an extensive analysis of the innovative EC judicial review with respect to TBT. When discussing some key principles (for example, the least-restrictive means principle) developed in this case law, this analysis is no doubt illuminating and helpful. But the GATT/WTO will not avail of a supreme, supranational court as the last resort of a sophisticated and elaborate machine for realizing compliance throughout the internal market. The welcome improvements of the dispute settlement procedures, accomplished in the Uruguay Round, cannot possibly lead to a similar rigor and effectiveness. The EC Court and the EC Court of First Instance deal with hundreds of cases a year, and these rulings, in turn, determine national judicial review and shape EC regulation of policies as well as monitoring, implementation, and compliance procedures executed by the Commission and member states. This point is not just a legal one—a careful reflection about the EC machinery demonstrates beyond any doubt that the transaction costs of policing, removing, and preventing TBT are very considerable. This *is* true despite the fact that costs are already drastically lowered by the willingness of member states to accept supreme EC judicial review and to collaborate actively and permanently (both with the EC level and among one another) to keep the internal market free from such barriers.

Dispute settlement is in an entirely different class of activity and scope, and hence its effects on trade and business are commensurately smaller. Not only does GATT encourage pragmatic bilateral resolution of whatever "dispute" there is, but the last-resort function of dispute settlement will only be invoked for rather extreme cases. Although it is hoped to build case law, especially confirming the application of certain regulatory principles, the practical effect of such "case-law" is not at all comparable to the economic and regulatory impact it would have in the EC system. This is fully understandable in a WTO of sovereign states. Nevertheless, in a discussion emphasizing regulatory principles, the expected weak actual impact compared with the case of the EC stands in sharp contrast with the analytical similarity of some of those principles between EC and GATT. The combination of similar principles and yet little impact might cause great disillusions among businesses and traders who are interested in tangible effects of the codes.

A second reason why an emphasis on judicial review may engender problems of interpretation is found in the great importance of the other two pillars of the EC way of removing TBT: standardization and regulation at one or two levels of government. A crucial lesson from the EC experience is that EC regulation can greatly—often decisively—add to the incentives to promulgate European standards for health and safety. Conversely, a credible and appropriate linkage between standardization and regulation may greatly facilitate decision-making at the regulatory level, with a view to remove TBT.[1] Thus in considering whether the EC experience could provide lessons for enhancing the effectiveness of approaches to remove TBT at the world level, the entire web of interactions within the EC standards-regulation-judicial review triangle would have to be inspected more closely. Although the GATT TBT Agreement comprises an encouragement to use world standards, the questions, inspired by the EC experience, are how exactly is this done, what is the linkage with common regulation, if any, and what is the probable impact on barrier removal if health and safety and environment standards are not linked to common regulation.

The presentation proceeds as follows.[2] First, an exhaustive system of seven elements for TBT removal and prevention as has emerged in the EC is formulated. Second, this stylized system is briefly discussed against the backdrop of the new regulatory strategy of the EC, which reflects some fundamental principles for the design of the single market. Third, the question is addressed whether and to what extent this ambitious approach to eliminate TBT can be transposed, in a truncated and amended form, to the world level. The aim of going through these stages is to identify carefully what the possibilities and impossibilities are of removing and preventing TBT in the GATT/WTO.

Stylizing the EC System: Seven Elements

The three types of TBT are regulations, standards, and conformity assessment. But because there are two distinct tracks—the mandatory and voluntary ones—it *is* useful to distinguish five such barriers in total. The mandatory track may involve barriers caused by national regulation, national standards (to which, in the EC, national regulations refer), and conformity assessment. The voluntary track lacks the regulations, but national standards (not connected to regulations) and

1. For elaboration of these points, see, for example, Pelkmans (1990); Egan (1995).
2. The following draws from recent work in CEPS, for example, Pelkmans and Bohan (1994); Pelkmans and Sun (1994); Sun and Pelkmans (1995); see also Majone (1994).

conformity assessment with respect to those standards may nevertheless create cost-increasing barriers when accessing a national market.

The seven elements refer to the regulatory track, as this was by far the most urgent and costly problem to be resolved. The main purpose of the EC approach consists of the accomplishment of a single market. Hence it may serve as an ideal benchmark for the removal and prevention of TBT. An interesting condition is to pursue this removal and prevention in an economic and administrative least-cost manner without, however, impinging on justified regulatory objectives of the member states. The least-cost condition makes it possible also to facilitate the voluntary track by linkages giving rise to economies-of-scope, in particular in conformity assessment. This stylized EC system is an ideal benchmark, but it is not unique. There are similarities and differences with the U.S. system for its own single market. The EC system is more centralized in some respects and based on a somewhat different philosophy about public-private complementarity.[3] Given that the EC is not a federal state, at the most quasi-federal in its approach to the single market, it might be more instructive for world trade than the U.S. system.[4] The seven elements are summarized in table 1.

In principle, the system as described above is complete in the sense that all TBT can be removed and prevented. But exhaustive removal and prevention is neither sensible nor feasible in practice. Even within the United States, some TBT have remained in place, as Sykes points out. It is also not sensible because removal is not purely beneficial—when market failures justify regulation and preferences (and their weight to citizens) between member states differ greatly, approximation or imposed mutual acceptance may entail high welfare losses for some. However, if the seven notions are carefully pursued and their implications present no major problem after a period of adjustment, eventually the single market will, for all practical purposes, be free from TBT.[5]

3. Egan (1995).
4. Pelkmans (forthcoming).
5. Note that the implications may, at times, present problems. For instance, approximation may fail in Council of Parliament; writing European standards may prove to be difficult and slow; certifiers are not yet accredited but appointed by member states and merely "notified" to the EC (hence, "notified bodies"); and mutual acceptance of certification for products not following the referred standard may not be easy.

Table 1. *Elements of the Regulatory Track*

Item	Notion	Main Implication
1.	Approximation for "equivalence" of "justified" protection only; regulatory principle of "mutual acceptance"	National regulations should be approximated with respect to "essential requirements" (that is, objectives of regulatory protection) only; "equivalence" of "justified" protection (see article 36 EC and "rule of reason") and any unjustified protection (see article 30 and *Cassis de Dijon*-type case law) must imply "mutual acceptance," hence market access
2.	Maximum flexibility for alternative instruments or technical specifications, as long as "essential requirements" are met	Avoid detail, let alone technical uniformity, in the "essential requirements" for all but the most extreme risks; reference to European standards; the standards themselves should be "performance," not "design" oriented; referred standards meet essential requirements, hence imply access to any national market in EC; even the referred performance standard is not mandatory, but other solutions are subject to conformity assessment directly based on "essential requirements"
3.	Use and promote hierarchy of world, European, and national standards	National standards can serve as a temporary last resort for reference in approximation; European standards to be based on world standards, when possible; pursue tight coordination with ISO/IEC when writing new European standards; subsidize priorities in referred standard writing
4.	Remove conformity assessment barriers via approximation and confidence building	Because testing requirements will be written into the referred European standards, they are uniform; therefore approximate first the certification requirements in "modules" according to risk; prescribe quality standards for testers, provide common criteria for accrediting certifiers; such confidence must imply "mutual acceptance" of certification among member states and of qualified test houses subcontracted by certifiers; establish permanent coordination for the mutual acceptance of assessment of products not following referred standards
5.	Efficient decisionmaking	Qualified majority voting for approximation; opting out only possible after meeting severe and special conditions, subject to Court review; qualified majority voting in standard bodies; referred European standards replace national standards
6.	Credible and binding judicial review	Judicial review is a vital element in that it determines when regulatory barriers are "unjustified" (article 30) so free trade is achieved directly; it also determines whether and to what extent nonregulatory protection is justified, thereby limiting approximation to these areas; review is binding and builds cumulative case law at EC and national level
7.	Prevent new TBT from arising	Notification is mandatory (non-notification is treaty infringement) and actively monitored; network of national coordinators; quick response/feedback system with extensive powers for shorter and longer standstills of national drafting of laws, and option to approximate/regulate at EC level instead

New Regulatory Strategy of the EC

The Community has gone through a learning-by-doing process of developing a new regulatory strategy during the period of "completing" its single market by the end of 1992.[6] Table 1 has to be understood against the backdrop of that strategy. For present purposes, the latter can be summarized in the regulatory quintet, a group of five principles of economic regulation specified in table 2 (for goods only).

Before the single market program, which heavily emphasized the removal of TBT, only "free movement" was applied, with many exceptions or derogations. A first breakthrough was prompted by the judicial mutual acceptance in *Cassis de Dijon*. Minimum harmonization and its corollary, regulatory mutual acceptance, constituted the second breakthrough. This exposure of national differences in regulation to cross-border competition in the goods market was further enhanced by the removal of internal frontiers. Altogether, this frontal attack of, especially, TBT was balanced by the subsidiarity principle: Any shift to EC regulatory activity has to be explicitly justified.

Although minimum harmonization and mutual recognition or, better, acceptance appear in both tables 1 and 2, the other three principles do not. Without the latter, however, the technicalities of table 1 might obscure that there are obligations, in EC 1992, to eliminate internal frontiers, to overcome the exceptions to free movement, and to minimize approximation to what was justifiable under subsidiarity. Those three principles explain the enormous pressure behind the "new" approach to technical harmonization with reference to standards and the "global" approach to conformity assessment. These pressures come on top of the judicial review since *Cassis de Dijon*.

This crucial insight casts some doubt on whether the success of the elaborate EC system is merely due to its logic and innovativeness. If it were only for the latter two, perhaps much of it could be transposed to GATT, although sovereign states would not accept all the elements of table 1.

6. Pelkmans and Sun (1994).

Table 2. *Regulatory Quintet of the EC's Single Market*

Principle	Main Implication
Free movement	Ability (both de jure and de facto) of goods to move across national borders in the international market
Minimum harmonization	Approximation only of the "essential requirements" (see notion 1, table 1)
Mutual recognition	Widely used jargon for what is, in effect, a "mutual acceptance" notion in two distinct ways: (1) as a principle in judicial review since *Cassis de Dijon* (see table 1, main implications of notion 1, for *unjustified* regulatory barriers) (2) as a regulatory principle, a corollary of the minimum harmonization principle; beyond approximated "essential requirements," any product specifications (or the lack thereof) induced by regulation (or the lack thereof) of other member states must be accepted (see table 1, main implications of notions 1 and 4)
Subsidiarity	Based on the functional criteria of negative and positive spillovers across national borders as well as scale, regulatory powers may be assigned to the EC rather than the national level of government; for the single market, barriers will usually imply negative externalities, hence a need to solve it at EC level, but there are costs, hence limits, to suppressing national regulatory autonomy
No internal frontiers	Since Single European Act, note that the "free movement" principle did not require the dismantling of frontiers and that the frontiers kept many exceptions alive

Comparing the GATT and EC Approaches

However, the GATT/WTO does not have or foresee a general free movement principle, let alone that the frontiers will have to go. But because that is so, the logic of introducing subsidiarity as a functional assignment principle also becomes irrelevant. After all, sovereign countries have regulatory autonomy and do not accept a general assignment principle of regulation beyond national level. They might agree to some approximation, but only ad hoc, and with both unanimity and ample opting-out. It is for these fundamental reasons that Alan Sykes emphasizes a series of general (TBT Agreement) principles of economic regulation for the contracting parties as the basis for bilateral consultations after complaints and for dispute settlement. He shows that, in a way, nondiscrimination, national treatment, performance versus design methods in referred standards, notification procedures on draft laws, and even mutual recognition can be said to be corollaries of the "least-restrictive means" principle, adopted in the TBT Agreement. The entire series has found some place in the new TBT Agreement.

A careful look at table 1 reveals that the least-restrictive means principle is not explicitly listed. The EC baptizes it the "proportionality" principle and it is subsumed in the word *justified* protection in the main implications of notion 1. Disproportionate or too restrictive means are not justified even if the objectives are. The difference between Sykes's correct emphasis on this principle in the TBT Agreement and for GATT dispute settlement on the one hand and the EC approach on the other is that the principle is central in GATT and secondary in the EC. This crucial difference is understandable: as so many TBT persist under the GATT TBT Agreement, it is key to subject them to the least-restrictive means condition. Central in the EC are free movement and no frontiers on the one hand and approximation, subject to subsidiarity, on the other. Both lead directly to elimination of TBT. Even remaining barriers are first judged on whether their objectives are "justified," and only then the proportionality principle is imposed. The economic, competition, and trade implications of the EC system are therefore radically different. Moreover, the corollaries of what is central in the EC are also far-reaching and eliminate a second layer of barriers: mandated European standards for reference (the incentive here is not the subsidy but the guarantee of market access) and elaborate confidence building measures to realize mutual acceptance of tests from qualified test houses and mutual recognition of certificates from notified bodies.

It is in this light that Sykes's conclusion (chapter 4) about the new GATT TBT Agreement should be read:

> But the GATT system can hardly be expected to eliminate technical barriers problems. The obligations of signatories to police the practices of subsidiary governments are at most limited, and it remains to be seen how effectively the Code of Good Practice will solve difficulties with private entities. The obligations respecting harmonization and mutual recognition remain on the whole

weakly worded and thus qualified by considerable deference to national regulators who may not wish to accept them in given instances. The likely degree of movement toward mutual recognition and harmonization will thus be uncertain.

As Sykes writes in the same chapter, the new TBT and SPM agreements coupled with the WTO dispute settlements procedures "have the *potential* to contribute substantially to a reduction of technical barriers. It remains to be seen how diligently nations comply with the new agreements, however."

Could the EC Approach Be Transposed to GATT?

What elements of the EC approach could possibly be transposed to GATT? To answer this question in brief, table 1 can be used as a checklist, bearing in mind, however, that three principles of the EC regulatory strategy (table 2) do not apply.

1. *Approximation and mutual acceptance:* The new GATT TBT Agreement has no approximation provision. It merely disciplines national regulations. This leaves many TBT in place, in particular those justified by health, safety, or the environment (and, as the agreement notes, national security). There are encouragements to "harmonize" via international standards writing (article 2.6) and practice mutual acceptance (article 2.7). Not only have the encouragements proved to be ineffective since 1980 (as they existed before), they turn the lessons from the EC experience on their head. Without approximation, reference to standards hangs in the air as the essential requirements are unspecified at GATT level. It implies that a general boost for world standards will not be induced by the agreement and that the world standards that are (or have already been) written may not actually be used as referred standards. Because this is so, regulatory mutual acceptance will not work, and its very weak encouragement is practically an empty article without incentives. The disciplines imposed on "justified" national regulation are better developed in the agreement, but their effectiveness remains to be seen (as Sykes explains in detail).

2. *Maximum flexibility for the means:* Only the preference of performance standards is expressed clearly. Reference to world standards

cannot be expected as a rule because the essential requirements are not given. Because there is no free movement obligation to begin with, the logic of the "new approach" of the EC providing market access breaks down completely. What might keep the TBT from being too costly are the principles as discussed by Sykes, but this is anything but certain.

3. *Hierarchy of world, European, and national standards:* Quite apart from the very weak stimulus the GATT Agreement gives to the writing of world standards, the use of world standards can hardly be expected without further market incentives. World standards cannot normally be used for reference in regulation because essential requirements are lacking and regulators cannot therefore "presume" conformity with those requirements. If world standards would be used by companies, a heavier form of conformity assessment may well follow. But the usual company response will be to align with national health, safety, and environmental standards.

Lacking an approximation incentive to align national standards to world standards, a rule about the hierarchy of world above national standards might nevertheless still be helpful. The rule could be that, for ISO/IEC members, world standards must replace divergent national standards for all member bodies or at least for those who vote yes. However, even this modest obligation does not exist in ISO: A yes vote does not oblige the voting body, and the world standard may, or may only partly, or may not be adopted. The Code of Good Practice addresses this problem in persuasive but noncommittal language in articles F, G, and H, but the credibility of these provisions is in doubt, to say the least.

To see this, one does not have to refer to suspected slow movers among the developing countries. The United States itself has very few national standards based on world standards.[7] Can one seriously imagine that, even with the code in force ANSI would use world standards (article F) much more often and that, for example, ANSI would "make every effort to avoid duplication of, or overlap with, the work of other standardizing bodies in the national territory"? ANSI

---

7. The reports vary from ½ percent to perhaps up to 10 percent. There are historical reasons, but also the "outvoting" of the United States by many relatively small European countries in ISO/IEC has played a role. See Pelkmans and Bohan (1994).

has no power to do the latter (it represents the United States in ISO, but its network covers less than one-third of the U.S. standards) and would provoke an upheaval if it were to attempt the former in a rapid and nonvoluntary fashion.

There is also a quality problem. Many world standards are not product standards but make classifications, define uniform terminology, and so on. When they might affect trade directly, by dealing with products, they often allow "options" that reduce the value of a standard. As Sykes notes, there are persistent complaints about the quality of the Codex Alimentarius standards; also ISO standards often do not represent "the state of the art" due to compromises and slowness (average duration once was 12 years!). Worse still, many product standards are *never* written at world level precisely because approximation is lacking and national standards have little choice but to be aligned to national regulatory traditions.

All in all, the agreements and the code do not establish a true hierarchy and provide few genuine incentives that would lead one to expect world standards to become prominent.

4. *Remove conformity assessment:* Apart from national treatment and some encouragement to negotiate mutual recognition agreements, little is done to build confidence. This will remain a bilateral issue.

5. *Efficient decisionmaking:* Again, most of what the EC does here does not apply. As noted above (under 3), the ISO voting should, at the very least, oblige the yes voters.

6. *Binding judicial review:* Sykes's study is an insightful guide of the scope and potential of the now more judicial dispute settlement in the WTO, based on the TBT and SPM agreements. This is definite progress. But the gap with the EC remains huge. Whereas in GATT/ WTO, a dispute will be reserved for extreme violations, the EC judicial review shoots down TBT as a routine matter. More important, the Commission as the "guardian of the treaty" uses a (cooperative) carrot and (infringement) stick policy, based on extensive monitoring and permanent consultations with member states, before judicial review comes into play. And this far-stricter regime applies to a much narrower product scope than GATT, precisely because the toughest problems have typically been approximated in the EC. A subtle but crucial point is that the no-frontiers principle has, in combination with mutual acceptance, greatly enhanced the potential for regulatory competition between

member states, causing TBT to reduce without any interference by council or Commission.

7. *Prevent new barriers from arising:* The GATT notification system helps only little to prevent new TBT from arising. Comparison with notion 7 of table 1 immediately clarifies why. It is unclear whether non-notification is "actionable" in GATT, and in any event, there is no "guardian" to pursue it. Active monitoring is not done, but it is also not clear to me what exactly the follow-up is of the inflow of notifications (it would seem, very little). If a problem is spotted, there are no standstill provisions, and only the most extreme cases might be shifted to dispute settlements procedures (while approximation as a solution is not available).[8] Sykes rightly observes that little more can be done than raise the political costs of introducing new TBT. On this account alone and given the strong tendencies to regulate nowadays, TBT in the world increase secularly despite the GATT efforts. Their being hardly visible and difficult to measure lead me to underscore strongly Sykes's call for much more systematic economic study of TBT trends and impact.

Virtuous Interaction of EC and GATT

But the news is not only disappointing. EC 1992 has engendered some shock waves and repercussions that do have a positive effect on the removal and prevention of TBT worldwide. There are several reasons.

First, as an aftermath of the "fortress Europe" campaign, U.S. Secretary of Commerce Mosbacher concluded bilateral arrangements with the EC on the EC reliance on world standards. For existing standards, the European problem, although not trivial, is less problematic for the United States as national or CEN/CENELEC standards are based on world standards in many cases (ranging from some 25 percent in some EC countries to more than 70 percent for CENELEC standards). For mandated standards flowing from EC 1992, CEN/CENELEC has arranged a tight coordination with ISO/IEC in terms of calendars (scarce!), expertise, and scope. In other words, the EC activism reverses the top-down logic of the previous section and, in doing so, strengthens the

8. But the EC system has shown that about one-third of the cases give rise to amendments or standstills!

actual impact of GATT and ISO/IEC. The reason is as simple as it is forceful: The EC mandates new standards after approximation, so the essential requirements are known in fairly general terms. Given the tight coordination between CEN and ISO, any consensus standard at the world level will then incorporate the attractive incentive of having access to the big EC market. This overcomes the greatest weakness of the GATT TBT removal.

Second, the EC approach is rapidly being extended to a pan-European environment. Not only European Free Trade Association countries have aligned themselves (in the European Economic Area Treaty), but the six central and east European associated countries are in the process of doing so, too. Turkey will do so after its customs union with the EC in 1996. This will further strengthen the incentives for world standards promulgation in third world countries.

Third, in response to EC 1992, the United States has gone through a period of introspection about its own standards and conformity assessment system. Although no major changes have been adopted, it has (1) greatly increased the awareness that, in the new situation, a reliance on world standards may (at times) be critical for U.S. competitiveness, (2) led to greater attention for confidence-building measures (especially quality standards), facilitating the mutual acceptance of tests and certification, and (3) prompted serious negotiations between the United States and the EC about mutual recognition agreements for a range of products with significant health or safety risks.

If this greatly increased cooperative effort can firmly remain in the GATT and ISO context, the possible drawback of a world of trade blocs with few TBT inside and entrenched ones between them may be avoided, while the number of TBT and their costs might finally be on the way down.

Appendix

Technical Barriers Agreements Concluded during the Uruguay Round

Agreement on Technical Barriers to Trade

Members,

Having regard to the Uruguay Round of Multilateral Trade Negotiations;

Desiring to further the objectives of GATT 1994;

Recognizing the important contribution that international standards and conformity assessment systems can make in this regard by improving efficiency of production and facilitating the conduct of international trade;

Desiring therefore to encourage the development of such international standards and conformity assessment systems;

Desiring however to ensure that technical regulations and standards, including packaging, marking and labelling requirements, and procedures for assessment of conformity with technical regulations and standards do not create unnecessary obstacles to international trade;

Recognizing that no country should be prevented from taking measures necessary to ensure the quality of its exports, or for the protection of human, animal or plant life or health, of the environment, or for the prevention of deceptive practices, at the levels it considers appropriate, subject to the requirement that they are not applied in a manner which would constitute a means of arbitrary or unjustifiable discrimination between countries where the same conditions prevail or a disguised restriction on international trade, and are otherwise in accordance with the provisions of this Agreement;

Recognizing that no country should be prevented from taking measures necessary for the protection of its essential security interest;

Recognizing the contribution which international standardization can make to the transfer of technology from developed to developing countries;

Recognizing that developing countries may encounter special difficulties in the formulation and application of technical regulations and standards and procedures for assessment of conformity with technical regulations and standards, and desiring to assist them in their endeavours in this regard;

Hereby *agree* as follows:

Article 1
General Provisions

1.1 General terms for standardization and procedures for assessment of conformity shall normally have the meaning given to them by definitions adopted within the United Nations system and by international standardizing bodies taking into account their context and in the light of the object and purpose of this Agreement.

1.2 However, for the purposes of this Agreement the meaning of the terms given in Annex 1 applies.

1.3 All products, including industrial and agricultural products, shall be subject to the provisions of this Agreement.

1.4 Purchasing specifications prepared by governmental bodies for production or consumption requirements of governmental bodies are not subject to the provisions of this Agreement but are addressed in the Agreement on Government Procurement, according to its coverage.

1.5 The provisions of this Agreement do not apply to sanitary and phytosanitary measures as defined in Annex A of the Agreement on the Application of Sanitary and Phytosanitary Measures.

1.6 All references in this Agreement to technical regulations, standards and conformity assessment procedures shall be construed to include any amendments thereto and any additions to the rules or the product coverage thereof, except amendments and additions of an insignificant nature.

Technical Regulations and Standards

Article 2
Preparation, Adoption and Application of Technical Regulations by Central Government Bodies

With respect to their central government bodies:

2.1 Members shall ensure that in respect of technical regulations, products imported from the territory of any Member shall be accorded treatment no less favourable than that accorded to like products of national origin and to like products originating in any other country.

2.2 Members shall ensure that technical regulations are not prepared, adopted or applied with a view to or with the effect of creating unnecessary obstacles to international trade. For this purpose, technical regulations shall not be more trade-restrictive than necessary to fulfil a legitimate objective, taking account of the risks non-fulfilment would create. Such legitimate objectives are, *inter alia:* national security requirements; the prevention of deceptive practices; protection of human health or safety, animal or plant life or health, or the environment. In assessing such risks, relevant elements of consideration are, *inter alia:* available scientific and technical information, related processing technology or intended end-uses of products.

2.3 Technical regulations shall not be maintained if the circumstances or objectives giving rise to their adoption no longer exist or if the changed circumstances or objectives can be addressed in a less trade-restrictive manner.

2.4 Where technical regulations are required and relevant international standards exist or their completion is imminent, Members shall use them, or the relevant parts of them, as a basis for their technical regulations except when such international standards or relevant parts would be an ineffective or inappropriate means for the fulfilment of the legitimate objectives pursued, for instance because of fundamental climatic or geographical factors or fundamental technological problems.

2.5 A Member preparing, adopting or applying a technical regulation which may have a significant effect on trade of other Members shall, upon the request of another Member, explain the justification for that technical regulation in terms of the provisions of paragraphs

2 to 4. Whenever a technical regulation is prepared, adopted or applied for one of the legitimate objectives explicitly mentioned in paragraph 2, and is in accordance with relevant international standards, it shall be rebuttably presumed not to create an unnecessary obstacle to international trade.

2.6 With a view to harmonizing technical regulations on as wide a basis as possible, Members shall play a full part, within the limits of their resources, in the preparation by appropriate international standardizing bodies of international standards for products for which they either have adopted, or expect to adopt, technical regulations.

2.7 Members shall give positive consideration to accepting as equivalent technical regulations of other Members, even if these regulations differ from their own, provided they are satisfied that these regulations adequately fulfil the objectives of their own regulations.

2.8 Wherever appropriate, Members shall specify technical regulations based on product requirements in terms of performance rather than design or descriptive characteristics.

2.9 Whenever a relevant international standard does not exist or the technical content of a proposed technical regulation is not in accordance with the technical content of relevant international standards, and if the technical regulation may have a significant effect on trade of other Members, Members shall:

2.9.1   publish a notice in a publication at an early appropriate stage, in such a manner as to enable interested parties in other Members to become acquainted with it, that they propose to introduce a particular technical regulation;

2.9.2   notify other Members through the Secretariat of the products to be covered by the proposed technical regulation, together with a brief indication of its objective and rationale. Such notifications shall take place at an early appropriate stage, when amendments can still be introduced and comments taken into account;

2.9.3   upon request, provide to other Members particulars or copies of the proposed technical regulation and, whenever possible, identify the parts which in substance deviate from relevant international standards;

2.9.4   without discrimination, allow reasonable time for other Members to make comments in writing, discuss these comments upon request, and take these written comments and the results of these discussions into account.

2.10 Subject to the provisions in the lead-in to paragraph 9, where urgent problems of safety, health, environmental protection or national security arise or threaten to arise for a Member, that Member may omit such of the steps enumerated in paragraph 9 as it finds necessary, provided that the Member, upon adoption of a technical regulation, shall:

2.10.1   notify immediately other Members through the Secretariat of the particular technical regulation and the products covered, with a brief indication of the objective and the rationale of the technical regulation, including the nature of the urgent problems;

2.10.2   upon request, provide other Members with copies of the technical regulation;

2.10.3   without discrimination, allow other Members to present their comments in writing, discuss these comments upon request, and take these written comments and the results of these discussions into account.

2.11 Members shall ensure that all technical regulations which have been adopted are published promptly or otherwise made available in such a manner as to enable interested parties in other Members to become acquainted with them.

2.12 Except in those urgent circumstances referred to in paragraph 10, Members shall allow a reasonable interval between the publication of technical regulations and their entry into force in order to allow time for producers in exporting Members, and particularly in developing country Members, to adapt their products or methods of production to the requirements of the importing Member.

Article 3
Preparation, Adoption and Application of Technical Regulations by Local Government Bodies and Non-Governmental Bodies

With respect to their local government and non-governmental bodies within their territories:

3.1 Members shall take such reasonable measures as may be available to them to ensure compliance by such bodies with the provisions of Article 2, with the exception of the obligation to notify as referred to in paragraphs 9.2 and 10.1 of Article 2.

3.2 Members shall ensure that the technical regulations of local governments on the level directly below that of the central government in Members are notified in accordance with the provisions of paragraphs 9.2 and 10.1 of Article 2, noting that notification shall not be required for technical regulations the technical content of which is substantially the same as that of previously notified technical regulations of central government bodies of the Member concerned.

3.3 Members may require contact with other Members, including the notifications, provision of information, comments and discussions referred to in paragraphs 9 and 10 of Article 2, to take place through the central government.

3.4 Members shall not take measures which require or encourage local government bodies or non-governmental bodies within their territories to act in a manner inconsistent with the provisions of Article 2.

3.5 Members are fully responsible under this Agreement for the observance of all provisions of Article 2. Members shall formulate and implement positive measures and mechanisms in support of the observance of the provisions of Article 2 by other than central government bodies.

Article 4
Preparation, Adoption and Application of Standards

4.1 Members shall ensure that their central government standardizing bodies accept and comply with the Code of Good Practice for the Preparation, Adoption and Application of Standards in Annex 3 to this Agreement (referred to in this Agreement as the "Code of Good Practice"). They shall take such reasonable measures as may be available to them to ensure that local government and non-governmental standardizing bodies within their territories, as well as regional standardizing bodies of which they or one or more bodies within their territories are members, accept and comply with this Code of Good Practice. In addition, Members shall not take measures which have the effect of, directly or indirectly, requiring or encouraging such standardizing bodies to act in a manner inconsistent with the Code of Good Practice. The obligations of Members with respect to compliance of standardizing bodies with the provisions of the Code of Good Practice shall apply irrespective of whether or not a standardizing body has accepted the Code of Good Practice.

4.2 Standardizing bodies that have accepted and are complying with the Code of Good Practice shall be acknowledged by the Members as complying with the principles of this Agreement.

Conformity with Technical Regulations and Standards

Article 5
Procedures for Assessment of Conformity by
Central Government Bodies

5.1 Members shall ensure that, in cases where a positive assurance of conformity with technical regulations or standards is required, their central government bodies apply the following provisions to products originating in the territories of other Members:

5.1.1 conformity assessment procedures are prepared, adopted and applied so as to grant access for suppliers of like products originating in the territories of other Members under conditions no less favourable than those accorded to suppliers of like products of national origin or originating in any other country, in a comparable situation; access entails suppliers' right to an assessment of conformity under the rules of the procedure, including, when foreseen by this procedure, the possibility to have conformity assessment activities undertaken at the site of facilities and to receive the mark of the system;

5.1.2 conformity assessment procedures are not prepared, adopted or applied with a view to or with the effect of creating unnecessary obstacles to international trade. This means, *inter alia*, that conformity assessment procedures shall not be more strict or be applied more strictly than is necessary to give the importing Member adequate confidence that products conform with the applicable technical regulations or standards, taking account of the risks non-conformity would create.

5.2 When implementing the provisions of paragraph 1, Members shall ensure that:

5.2.1   conformity assessment procedures are undertaken and completed as expeditiously as possible and in a no less favourable order for products originating in the territories of other Members than for like domestic products;

5.2.2   the standard processing period of each conformity assessment procedure is published or that the anticipated processing period is communicated to the applicant upon request; when receiving an application, the competent body promptly examines the completeness of the documentation and informs the applicant in a precise and complete manner of all deficiencies; the competent body transmits as soon as possible the results of the assessment in a precise and complete manner to the applicant so that corrective action may be taken if necessary; even when the application has deficiencies, the competent body proceeds as far as practicable with the conformity assessment if the applicant so requests; and that, upon request, the applicant is informed of the stage of the procedure, with any delay being explained;

5.2.3   information requirements are limited to what is necessary to assess conformity and determine fees;

5.2.4   the confidentiality of information about products originating in the territories of other Members arising from or supplied in connection with such conformity assessment procedures is respected in the same way as for domestic products and in such a manner that legitimate commercial interests are protected;

5.2.5   any fees imposed for assessing the conformity of products originating in the territories of other Members are equitable in relation to any fees chargeable for assessing the conformity of like products of national origin or originating in any other country, taking into account communication, transportation and other costs arising from differences between location of facilities of the applicant and the conformity assessment body;

5.2.6   the siting of facilities used in conformity assessment procedures and the selection of samples are not such as to cause unnecessary inconvenience to applicants or their agents;

5.2.7   whenever specifications of a product are changed subsequent to the determination of its conformity to the applicable technical regulations or standards, the conformity assessment procedure for the modified product is limited to what is necessary to determine whether adequate confidence exists that the product still meets the technical regulations or standards concerned;

5.2.8   a procedure exists to review complaints concerning the operation of a conformity assessment procedure and to take corrective action when a complaint is justified.

5.3 Nothing in paragraphs 1 and 2 shall prevent Members from carrying out reasonable spot checks within their territories.

5.4 In cases where a positive assurance is required that products conform with technical regulations or standards, and relevant guides or recommendations issued by international standardizing bodies exist or their completion is imminent, Members shall ensure that central government bodies use them, or the relevant parts of them, as a basis for their conformity assessment procedures, except where, as duly explained upon request, such guides or recommendations or relevant parts are inappropriate for the Members concerned, for, *inter alia,* such reasons as: national security requirements; the prevention of deceptive practices; protection of human health or safety, animal or plant life or health, or the environment; fundamental climatic or other geographical factors; fundamental technological or infrastructural problems.

5.5 With a view to harmonizing conformity assessment procedures on as wide a basis as possible, Members shall play a full part, within the limits of their resources, in the preparation by appropriate international standardizing bodies of guides and recommendations for conformity assessment procedures.

5.6 Whenever a relevant guide or recommendation issued by an international standardizing body does not exist or the technical content of a proposed conformity assessment procedure is not in accordance with relevant guides and recommendations issued by international standardizing bodies, and if the conformity assessment procedure may have a significant effect on trade of other Members, Members shall:

5.6.1   publish a notice in a publication at an early appropriate stage, in such a manner as to enable interested parties in other Members to become acquainted with it, that they propose to introduce a particular conformity assessment procedure;

5.6.2   notify other Members through the Secretariat of the products to be covered by the proposed conformity assessment procedure, together with a brief indication of its objective and rationale. Such notifications shall take place at an early appropriate stage, when amendments can still be introduced and comments taken into account;

5.6.3   upon request, provide to other Members particulars or copies of the proposed procedure and, whenever possible, identify the parts which in substance deviate from relevant guides or recommendations issued by international standardizing bodies;

5.6.4   without discrimination, allow reasonable time for other Members to make comments in writing, discuss these comments upon request, and take these written comments and the results of these discussions into account.

5.7 Subject to the provisions in the lead-in to paragraph 6, where urgent problems of safety, health, environmental protection or national security arise or threaten to arise for a Member, that Member may omit such of the steps enumerated in paragraph 6 as it finds necessary, provided that the Member, upon adoption of the procedure, shall:

5.7.1   notify immediately other Members through the Secretariat of the particular procedure and the products covered, with a brief indication of the objective and the rationale of the procedure, including the nature of the urgent problems;

5.7.2   upon request, provide other Members with copies of the rules of the procedure;

5.7.3   without discrimination, allow other Members to present their comments in writing, discuss these comments upon request, and take these written comments and the results of these discussions into account.

5.8 Members shall ensure that all conformity assessment procedures which have been adopted are published promptly or otherwise made available in such a manner as to enable interested parties in other Members to become acquainted with them.

5.9 Except in those urgent circumstances referred to in paragraph 7, Members shall allow a reasonable interval between the publication of requirements concerning conformity assessment procedures and their entry into force in order to allow time for producers in exporting Members, and particularly in developing country Members, to adapt their products or methods of production to the requirements of the importing Member.

Article 6
Recognition of Conformity Assessment by Central Government Bodies

With respect to their central government bodies:

6.1 Without prejudice to the provisions of paragraphs 3 and 4, Members shall ensure, whenever possible, that results of conformity assessment procedures in other Members are accepted, even when those procedures differ from their own, provided they are satisfied that those procedures offer an assurance of conformity with applicable technical regulations or standards equivalent to their own procedures. It is recognized that prior consultations may be necessary in order to arrive at a mutually satisfactory understanding regarding, in particular:

6.1.1   adequate and enduring technical competence of the relevant conformity assessment bodies in the exporting Member, so that confidence in the continued reliability of their conformity assessment results can exist; in this regard, verified compliance, for instance through accreditation, with relevant guides or recommendations issued by international standardizing bodies shall be taken into account as an indication of adequate technical competence;

6.1.2   limitation of the acceptance of conformity assessment results to those produced by designated bodies in the exporting Member.

6.2 Members shall ensure that their conformity assessment procedures permit, as far as practicable, the implementation of the provisions in paragraph 1.

6.3 Members are encouraged, at the request of other Members, to be willing to enter into negotiations for the conclusion of agreements for the mutual recognition of results of each other's conformity assessment procedures. Members may require that such agreements fulfil the criteria of paragraph 1 and give mutual satisfaction regarding their potential for facilitating trade in the products concerned.

6.4 Members are encouraged to permit participation of conformity assessment bodies located in the territories of other Members in their conformity assessment procedures under conditions no less favourable than those accorded to bodies located within their territory or the territory of any other country.

Article 7
Procedures for Assessment of Conformity by Local Government Bodies

With respect to their local government bodies within their territories:

7.1 Members shall take such reasonable measures as may be available to them to ensure compliance by such bodies with the provisions of Articles 5 and 6, with the exception of the obligation to notify as referred to in paragraphs 6.2 and 7.1 of Article 5.

7.2 Members shall ensure that the conformity assessment procedures of local governments on the level directly below that of the central government in Members are notified in accordance with the provisions of paragraphs 6.2 and 7.1 of Article 5, noting that notifications shall not be required for conformity assessment procedures the technical content of which is substantially the same as that of previously notified conformity assessment procedures of central government bodies of the Members concerned.

7.3 Members may require contact with other Members, including the notifications, provision of information, comments and discussions referred to in paragraphs 6 and 7 of Article 5, to take place through the central government.

7.4 Members shall not take measures which require or encourage local government bodies within their territories to act in a manner inconsistent with the provisions of Articles 5 and 6.

7.5 Members are fully responsible under this Agreement for the observance of all provisions of Articles 5 and 6. Members shall formulate and implement positive measures and mechanisms in support of the observance of the provisions of Articles 5 and 6 by other than central government bodies.

Article 8
Procedures for Assessment of Conformity by Non-Governmental Bodies

8.1 Members shall take such reasonable measures as may be available to them to ensure that non-governmental bodies within their territories which operate conformity assessment procedures comply with the provisions of Articles 5 and 6, with the exception of the obligation to notify proposed conformity assessment procedures. In addition, Members shall not take measures which have the effect of, directly or indirectly, requiring or encouraging such bodies to act in a manner inconsistent with the provisions of Articles 5 and 6.

8.2 Members shall ensure that their central government bodies rely on conformity assessment procedures operated by non-governmental bodies only if these latter bodies comply with the provisions of Articles 5 and 6, with the exception of the obligation to notify proposed conformity assessment procedures.

Article 9
International and Regional Systems

9.1 Where a positive assurance of conformity with a technical regulation or standard is required, Members shall, wherever practicable, formulate and adopt international systems for conformity assessment and become members thereof or participate therein.

9.2 Members shall take such reasonable measures as may be available to them to ensure that international and regional systems for conformity assessment in which relevant bodies within their territories are members or participants comply with the provisions of Articles 5 and 6. In addition, Members shall not take any measures which have the effect of, directly or indirectly, requiring or encouraging such systems to act in a manner inconsistent with any of the provisions of Articles 5 and 6.

9.3 Members shall ensure that their central government bodies rely on international or regional conformity assessment systems only to the extent that these systems comply with the provisions of Articles 5 and 6, as applicable.

Information and Assistance

Article 10
Information About Technical Regulations, Standards and Conformity Assessment Procedures

10.1   Each Member shall ensure that an enquiry point exists which is able to answer all reasonable enquiries from other Members and interested parties in other Members as well as to provide the relevant documents regarding:

10.1.1   any technical regulations adopted or proposed within its territory by central or local government bodies, by non-governmental bodies which have legal power to enforce a technical regulation, or by regional standardizing bodies of which such bodies are members or participants;

10.1.2   any standards adopted or proposed within its territory by central or local government bodies, or by regional standardizing bodies of which such bodies are members or participants;

10.1.3   any conformity assessment procedures, or proposed conformity assessment procedures, which are operated within its territory by central or local government bodies, or by non-governmental bodies which have legal power to enforce a technical regulation, or by regional bodies of which such bodies are members or participants;

10.1.4   the membership and participation of the Member, or of relevant central or local government bodies within its territory, in international and regional standardizing bodies and conformity assessment systems, as well as in bilateral and multilateral arrangements within the scope of this Agreement; it shall also be able to provide reasonable information on the provisions of such systems and arrangements;

10.1.5   the location of notices published pursuant to this Agreement, or the provision of information as to where such information can be obtained; and

10.1.6   the location of the enquiry points mentioned in paragraph 3.

10.2 If, however, for legal or administrative reasons more than one enquiry point is established by a Member, that Member shall provide to the other Members complete and unambiguous information on the scope of responsibility of each of these enquiry points. In addition, that Member shall ensure that any enquiries addressed to an incorrect enquiry point shall promptly be conveyed to the correct enquiry point.

10.3 Each Member shall take such reasonable measures as may be available to it to ensure that one or more enquiry points exist which are able to answer all reasonable enquiries from other Members and interested parties in other Members as well as to provide the relevant documents or information as to where they can be obtained regarding:

10.3.1   any standards adopted or proposed within its territory by non-governmental standardizing bodies, or by regional standardizing bodies of which such bodies are members or participants; and

10.3.2   any conformity assessment procedures, or proposed conformity assessment procedures, which are operated within its territory by non-governmental bodies, or by regional bodies of which such bodies are members or participants;

10.3.3   the membership and participation of relevant non-governmental bodies within its territory in international and regional standardizing bodies and conformity assessment systems, as well as in bilateral and multilateral arrangements within the scope of this Agreement; they shall also be able to provide reasonable information on the provisions of such systems and arrangements.

10.4 Members shall take such reasonable measures as may be available to them to ensure that where copies of documents are requested by other Members or by interested parties in other Members, in accordance with the provisions of this Agreement, they are supplied at an equitable price (if any) which shall, apart from the real cost of delivery, be the same for the nationals[1] of the Member concerned or of any other Member.

---

1. "Nationals" here shall be deemed, in the case of a separate customs territory Member of the WTO, to mean persons, natural or legal, who are domiciled or who have a real and effective industrial or commercial establishment in that customs territory.

10.5 Developed country Members shall, if requested by other Members, provide, in English, French or Spanish, translations of the documents covered by a specific notification or, in case of voluminous documents, of summaries of such documents.

10.6 The Secretariat shall, when it receives notifications in accordance with the provisions of this Agreement, circulate copies of the notifications to all Members and interested international standardizing and conformity assessment bodies, and draw the attention of developing country Members to any notifications relating to products of particular interest to them.

10.7 Whenever a Member has reached an agreement with any other country or countries on issues related to technical regulations, standards or conformity assessment procedures which may have a significant effect on trade, at least one Member party to the agreement shall notify other Members through the Secretariat of the products to be covered by the agreement and include a brief description of the agreement. Members concerned are encouraged to enter, upon request, into consultations with other Members for the purposes of concluding similar agreements or of arranging for their participation in such agreements.

10.8 Nothing in this Agreement shall be construed as requiring:

10.8.1   the publication of texts other than in the language of the Member;

10.8.2   the provision of particulars or copies of drafts other than in the language of the Member except as stated in paragraph 5; or

10.8.3   Members to furnish any information, the disclosure of which they consider contrary to their essential security interests.

10.9 Notifications to the Secretariat shall be in English, French or Spanish.

10.10 Members shall designate a single central government authority that is responsible for the implementation on the national level of the provisions concerning notification procedures under this Agreement except those included in Annex 3.

10.11 If, however, for legal or administrative reasons the responsibility for notification procedures is divided among two or more central government authorities, the Member concerned shall provide to the other Members complete and unambiguous information on the scope of responsibility of each of these authorities.

Article 11
Technical Assistance to Other Members

11.1 Members shall, if requested, advise other Members, especially the developing country Members, on the preparation of technical regulations.

11.2 Members shall, if requested, advise other Members, especially the developing country Members, and shall grant them technical assistance on mutually agreed terms and conditions regarding the establishment of national standardizing bodies, and participation in the international standardizing bodies, and shall encourage their national standardizing bodies to do likewise.

11.3 Members shall, if requested, take such reasonable measures as may be available to them to arrange for the regulatory bodies within their territories to advise other Members, especially the developing country Members, and shall grant them technical assistance on mutually agreed terms and conditions regarding:

11.3.1   the establishment of regulatory bodies, or bodies for the assessment of conformity with technical regulations; and

11.3.2   the methods by which their technical regulations can best be met.

11.4 Members shall, if requested, take such reasonable measures as may be available to them to arrange for advice to be given to other Members, especially the developing country Members, and shall grant them technical assistance on mutually agreed terms and conditions regarding the establishment of bodies for the assessment of conformity with standards adopted within the territory of the requesting Member.

11.5 Members shall, if requested, advise other Members, especially the developing country Members, and shall grant them technical assistance on mutually agreed terms and conditions regarding the steps that should be taken by their producers if they wish to have access to systems for conformity assessment operated by governmental or non-governmental bodies within the territory of the Member receiving the request.

11.6 Members which are members or participants of international or regional systems for conformity assessment shall, if requested, advise other Members, especially the developing country Members, and shall grant them technical assistance on mutually agreed terms and conditions regarding the establishment of the institutions and legal framework which would enable them to fulfil the obligations of membership or participation in such systems.

11.7 Members shall, if so requested, encourage bodies within their territories which are members or participants of international or regional systems for conformity assessment to advise other Members, especially the developing country Members, and should consider requests for technical assistance from them regarding the establishment of the institutions which would enable the relevant bodies within their territories to fulfil the obligations of membership or participation.

11.8 In providing advice and technical assistance to other Members in terms of paragraphs 1 to 7, Members shall give priority to the needs of the least-developed country Members.

Article 12
Special and Differential Treatment of
Developing Country Members

12.1 Members shall provide differential and more favourable treatment to developing country Members to this Agreement, through the following provisions as well as through the relevant provisions of other Articles of this Agreement.

12.2 Members shall give particular attention to the provisions of this Agreement concerning developing country Members' rights and obligations and shall take into account the special development, financial and trade needs of developing country Members in the implementation of this Agreement, both nationally and in the operation of this Agreement's institutional arrangements.

12.3 Members shall, in the preparation and application of technical regulations, standards and conformity assessment procedures, take account of the special development, financial and trade needs of developing country Members, with a view to ensuring that such technical regulations, standards and conformity assessment procedures do not create unnecessary obstacles to exports from developing country Members.

12.4 Members recognize that, although international standards, guides or recommendations may exist, in their particular technological and socio-economic conditions, developing country Members adopt certain technical regulations, standards or conformity assessment procedures aimed at preserving indigenous technology and production methods and processes compatible with their development needs. Members therefore recognize that developing country Members should not be expected to use international standards as a basis for their technical regulations or standards, including test methods, which are not appropriate to their development, financial and trade needs.

12.5 Members shall take such reasonable measures as may be available to them to ensure that international standardizing bodies and international systems for conformity assessment are organized and operated in a way which facilitates active and representative participation of relevant bodies in all Members, taking into account the special problems of developing country Members.

12.6 Members shall take such reasonable measures as may be available to them to ensure that international standardizing bodies, upon request of developing country Members, examine the possibility of, and, if practicable, prepare international standards concerning products of special interest to developing country Members.

12.7 Members shall, in accordance with the provisions of Article 11, provide technical assistance to developing country Members to ensure that the preparation and application of technical regulations, standards and conformity assessment procedures do not create unnecessary obstacles to the expansion and diversification of exports from developing country Members. In determining the terms and conditions of the technical assistance, account shall be taken of the stage of development of the requesting Members and in particular of the least-developed country Members.

12.8 It is recognized that developing country Members may face special problems, including institutional and infrastructural problems, in the field of preparation and application of technical regulations, standards and conformity assessment procedures. It is further recognized that the special development and trade needs of developing country Members, as well as their stage of technological development, may hinder their ability to discharge fully their obligations under this Agreement. Members, therefore, shall take this fact fully into account. Accordingly, with a view to ensuring that developing country Members are able to comply with this Agreement, the Committee on Technical Barriers to Trade provided for in Article 13 (referred to in this Agreement as the "Committee") is enabled to grant, upon request, specified, time-limited exceptions in whole or in part from obligations under this Agreement. When considering such requests the Committee shall take into account the special problems, in the field of preparation and application of technical regulations, standards and conformity assessment procedures, and the special development and trade needs of the developing country Member, as well as its stage of technological development, which may hinder its ability to discharge fully its obligations under this Agreement. The Committee shall, in particular, take into account the special problems of the least-developed country Members.

12.9 During consultations, developed country Members shall bear in mind the special difficulties experienced by developing country Members in formulating and implementing standards and technical regulations and conformity assessment procedures, and in their desire to assist developing country Members with their efforts in this direction, developed country Members shall take account of the special needs of the former in regard to financing, trade and development.

12.10 The Committee shall examine periodically the special and differential treatment, as laid down in this Agreement, granted to developing country Members on national and international levels.

Institutions, Consultation and Dispute Settlement

Article 13
The Committee on Technical Barriers to Trade

13.1 A Committee on Technical Barriers to Trade is hereby established, and shall be composed of representatives from each of the Members. The Committee shall elect its own Chairman and shall meet as necessary, but no less than once a year, for the purpose of affording Members the opportunity of consulting on any matters relating to the operation of this Agreement or the furtherance of its objectives, and shall carry out such responsibilities as assigned to it under this Agreement or by the Members.

13.2 The Committee shall establish working parties or other bodies as may be appropriate, which shall carry out such responsibilities as may be assigned to them by the Committee in accordance with the relevant provisions of this Agreement.

13.3 It is understood that unnecessary duplication should be avoided between the work under this Agreement and that of governments in other technical bodies. The Committee shall examine this problem with a view to minimizing such duplication.

Article 14
Consultation and Dispute Settlement

14.1 Consultations and the settlement of disputes with respect to any matter affecting the operation of this Agreement shall take place under the auspices of the Dispute Settlement Body and shall follow, *mutatis mutandis,* the provisions of Articles XXII and XXIII of GATT 1994, as elaborated and applied by the Dispute Settlement Understanding.

14.2 At the request of a party to a dispute, or at its own initiative, a panel may establish a technical expert group to assist in questions of a technical nature, requiring detailed consideration by experts.

14.3 Technical expert groups shall be governed by the procedures of Annex 2.

14.4 The dispute settlement provisions set out above can be invoked in cases where a Member considers that another Member has not achieved satisfactory results under Articles 3, 4, 7, 8 and 9 and its trade interests are significantly affected. In this respect, such results shall be equivalent to those as if the body in question were a Member.

FINAL PROVISIONS

Article 15
Final Provisions

Reservations

15.1 Reservations may not be entered in respect of any of the provisions of this Agreement without the consent of the other Members.

Review

15.2 Each Member shall, promptly after the date on which the WTO Agreement enters into force for it, inform the Committee of measures in existence or taken to ensure the implementation and administration of this Agreement. Any changes of such measures thereafter shall also be notified to the Committee.

15.3 The Committee shall review annually the implementation and operation of this Agreement taking into account the objectives thereof.

15.4 Not later than the end of the third year from the date of entry into force of the WTO Agreement and at the end of each three-year period thereafter, the Committee shall review the operation and implementation of this Agreement, including the provisions relating to transparency, with a view to recommending an adjustment of the rights and obligations of this Agreement where necessary to ensure mutual economic advantage and balance of rights and obligations, without prejudice to the provisions of Article 12. Having regard, *inter alia,* to the experience gained in the implementation of the Agreement, the Committee shall, where appropriate, submit proposals for amendments to the text of this Agreement to the Council for Trade in Goods.

Annexes

15.5 The annexes to this Agreement constitute an integral part thereof.

Annex 1
Terms and Their Definitions for the Purpose of this Agreement

The terms presented in the sixth edition of the ISO/IEC Guide 2: 1991, General Terms and Their Definitions Concerning Standardization and Related Activities, shall, when used in this Agreement, have the same meaning as given in the definitions in the said Guide taking into account that services are excluded from the coverage of this Agreement.

For the purpose of this Agreement, however, the following definitions shall apply:

1. *Technical regulation*

Document which lays down product characteristics or their related processes and production methods, including the applicable administrative provisions, with which compliance is mandatory. It may also include or deal exclusively with terminology, symbols, packaging, marking or labelling requirements as they apply to a product, process or production method.

Explanatory note

The definition in ISO/IEC Guide 2 is not self-contained, but based on the so-called "building block" system.

2. *Standard*

Document approved by a recognized body, that provides, for common and repeated use, rules, guidelines or characteristics for products or related processes and production methods, with which compliance is not mandatory. It may also include or deal exclusively with terminology, symbols, packaging, marking or labelling requirements as they apply to a product, process or production method.

Explanatory note

The terms as defined in ISO/IEC Guide 2 cover products, processes and services. This Agreement deals only with technical regulations, standards and conformity assessment procedures related to products or processes and production methods. Standards as defined by ISO/ IEC Guide 2 may be mandatory or voluntary. For the purpose of this Agreement standards are defined as voluntary and technical regulations as mandatory documents. Standards prepared by the international standardization community are based on consensus. This Agreement covers also documents that are not based on consensus.

3. *Conformity assessment procedures*

Any procedure used, directly or indirectly, to determine that relevant requirements in technical regulations or standards are fulfilled.

Explanatory note

Conformity assessment procedures include, *inter alia,* procedures for sampling, testing and inspection; evaluation, verification and assurance of conformity; registration, accreditation and approval as well as their combinations.

4. *International body or system*

Body or system whose membership is open to the relevant bodies of at least all Members.

5. *Regional body or system*

Body or system whose membership is open to the relevant bodies of only some of the Members.

6. *Central government body*

Central government, its ministries and departments or any body subject to the control of the central government in respect of the activity in question.

Explanatory note:

In the case of the European Communities the provisions governing central government bodies apply. However, regional bodies or conformity assessment systems may be established within the European Communities, and in such cases would be subject to the provisions of this Agreement on regional bodies or conformity assessment systems.

7. *Local government body*

Government other than a central government (e.g. states, provinces, Länder, cantons, municipalities, etc.), its ministries or departments or any body subject to the control of such a government in respect of the activity in question.

8. *Non-governmental body*

Body other than a central government body or a local government body, including a non-governmental body which has legal power to enforce a technical regulation.

Annex 2
Technical Expert Groups

The following procedures shall apply to technical expert groups established in accordance with the provisions of Article 14.

1. Technical expert groups are under the panel's authority. Their terms of reference and detailed working procedures shall be decided by the panel, and they shall report to the panel.

2. Participation in technical expert groups shall be restricted to persons of professional standing and experience in the field in question.

3. Citizens of parties to the dispute shall not serve on a technical expert group without the joint agreement of the parties to the dispute, except in exceptional circumstances when the panel considers that the need for specialized scientific expertise cannot be fulfilled otherwise. Government officials of parties to the dispute shall not serve on a technical expert group. Members of technical expert groups shall serve in their individual capacities and not as government representatives, nor as representatives of any organization. Governments or

organizations shall therefore not give them instructions with regard to matters before a technical expert group.

4. Technical expert groups may consult and seek information and technical advice from any source they deem appropriate. Before a technical expert group seeks such information or advice from a source within the jurisdiction of a Member, it shall inform the government of that Member. Any Member shall respond promptly and fully to any request by a technical expert group for such information as the technical expert group considers necessary and appropriate.

5. The parties to a dispute shall have access to all relevant information provided to a technical expert group, unless it is of a confidential nature. Confidential information provided to the technical expert group shall not be released without formal authorization from the government, organization or person providing the information. Where such information is requested from the technical expert group but release of such information by the technical expert group is not authorized, a non-confidential summary of the information will be provided by the government, organization or person supplying the information.

6. The technical expert group shall submit a draft report to the Members concerned with a view to obtaining their comments, and taking them into account, as appropriate, in the final report, which shall also be circulated to the Members concerned when it is submitted to the panel.

Annex 3
Code of Good Practice for the Preparation, Adoption and Application of Standards

General Provisions

A. For the purposes of this Code the definitions in Annex 1 of this Agreement shall apply.

B. This Code is open to acceptance by any standardizing body within the territory of a Member of the WTO, whether a central government body, a local government body, or a non-governmental body; to any governmental regional standardizing body one or more members of which are Members of the WTO; and to any non-governmental regional standardizing body one or more members of which are situated within the territory of a Member of the WTO (referred to in this Code collectively as "standardizing bodies" and individually as "the standardizing body").

C. Standardizing bodies that have accepted or withdrawn from this Code shall notify this fact to the ISO/IEC Information Centre in Geneva. The notification shall include the name and address of the body concerned and the scope of its current and expected standardization activities. The notification may be sent either directly to the ISO/IEC Information Centre, or through the national member body of ISO/IEC or, preferably, through the relevant national member or international affiliate of ISONET, as appropriate.

Substantive Provisions

D. In respect of standards, the standardizing body shall accord treatment to products originating in the territory of any other Member of the WTO no less favourable than that accorded to like products of national origin and to like products originating in any other country.

E. The standardizing body shall ensure that standards are not prepared, adopted or applied with a view to, or with the effect of, creating unnecessary obstacles to international trade.

F. Where international standards exist or their completion is imminent, the standardizing body shall use them, or the relevant parts of them, as a basis for the standards it develops, except where such international standards or relevant parts would be ineffective or inappropriate, for instance, because of an insufficient level of protection or fundamental climatic or geographical factors or fundamental technological problems.

G. With a view to harmonizing standards on as wide a basis as possible, the standardizing body shall, in an appropriate way, play a full part, within the limits of its resources, in the preparation by relevant international standardizing bodies of international standards regarding subject matter for which it either has adopted, or expects to adopt, standards. For standardizing bodies within the territory of a Member, participation in a particular international standardization activity shall, whenever possible, take place through one delegation representing all standardizing bodies in the territory that have adopted, or expect to adopt, standards for the subject matter to which the international standardization activity relates.

H. The standardizing body within the territory of a Member shall make every effort to avoid duplication of, or overlap with, the work of other standardizing bodies in the national territory or with the work of relevant international or regional standardizing bodies. They shall also make every effort to achieve a national consensus on the standards they develop. Likewise the regional standardizing body shall make every effort to avoid duplication of, or overlap with, the work of relevant international standardizing bodies.

I. Wherever appropriate, the standardizing body shall specify standards based on product requirements in terms of performance rather than design or descriptive characteristics.

J. At least once every six months, the standardizing body shall publish a work programme containing its name and address, the standards it is currently preparing and the standards which it has adopted in the preceding period. A standard is under preparation from the moment a decision has been taken to develop a standard until that standard has been adopted. The titles of specific draft standards shall, upon request, be provided in English, French or Spanish. A notice of the existence of the work programme shall be published in a national or, as the case may be, regional publication of standardization activities.

The work programme shall for each standard indicate, in accordance with any ISONET rules, the classification relevant to the subject matter, the stage attained in the standard's development, and the references of any international standards taken as a basis. No later than at the time of publication of its work programme, the standardizing body shall notify the existence thereof to the ISO/IEC Information Centre in Geneva.

The notification shall contain the name and address of the standardizing body, the name and issue of the publication in which the work programme is published, the period to which the work programme applies, its price (if any), and how and where it can be obtained. The notification may be sent directly to the ISO/IEC Information Centre, or, preferably, through the relevant national member or international affiliate of ISONET, as appropriate.

K. The national member of ISO/IEC shall make every effort to become a member of ISONET or to appoint another body to become a member as well as to acquire the most advanced membership type possible for the ISONET member. Other standardizing bodies shall make every effort to associate themselves with the ISONETmember.

L. Before adopting a standard, the standardizing body shall allow a period of at least 60 days for the submission of comments on the draft standard by interested parties within the territory of a Member of the WTO. This period may, however, be shortened in cases where urgent problems of safety, health or environment arise or threaten to arise. No later than at the start of the comment period, the standardizing body shall publish a notice announcing the period for commenting in the publication referred to in paragraph J. Such notification shall include, as far as practicable, whether the draft standard deviates from relevant international standards.

M. On the request of any interested party within the territory of a Member of the WTO, the standardizing body shall promptly provide, or arrange to provide, a copy of a draft standard which it has submitted for comments. Any fees charged for this service shall, apart from the real cost of delivery, be the same for foreign and domestic parties.

N. The standardizing body shall take into account, in the further processing of the standard, the comments received during the period for commenting. Comments received through standardizing bodies that have accepted this Code of Good Practice shall, if so requested, be replied to as promptly as possible. The reply shall include an explanation why a deviation from relevant international standards is necessary.

O. Once the standard has been adopted, it shall be promptly published.

P. On the request of any interested party within the territory of a Member of the WTO, the standardizing body shall promptly provide, or arrange to provide, a copy of its most recent work programme or of a standard which it produced. Any fees charged for this service shall, apart from the real cost of delivery, be the same for foreign and domestic parties.

Q. The standardizing body shall afford sympathetic consideration to, and adequate opportunity for, consultation regarding representations with respect to the operation of this Code presented by standardizing bodies that have accepted this Code of Good Practice. It shall make an objective effort to solve any complaints.

Agreement on the Application of
Sanitary And Phytosanitary Measures

Members,

Reaffirming that no Member should be prevented from adopting or enforcing measures necessary to protect human, animal or plant life or health, subject to the requirement that these measures are not applied in a manner which would constitute a means of arbitrary or unjustifiable discrimination between Members where the same conditions prevail or a disguised restriction on international trade;

Desiring to improve the human health, animal health and phytosanitary situation in all Members;

Noting that sanitary and phytosanitary measures are often applied on the basis of bilateral agreements or protocols;

Desiring the establishment of a multilateral framework of rules and disciplines to guide the development, adoption and enforcement of sanitary and phytosanitary measures in order to minimize their negative effects on trade;

Recognizing the important contribution that international standards, guidelines and recommendations can make in this regard;

Desiring to further the use of harmonized sanitary and phytosanitary measures between Members, on the basis of international standards, guidelines and recommendations developed by the relevant international organizations, including the Codex Alimentarius Commission, the International Office of Epizootics, and the relevant international and regional organizations operating within the framework of the International Plant Protection Convention, without requiring Members to change their appropriate level of protection of human, animal or plant life or health;

Recognizing that developing country Members may encounter special difficulties in complying with the sanitary or phytosanitary measures of importing Members, and as a consequence in access to markets, and also in the formulation and application of sanitary or phytosanitary measures in their own territories, and desiring to assist them in their endeavours in this regard;

Desiring therefore to elaborate rules for the application of the provisions of GATT 1994 which relate to the use of sanitary or phytosanitary measures, in particular the provisions of Article XX(b)[2];

Hereby agree as follows:

Article 1
General Provisions

1. This Agreement applies to all sanitary and phytosanitary measures which may, directly or indirectly, affect international trade. Such measures shall be developed and applied in accordance with the provisions of this Agreement.

2. For the purposes of this Agreement, the definitions provided in Annex A shall apply.

3. The annexes are an integral part of this Agreement.

4. Nothing in this Agreement shall affect the rights of Members under the Agreement on Technical Barriers to Trade with respect to measures not within the scope of this Agreement.

Article 2
Basic Rights and Obligations

1. Members have the right to take sanitary and phytosanitary measures necessary for the protection of human, animal or plant life or health, provided that such measures are not inconsistent with the provisions of this Agreement.

2. Members shall ensure that any sanitary or phytosanitary measure is applied only to the extent necessary to protect human, animal or plant life or health, is based on scientific principles and is not maintained without sufficient scientific evidence, except as provided for in paragraph 7 of Article 5.

3. Members shall ensure that their sanitary and phytosanitary measures do not arbitrarily or unjustifiably discriminate between Members where identical or similar conditions prevail, including between their own territory and that of other Members. Sanitary and phytosanitary measures shall not be applied in a manner which would constitute a disguised restriction on international trade.

---

2. In this Agreement, reference to Article XX(b) includes also the chapeau of that Article.

4. Sanitary or phytosanitary measures which conform to the relevant provisions of this Agreement shall be presumed to be in accordance with the obligations of the Members under the provisions of GATT 1994 which relate to the use of sanitary or phytosanitary measures, in particular the provisions of Article XX(b).

Article 3
Harmonization

1. To harmonize sanitary and phytosanitary measures on as wide a basis as possible, Members shall base their sanitary or phytosanitary measures on international standards, guidelines or recommendations, where they exist, except as otherwise provided for in this Agreement, and in particular in paragraph 3.

2. Sanitary or phytosanitary measures which conform to international standards, guidelines or recommendations shall be deemed to be necessary to protect human, animal or plant life or health, and presumed to be consistent with the relevant provisions of this Agreement and of GATT 1994.

3. Members may introduce or maintain sanitary or phytosanitary measures which result in a higher level of sanitary or phytosanitary protection than would be achieved by measures based on the relevant international standards, guidelines or recommendations, if there is a scientific justification, or as a consequence of the level of sanitary or phytosanitary protection a Member determines to be appropriate in accordance with the relevant provisions of paragraphs 1 through 8 of Article 5.[3] Notwithstanding the above, all measures which result in a level of sanitary or phytosanitary protection different from that which would be achieved by measures based on international standards, guidelines or recommendations shall not be inconsistent with any other provision of this Agreement.

4. Members shall play a full part, within the limits of their resources, in the relevant international organizations and their subsidiary bodies, in particular the Codex Alimentarius Commission, the

3. For the purposes of paragraph 3 of Article 3, there is a scientific justification if, on the basis of an examination and evaluation of available scientific information in conformity with the relevant provisions of this Agreement, a Member determines that the relevant international standards, guidelines or recommendations are not sufficient to achieve its appropriate level of sanitary or phytosanitary protection.

International Office of Epizootics, and the international and regional organizations operating within the framework of the International Plant Protection Convention, to promote within these organizations the development and periodic review of standards, guidelines and recommendations with respect to all aspects of sanitary and phytosanitary measures.

5. The Committee on Sanitary and Phytosanitary Measures provided for in paragraphs 1 and 4 of Article 12 (referred to in this Agreement as the "Committee") shall develop a procedure to monitor the process of international harmonization and coordinate efforts in this regard with the relevant international organizations.

Article 4
Equivalence

1. Members shall accept the sanitary or phytosanitary measures of other Members as equivalent, even if these measures differ from their own or from those used by other Members trading in the same product, if the exporting Member objectively demonstrates to the importing Member that its measures achieve the importing Member's appropriate level of sanitary or phytosanitary protection. For this purpose, reasonable access shall be given, upon request, to the importing Member for inspection, testing and other relevant procedures.

2. Members shall, upon request, enter into consultations with the aim of achieving bilateral and multilateral agreements on recognition of the equivalence of specified sanitary or phytosanitary measures.

Article 5
Assessment of Risk and Determination of the Appropriate Level of Sanitary or Phytosanitary Protection

1. Members shall ensure that their sanitary or phytosanitary measures are based on an assessment, as appropriate to the circumstances, of the risks to human, animal or plant life or health, taking into account risk assessment techniques developed by the relevant international organizations.

2. In the assessment of risks, Members shall take into account available scientific evidence; relevant processes and production methods; relevant inspection, sampling and testing methods; prevalence of

specific diseases or pests; existence of pest- or disease-free areas; relevant ecological and environmental conditions; and quarantine or other treatment.

3. In assessing the risk to animal or plant life or health and determining the measure to be applied for achieving the appropriate level of sanitary or phytosanitary protection from such risk, Members shall take into account as relevant economic factors: the potential damage in terms of loss of production or sales in the event of the entry, establishment or spread of a pest or disease; the costs of control or eradication in the territory of the importing Member; and the relative cost-effectiveness of alternative approaches to limiting risks.

4. Members should, when determining the appropriate level of sanitary or phytosanitary protection, take into account the objective of minimizing negative trade effects.

5. With the objective of achieving consistency in the application of the concept of appropriate level of sanitary or phytosanitary protection against risks to human life or health, or to animal and plant life or health, each Member shall avoid arbitrary or unjustifiable distinctions in the levels it considers to be appropriate in different situations, if such distinctions result in discrimination or a disguised restriction on international trade. Members shall cooperate in the Committee, in accordance with paragraphs 1, 2 and 3 of Article 12, to develop guidelines to further the practical implementation of this provision. In developing the guidelines, the Committee shall take into account all relevant factors, including the exceptional character of human health risks to which people voluntarily expose themselves.

6. Without prejudice to paragraph 2 of Article 3, when establishing or maintaining sanitary or phytosanitary measures to achieve the appropriate level of sanitary or phytosanitary protection, Members shall ensure that such measures are not more trade-restrictive than required to achieve their appropriate level of sanitary or phytosanitary protection, taking into account technical and economic feasibility.[4]

7. In cases where relevant scientific evidence is insufficient, a Member may provisionally adopt sanitary or phytosanitary measures on the basis of available pertinent information, including that from

4. For purposes of paragraph 6 of Article 5, a measure is not more trade-restrictive than required unless there is another measure, reasonably available taking into account technical and economic feasibility, that achieves the appropriate level of sanitary or phytosanitary protection and is significantly less restrictive to trade.

the relevant international organizations as well as from sanitary or phytosanitary measures applied by other Members. In such circumstances, Members shall seek to obtain the additional information necessary for a more objective assessment of risk and review the sanitary or phytosanitary measure accordingly within a reasonable period of time.

8. When a Member has reason to believe that a specific sanitary or phytosanitary measure introduced or maintained by another Member is constraining, or has the potential to constrain, its exports and the measure is not based on the relevant international standards, guidelines or recommendations, or such standards, guidelines or recommendations do not exist, an explanation of the reasons for such sanitary or phytosanitary measure may be requested and shall be provided by the Member maintaining the measure.

Article 6
Adaptation to Regional Conditions, Including Pest- or Disease-Free Areas and Areas of Low Pest or Disease Prevalence

1. Members shall ensure that their sanitary or phytosanitary measures are adapted to the sanitary or phytosanitary characteristics of the area—whether all of a country, part of a country, or all or parts of several countries—from which the product originated and to which the product is destined. In assessing the sanitary or phytosanitary characteristics of a region, Members shall take into account, *inter alia,* the level of prevalence of specific diseases or pests, the existence of eradication or control programmes, and appropriate criteria or guidelines which may be developed by the relevant international organizations.

2. Members shall, in particular, recognize the concepts of pest- or disease-free areas and areas of low pest or disease prevalence. Determination of such areas shall be based on factors such as geography, ecosystems, epidemiological surveillance, and the effectiveness of sanitary or phytosanitary controls.

3. Exporting Members claiming that areas within their territories are pest- or disease-free areas or areas of low pest or disease prevalence shall provide the necessary evidence thereof in order to objectively demonstrate to the importing Member that such areas are, and are likely to remain, pest-or disease-free areas or areas of low pest or disease prevalence, respectively. For this purpose, reasonable access

shall be given, upon request, to the importing Member for inspection, testing and other relevant procedures.

Article 7
Transparency

Members shall notify changes in their sanitary or phytosanitary measures and shall provide information on their sanitary or phytosanitary measures in accordance with the provisions of Annex B.

Article 8
Control, Inspection and Approval Procedures

Members shall observe the provisions of Annex C in the operation of control, inspection and approval procedures, including national systems for approving the use of additives or for establishing tolerances for contaminants in foods, beverages or feedstuffs, and otherwise ensure that their procedures are not inconsistent with the provisions of this Agreement.

Article 9
Technical Assistance

1.   Members agree to facilitate the provision of technical assistance to other Members, especially developing country Members, either bilaterally or through the appropriate international organizations. Such assistance may be, *inter alia,* in the areas of processing technologies, research and infrastructure, including in the establishment of national regulatory bodies, and may take the form of advice, credits, donations and grants, including for the purpose of seeking technical expertise, training and equipment to allow such countries to adjust to, and comply with, sanitary or phytosanitary measures necessary to achieve the appropriate level of sanitary or phytosanitary protection in their export markets.

2. Where substantial investments are required in order for an exporting developing country Member to fulfil the sanitary or phytosanitary requirements of an importing Member, the latter shall consider providing such technical assistance as will permit the developing country Member to maintain and expand its market access opportunities for the product involved.

Article 10
Special and Differential Treatment

1. In the preparation and application of sanitary or phytosanitary measures, Members shall take account of the special needs of developing country Members, and in particular of the least-developed country Members.

2. Where the appropriate level of sanitary or phytosanitary protection allows scope for the phased introduction of new sanitary or phytosanitary measures, longer time-frames for compliance should be accorded on products of interest to developing country Members so as to maintain opportunities for their exports.

3. With a view to ensuring that developing country Members are able to comply with the provisions of this Agreement, the Committee is enabled to grant to such countries, upon request, specified, time-limited exceptions in whole or in part from obligations under this Agreement, taking into account their financial, trade and development needs.

4. Members should encourage and facilitate the active participation of developing country Members in the relevant international organizations.

Article 11
Consultations and Dispute Settlement

1. The provisions of Articles XXII and XXIII of GATT 1994 as elaborated and applied by the Dispute Settlement Understanding shall apply to consultations and the settlement of disputes under this Agreement, except as otherwise specifically provided herein.

2. In a dispute under this Agreement involving scientific or technical issues, a panel should seek advice from experts chosen by the panel in consultation with the parties to the dispute. To this end, the panel may, when it deems it appropriate, establish an advisory technical experts group, or consult the relevant international organizations, at the request of either party to the dispute or on its own initiative.

3. Nothing in this Agreement shall impair the rights of Members under other international agreements, including the right to resort to the good offices or dispute settlement mechanisms of other international organizations or established under any international agreement.

Article 12
Administration

1. A Committee on Sanitary and Phytosanitary Measures is hereby established to provide a regular forum for consultations. It shall carry out the functions necessary to implement the provisions of this Agreement and the furtherance of its objectives, in particular with respect to harmonization. The Committee shall reach its decisions by consensus.

2. The Committee shall encourage and facilitate ad hoc consultations or negotiations among Members on specific sanitary or phytosanitary issues. The Committee shall encourage the use of international standards, guidelines or recommendations by all Members and, in this regard, shall sponsor technical consultation and study with the objective of increasing coordination and integration between international and national systems and approaches for approving the use of food additives or for establishing tolerances for contaminants in foods, beverages or feedstuffs.

3. The Committee shall maintain close contact with the relevant international organizations in the field of sanitary and phytosanitary protection, especially with the Codex Alimentarius Commission, the International Office of Epizootics, and the Secretariat of the International Plant Protection Convention, with the objective of securing the best available scientific and technical advice for the administration of this Agreement and in order to ensure that unnecessary duplication of effort is avoided.

4. The Committee shall develop a procedure to monitor the process of international harmonization and the use of international standards, guidelines or recommendations. For this purpose, the Committee should, in conjunction with the relevant international organizations, establish a list of international standards, guidelines or recommendations relating to sanitary or phytosanitary measures which the Committee determines to have a major trade impact. The list should include an indication by Members of those international standards, guidelines or recommendations which they apply as conditions for import or on the basis of which imported products conforming to these standards can enjoy access to their markets. For those cases in which a Member does not apply an international standard, guideline or recommendation as a condition for import, the Member should provide an indication of the reason therefor, and, in particular,

whether it considers that the standard is not stringent enough to provide the appropriate level of sanitary or phytosanitary protection. If a Member revises its position, following its indication of the use of a standard, guideline or recommendation as a condition for import, it should provide an explanation for its change and so inform the Secretariat as well as the relevant international organizations, unless such notification and explanation is given according to the procedures of Annex B.

5. In order to avoid unnecessary duplication, the Committee may decide, as appropriate, to use the information generated by the procedures, particularly for notification, which are in operation in the relevant international organizations.

6. The Committee may, on the basis of an initiative from one of the Members, through appropriate channels invite the relevant international organizations or their subsidiary bodies to examine specific matters with respect to a particular standard, guideline or recommendation, including the basis of explanations for non-use given according to paragraph 4.

7. The Committee shall review the operation and implementation of this Agreement three years after the date of entry into force of the WTO Agreement, and thereafter as the need arises. Where appropriate, the Committee may submit to the Council for Trade in Goods proposals to amend the text of this Agreement having regard, *inter alia,* to the experience gained in its implementation.

Article 13
Implementation

Members are fully responsible under this Agreement for the observance of all obligations set forth herein. Members shall formulate and implement positive measures and mechanisms in support of the observance of the provisions of this Agreement by other than central government bodies. Members shall take such reasonable measures as may be available to them to ensure that non-governmental entities within their territories, as well as regional bodies in which relevant entities within their territories are members, comply with the relevant provisions of this Agreement. In addition, Members shall not take measures which have the effect of, directly or indirectly, requiring or encouraging such regional or non-governmental entities, or local governmental bodies, to act in a manner inconsistent with the provisions of this Agreement. Members shall ensure that they rely on the services of non-governmental entities for implementing sanitary or phytosanitary measures only if these entities comply with the provisions of this Agreement.

Article 14
Final Provisions

The least-developed country Members may delay application of the provisions of this Agreement for a period of five years following the date of entry into force of the WTO Agreement with respect to their sanitary or phytosanitary measures affecting importation or imported products. Other developing country Members may delay application of the provisions of this Agreement, other than paragraph 8 of Article 5 and Article 7, for two years following the date of entry into force of the WTO Agreement with respect to their existing sanitary or phytosanitary measures affecting importation or imported products, where such application is prevented by a lack of technical expertise, technical infrastructure or resources.

Annex A
Definitions[5]

1. *Sanitary or phytosanitary measure*—Any measure applied:
   (a) to protect animal or plant life or health within the territory of the Member from risks arising from the entry, establishment or spread of pests, diseases, disease-carrying organisms or disease-causing organisms;
   (b) to protect human or animal life or health within the territory of the Member from risks arising from additives, contaminants, toxins or disease-causing organisms in foods, beverages or feedstuffs;
   (c) to protect human life or health within the territory of the Member from risks arising from diseases carried by animals, plants

5. For the purpose of these definitions, "animal" includes fish and wild fauna; "plant" includes forests and wild flora; "pests" include weeds; and "contaminants" include pesticide and veterinary drug residues and extraneous matter.

or products thereof, or from the entry, establishment or spread of pests; or

(d) to prevent or limit other damage within the territory of the Member from the entry, establishment or spread of pests. Sanitary or phytosanitary measures include all relevant laws, decrees, regulations, requirements and procedures including, *inter alia,* end product criteria; processes and production methods; testing, inspection, certification and approval procedures; quarantine treatments including relevant requirements associated with the transport of animals or plants, or with the materials necessary for their survival during transport; provisions on relevant statistical methods, sampling procedures and methods of risk assessment; and packaging and labelling requirements directly related to food safety.

2. *Harmonization*—The establishment, recognition and application of common sanitary and phytosanitary measures by different Members.

3. *International standards, guidelines and recommendations*

(a) for food safety, the standards, guidelines and recommendations established by the Codex Alimentarius Commission relating to food additives, veterinary drug and pesticide residues, contaminants, methods of analysis and sampling, and codes and guidelines of hygienic practice;

(b) for animal health and zoonoses, the standards, guidelines and recommendations developed under the auspices of the International Office of Epizootics;

(c) for plant health, the international standards, guidelines and recommendations developed under the auspices of the Secretariat of the International Plant Protection Convention in cooperation with regional organizations operating within the framework of the International Plant Protection Convention; and

(d) for matters not covered by the above organizations, appropriate standards, guidelines and recommendations promulgated by other relevant international organizations open for membership to all Members, as identified by the Committee.

4. *Risk assessment*—The evaluation of the likelihood of entry, establishment or spread of a pest or disease within the territory of an importing Member according to the sanitary or phytosanitary measures which might be applied, and of the associated potential biologi-

cal and economic consequences; or the evaluation of the potential for adverse effects on human or animal health arising from the presence of additives, contaminants, toxins or disease-causing organisms in food, beverages or feedstuffs.

5. *Appropriate level of sanitary or phytosanitary protection*—The level of protection deemed appropriate by the Member establishing a sanitary or phytosanitary measure to protect human, animal or plant life or health within its territory.

NOTE: Many Members otherwise refer to this concept as the "acceptable level of risk."

6. *Pest- or disease-free area*—An area, whether all of a country, part of a country, or all or parts of several countries, as identified by the competent authorities, in which a specific pest or disease does not occur.

NOTE: A pest- or disease-free area may surround, be surrounded by, or be adjacent to an area—whether within part of a country or in a geographic region which includes parts of or all of several countries -in which a specific pest or disease is known to occur but is subject to regional control measures such as the establishment of protection, surveillance and buffer zones which will confine or eradicate the pest or disease in question.

7. *Area of low pest or disease prevalence*—An area, whether all of a country, part of a country, or all or parts of several countries, as identified by the competent authorities, in which a specific pest or disease occurs at low levels and which is subject to effective surveillance, control or eradication measures.

Annex B
Transparency of Sanitary and Phytosanitary Regulations

Publication of regulations

1. Members shall ensure that all sanitary and phytosanitary regulations[6] which have been adopted are published promptly in such a manner as to enable interested Members to become acquainted with them.

---

6. Sanitary and phytosanitary measures such as laws, decrees or ordinances which are applicable generally.

2. Except in urgent circumstances, Members shall allow a reasonable interval between the publication of a sanitary or phytosanitary regulation and its entry into force in order to allow time for producers in exporting Members, and particularly in developing country Members, to adapt their products and methods of production to the requirements of the importing Member.

Enquiry points

3. Each Member shall ensure that one enquiry point exists which is responsible for the provision of answers to all reasonable questions from interested Members as well as for the provision of relevant documents regarding:

(a) any sanitary or phytosanitary regulations adopted or proposed within its territory;

(b) any control and inspection procedures, production and quarantine treatment, pesticide tolerance and food additive approval procedures, which are operated within its territory;

(c) risk assessment procedures, factors taken into consideration, as well as the determination of the appropriate level of sanitary or phytosanitary protection;

(d) the membership and participation of the Member, or of relevant bodies within its territory, in international and regional sanitary and phytosanitary organizations and systems, as well as in bilateral and multilateral agreements and arrangements within the scope of this Agreement, and the texts of such agreements and arrangements.

4. Members shall ensure that where copies of documents are requested by interested Members, they are supplied at the same price (if any), apart from the cost of delivery, as to the nationals[7] of the Member concerned.

Notification procedures

5. Whenever an international standard, guideline or recommendation does not exist or the content of a proposed sanitary or phytosanitary regulation is not substantially the same as the content of an international standard, guideline or recommendation, and if the reg-

---

7. When "nationals" are referred to in this Agreement, the term shall be deemed, in the case of a separate customs territory Member of the WTO, to mean persons, natural or legal, who are domiciled or who have a real and effective industrial or commercial establishment in that customs territory.

ulation may have a significant effect on trade of other Members, Members shall:

(a) publish a notice at an early stage in such a manner as to enable interested Members to become acquainted with the proposal to introduce a particular regulation;

(b) notify other Members, through the Secretariat, of the products to be covered by the regulation together with a brief indication of the objective and rationale of the proposed regulation. Such notifications shall take place at an early stage, when amendments can still be introduced and comments taken into account;

(c) provide upon request to other Members copies of the proposed regulation and, whenever possible, identify the parts which in substance deviate from international standards, guidelines or recommendations;

(d) without discrimination, allow reasonable time for other Members to make comments in writing, discuss these comments upon request, and take the comments and the results of the discussions into account.

6. However, where urgent problems of health protection arise or threaten to arise for a Member, that Member may omit such of the steps enumerated in paragraph 5 of this Annex as it finds necessary, provided that the Member:

(a) immediately notifies other Members, through the Secretariat, of the particular regulation and the products covered, with a brief indication of the objective and the rationale of the regulation, including the nature of the urgent problem(s);

(b) provides, upon request, copies of the regulation to other Members;

(c) allows other Members to make comments in writing, discusses these comments upon request, and takes the comments and the results of the discussions into account.

7. Notifications to the Secretariat shall be in English, French or Spanish.

8. Developed country Members shall, if requested by other Members, provide copies of the documents or, in case of voluminous documents, summaries of the documents covered by a specific notification in English, French or Spanish.

9. The Secretariat shall promptly circulate copies of the notification to all Members and interested international organizations and

draw the attention of developing country Members to any notifications relating to products of particular interest to them.

10. Members shall designate a single central government authority as responsible for the implementation, on the national level, of the provisions concerning notification procedures according to paragraphs 5, 6, 7 and 8 of this Annex.

General reservations

11. Nothing in this Agreement shall be construed as requiring:

(a) the provision of particulars or copies of drafts or the publication of texts other than in the language of the Member except as stated in paragraph 8 of this Annex; or

(b) Members to disclose confidential information which would impede enforcement of sanitary or phytosanitary legislation or which would prejudice the legitimate commercial interests of particular enterprises.

Annex C
Control, Inspection and Approval Procedures[8]

1. Members shall ensure, with respect to any procedure to check and ensure the fulfilment of sanitary or phytosanitary measures, that:

(a) such procedures are undertaken and completed without undue delay and in no less favourable manner for imported products than for like domestic products;

(b) the standard processing period of each procedure is published or that the anticipated processing period is communicated to the applicant upon request; when receiving an application, the competent body promptly examines the completeness of the documentation and informs the applicant in a precise and complete manner of all deficiencies; the competent body transmits as soon as possible the results of the procedure in a precise and complete manner to the applicant so that corrective action may be taken if necessary; even when the application has deficiencies, the competent body proceeds as far as practicable with the procedure if the applicant so requests;

---

8. Control, inspection and approval procedures include, *inter alia*, procedures for sampling, testing and certification.

and that upon request, the applicant is informed of the stage of the procedure, with any delay being explained;

(c) information requirements are limited to what is necessary for appropriate control, inspection and approval procedures, including for approval of the use of additives or for the establishment of tolerances for contaminants in food, beverages or feedstuffs;

(d) the confidentiality of information about imported products arising from or supplied in connection with control, inspection and approval is respected in a way no less favourable than for domestic products and in such a manner that legitimate commercial interests are protected;

(e) any requirements for control, inspection and approval of individual specimens of a product are limited to what is reasonable and necessary;

(f) any fees imposed for the procedures on imported products are equitable in relation to any fees charged on like domestic products or products originating in any other Member and should be no higher than the actual cost of the service;

(g) the same criteria should be used in the siting of facilities used in the procedures and the selection of samples of imported products as for domestic products so as to minimize the inconvenience to applicants, importers, exporters or their agents;

(h) whenever specifications of a product are changed subsequent to its control and inspection in light of the applicable regulations, the procedure for the modified product is limited to what is necessary to determine whether adequate confidence exists that the product still meets the regulations concerned; and

(i) a procedure exists to review complaints concerning the operation of such procedures and to take corrective action when a complaint is justified.

Where an importing Member operates a system for the approval of the use of food additives or for the establishment of tolerances for contaminants in food, beverages or feedstuffs which prohibits or restricts access to its domestic markets for products based on the absence of an approval, the importing Member shall consider the use of a relevant international standard as the basis for access until a final determination is made.

2. Where a sanitary or phytosanitary measure specifies control at the level of production, the Member in whose territory the production takes place shall provide the necessary assistance to facilitate such control and the work of the controlling authorities.

3. Nothing in this Agreement shall prevent Members from carrying out reasonable inspection within their own territories.

The Uruguay Round GATT agreements, including the Agreement on Technical Barriers to Trade (TBT) and the Agreement on the Application of Sanitary and Phytosanitary Measures (SPM) can be found in *Message from the President Transmitting the Uruguay Round Trade Agreements,* House Doc. 103-316, 103d Cong. 2d sess. (Government Printing Office, September 27, 1994).

References

Agege, Charles O. 1985. "Dumping of Dangerous American Products Overseas: Should Congress Sit and Watch?" *Journal of World Trade Law* 19 (July–August): 403–10.

Akerlof, George A. 1970. "The Market for 'Lemons': Quality Uncertainty and the Market Mechanism." *Quarterly Journal of Economics* 84 (August): 488–500.

Arnould, Richard J., and Henry Grabowski. 1981. "Auto Safety Regulation: An Analysis of Market Failure." *Bell Journal of Economics* 12 (Spring): 27–48.

Arrow, Kenneth. 1982. "Risk Perception in Psychology and Economics." *Economic Inquiry* 20 (January):1–9.

Baldwin, Robert E. 1988. *Trade Policy in a Changing World Economy.* University of Chicago Press.

Beales, Howard, Richard Craswell, and Steven C. Salop. 1981. "The Efficient Regulation of Consumer Information." *Journal of Law and Economics* 24 (December): 491–539.

Beales, J. Howard, and Timothy J. Muris. 1993. *State and Federal Regulation of National Advertising.* Washington: American Enterprise Institute.

Becker, Gary S. 1968. "Crime and Punishment: An Economic Approach." *Journal of Political Economy* 76 (March–April): 169–217.

———. 1976. "Comment on Peltzman." *Journal of Law and Economics* 19 (August): 245–48.

Berg, Sanford V. 1987. "Public Policy and Corporate Strategies in the AM Stereo Market." In *Product Standardization and Competitive Strategy,* edited by H. Landis Gabel, 149–170. North-Holland.

Besen, Stanley M., and Leland L. Johnson. 1986. *Compatibility Standards, Competition, and Innovation in the Broadcasting Industry.* Santa Monica, Calif.: Rand.

Besen, Stanley M., and Garth Saloner. 1989. "The Economics of Telecommunications Standards." In *Changing the Rules: Technological Change, International Competition, and Regulation in Communications,* edited by Robert W. Crandall and Kenneth Flamm, 177–220. Brookings.

215

Bork, Robert H. 1991. "Federalism and Federal Regulation: The Case of Product Labeling." Working Paper 46. Washington: Washington Legal Foundation. (July).

Braunstein, Yale M., and Lawrence J. White. 1985. "Setting Technical Compatibility Standards: An Economic Analysis." *Antitrust Bulletin* 30 (Summer): 337–55.

Bredahl, Maury E., and Kenneth W. Forsythe. 1989. "Harmonizing Phytosanitary and Sanitary Regulations." *World Economy* 12 (June): 189–206.

Calabresi, Guido, and A. Douglas Melamed. 1972. "Property Rules, Liability Rules and Inalienability: One View of the Cathedral." *Harvard Law Review* 85 (April): 1089–1128.

Carlton, Dennis W., and J. Mark Klamer. 1983. "The Need for Coordination among Firms, with Special Reference to Network Industries." *University of Chicago Law Review* 50 (Spring): 446–65.

Cecchini, Paolo, and others. 1988. *The European Challenge 1992: The Benefits of a Single Market.* Brookfield, Vt: Gower.

Center for European Policy Studies. 1992. "The European Community without Technical Barriers." Working Party Report 5. Brussels. (March).

Clark, Harry. 1988. "The Free Movement of Goods and Regulation for Public Health and Consumer Protection in the EEC: The West German 'Beer Purity' Case." *Virginia Journal of International Law* 28: 753–82.

Clarkson, Kenneth W., and Timothy J. Muris. 1982. "Letting Competition Serve Consumers," In *Instead of Regulation: Alternatives to Federal Regulatory Agencies,* edited by Robert W. Poole, Jr., 135–68. D.C. Heath.

Coase, R. H. 1960. "The Problem of Social Cost." *Journal of Law and Economics* 3 (October): 1–44.

———. 1972. "Durability and Monopoly." *Journal of Law and Economics* 15 (April): 143–50.

Coccodrilli, Fred. 1984. "Dispute Settlement Pursuant to the Agreement on Technical Barriers to Trade: The United States-Japan Metal Bat Dispute." *Fordham International Law Journal* 7 (Winter): 137–67.

Cochrane, Rexmond C. 1966. *Measures for Progress: A History of the National Bureau of Standards.* Department of Commerce, National Bureau of Standards.

Cooper, Richard N. 1994. *Environment and Resource Policies for the World Economy.* Brookings.

Costello, Declan. 1990. "The Internal Market." In *The Annual Review of European Community Affairs,* 55–57. London: Brassey's.

Dam, Kenneth W. 1970. *The GATT: Law and International Economic Organization.* University of Chicago Press.

David, Paul A. 1985. "Clio and the Economics of QWERTY." *American Economic Review* 75 (May): 332–37.

Dybvig, Philip H., and Chester S. Spatt. 1983. "Adoption Externalities as Public Goods." *Journal of Public Economics* 20 (March): 231–47.

Easterbrook, Frank H. 1983. "Antitrust and the Economics of Federalism." *Journal of Law and Economics* 26 (April): 23–50.

———. 1988. "The Constitution of Business." *George Mason University Law Review* 11 (Winter): 53–72.

Edelman, Peter B. 1988. "Japanese Product Standards as Non-Tariff Trade Barriers: When Regulatory Policy Becomes a Trade Issue." *Stanford Journal of International Law* 24 (Spring): 389–446.

Egan, Michelle. 1995. "Regulatory Barriers and Trade Liberalisation." CEPS Paper. Brussels: Centre for European Policy Studies.

Ehrenberg, Ronald G. 1994. *Labor Markets and Integrating National Economics.* Brookings.

Ellickson, Robert C. 1973. "Alternatives to Zoning: Covenants, Nuisance Rules, and Fines as Land Use Controls." *University of Chicago Law Review* 40 (Summer): 681–781.

Emerson, Michael, and others. 1988. *The Economics of 1992.* Oxford University Press.

Farrell, Joseph, and Garth Saloner. 1985. "Standardization, Compatibility and Innovation." *Rand Journal of Economics* 16 (Spring): 70–83.

———. 1986a. "Installed Base and Compatibility: Innovation, Product Preannouncements and Predation." *American Economic Review* 76 (December): 940–55.

———. 1986b. "Standardization and Variety." *Economic Letters* 20: 71–74.

———. 1987. "Competition, Compatibility and Standards: The Economics of Horses, Penguins and Lemmings." In *Product Standardization and Competitive Strategy,* edited by H. Landis Gabel, 1–21. New York: North-Holland.

———. 1988. "Coordination through Committees and Markets." *Rand Journal of Economics* 19 (Summer): 235–52.

Fischel, Daniel. 1987. "From MITE to CTS: State Anti-Takeover Statutes, the Williams Act, the Commerce Clause, and Insider Trading." *Supreme Court Review* 47: 47–95.

Froman, Michael. 1989. "International Trade: The United States-European Community Hormone Treated Beef Conflict." *Harvard International Law Journal* 30 (Spring): 549–56.

Gabel, H. Landis. 1987. *Product Standardization and Competitive Strategy.* North-Holland.

———. 1991. *Competitive Strategies for Product Standards.* McGraw Hill.

GATT Secretariat. 1994. *The Results of the Uruguay Round of Multilateral Trade Negotiations: The Legal Texts.* Geneva.

General Accounting Office. 1978. *Getting a Better Understanding of the Metric System—Implications if Adopted by the United States.* Government Printing Office.

Gorski, John J. 1991. "An FDA-EEC Perspective on the International Acceptance of Foreign Clinical Data." *California Western International Law Journal* 21 (Spring): 329–60.

Grabowski, Henry G., and John M. Vernon. 1978. "Consumer Product Safety Regulation." *American Economic Review* 68 (May): 284–89.

———. 1983. *The Regulation of Pharmaceuticals: Balancing the Benefits and Risks.* Washington: American Enterprise Institute.

Grossman, Sanford J. 1981. "The Informational Role of Warranties and Private Disclosure about Product Quality." *Journal of Law and Economics* 24 (December): 461–83.

Hamilton, Robert W. 1978. "The Role of Nongovernmental Standards in the Development of Mandatory Federal Standards Affecting Safety or Health." *Texas Law Review* 56 (November): 1329–50.

———. 1983. "Prospects for the Nongovernmental Development of Regulatory Standards." *American University Law Review* 32 (Winter): 455–69.

Hammonds, Holly. 1990. "A U.S. Perspective on the EC Hormones Directive." *Michigan Journal of International Law* 11 (Spring): 840–44.

Hemenway, David. 1975. *Industrywide Voluntary Product Standards.* Ballinger.

Hergert, Michael. 1987. "Technical Standards and Competition in the Microcomputer Industry." In *Product Standardization and Competitive Strategy,* edited by H. Landis Gabel, 67–89. North-Holland.

International Organization for Standardization. 1975. "ISO Memento: 1975."

———. 1994. *ISO 9000: International Standards for Quality Management,* 4th ed. Geneva.

International Trade Administration. 1982. *Metric Laws and Practices in International Trade: A Handbook for U.S. Exporters.* Department of Commerce.

———. 1989. *EC 1992: A Commerce Department Analysis of European Community Directives.* Department of Commerce.

Jackson, John H. 1969. *World Trade and the Law of GATT.* Bobbs-Merrill.

———. 1990. *Restructuring the GATT System.* New York: Council on Foreign Relations Press.

Katz, Michael L., and Carl Shapiro. 1985. "Network Externalities, Competition and Compatibility." *American Economic Review* 75 (June): 424–40.

———. 1986a. "Technology Adoption in the Presence of Network Externalities." *Journal of Political Economy* 94 (August): 822–41.

———. 1986b. "Product Compatibility Choice in a Market with Technological Progress." *Oxford Economic Papers* 38 (November supplement): 146–65.

Kay, David A. 1976a. *The International Regulation of Pesticide Residues in Food.* Washington: American Society of International Law.

———. 1976b. *The International Regulation of Pharmaceutical Drugs.* Washington: American Society of International Law.

Kindleberger, Charles P. 1983. "Standards as Public, Collective and Private Goods." *Kyklos* 36: 377–96.

Kitch, Edmund W. 1981. "Regulation and the American Common Market." In *Regulation, Federalism and Interstate Commerce,* edited by A. Dan Tarlock, 7–55. Oelgeschlager, Gunn, and Hain.

Klein, Benjamin, and Keith B. Leffler. 1981. "The Role of Market Forces in Assuring Contractual Performance." *Journal of Political Economy* 81 (August): 615–41.

Kreps, David, and Robert Wilson. 1982. "Reputation and Imperfect Information." *Journal of Economic Theory* 27 (August): 253–79.

Kurland, Philip B., and Ralph Lerner, eds. 1987. *The Founders' Constitution,* vol. II. University of Chicago Press.

Lawrence, Robert Z. Forthcoming. *Regionalism, Multilateralism, and Deeper Integration.* Brookings.

Lecraw, Donald J. 1984. "Some Economic Effects of Standards. *Applied Economics* 16 (August): 507–22.

———. 1987. "Japanese Standards: A Barrier to Trade?" In *Product Standardization and Competitive Strategy,* edited by H. Landis Gabel, 29–46. North-Holland.

Levmore, Saul. 1983. "Interstate Exploitation and Judicial Intervention." *Virginia Law Review* 69 (May): 563–631.

Lewis, Xavier. 1993. "The Protection of Consumers in European Community Law." In *Yearbook of European Law,* vol. 12. Oxford: Clarendon Press.

Liebowitz, S. J., and Stephen E. Margolis. 1990. "The Fable of the Keys." *Journal of Law and Economics* 33 (April): 1–26.

———. 1991. "Understanding Network Externalities." North Carolina State University. (November).

Link, Albert N. 1983. "Market Structure and Voluntary Product Standards." *Applied Economics* 15 (June): 393–401.

Lister, Bruce A. 1987. "Comparison of U.S. Laws and Regulations Concerning Labeling of Prepackaged Foods with the Codex Alimentarius Draft General Standard for Labeling of Prepackaged Foods." *Food, Drug and Cosmetic Law Journal* 42 (April): 174–83.

Majone, Giandomenico. 1994. "Comparing Strategies of Regulatory Rapprochement." In *Regulatory Cooperation for an Interdependent World.* Paris: OECD.

Martino, Robert A. 1941. *Standardization Activities of National Technical and Trade Associations.* Department of Commerce, National Bureau of Standards.

Matutes, Carmen, and Pierre Regibeau. 1988. "Mix and Match: Product Compatibility without Network Externalities." *Rand Journal of Economics* 19 (Summer): 221–34.

Meiners, Roger E. 1982. "What to Do about Hazardous Products." In *Instead of Regulation: Alternatives to Federal Regulatory Agencies,* edited by Robert W. Poole, Jr., 285–309. D.C. Heath.

Meng, Werner P. 1990. "The Hormone Conflict between the EEC and the United States within the Context of GATT." *Michigan Journal of International Law* 11 (Spring): 819–39.

Middlekauff, Roger D., and Philippe Shubik, eds. 1989. *International Food Regulation Handbook.* Marcel Dekker.

National Industrial Conference Board. 1929. *Industrial Standardization.* New York: NICB.

Nelson, Philip. 1974. "Advertising as Information." *Journal of Political Economy* 82 (July–August): 729–54.

Nicolaïdis, Kalypso. 1989. "Mutual Recognition: The Next Frontier of Multilateralism?" Paris: Project Prométhée Perspectives.

———. 1993a. "Mutual Recognition among Nations: The European Community and Trade in Services." Ph.D. dissertation, Harvard University.

———. 1993b. "Mutual Recognition, Regulatory Competition, and the Globalization of Professional Services." In *Coalitions and Competition: The Globalization of Professional Services,* edited by Yair Aharoni. New York: Routledge.

———. 1995. "International Trade in Information-based Services. The Uruguay Round and Beyond." In *The New Information Infrastructure: Strategies for U.S. Policy,* edited by William Drake. New York: Twentieth Century Fund.

Nusbaumer, Jacques. 1984. "The GATT Standards Code in Operation." *Journal of World Trade Law* 18 (November–December): 542–52.

Office of Technology Assessment. 1992. *Global Standards: Building Blocks for the Future.* U.S. Congress.

Ordover, Janusz A., Alan O. Sykes, and Robert D. Willig. 1983. "Predatory Systems Rivalry: A Reply." *Columbia Law Review* 83 (June): 1150–66.

Ordover, Janusz A., and Robert D. Willig. 1981. "An Economic Definition of Predation: Pricing and Product Innovation." *Yale Law Journal* 91 (November): 8–53.

Organization for Economic Cooperation and Development. 1991. *Consumers, Product Safety Standards, and International Trade.* Paris.

Overman, JoAnne R. 1992. *GATT Standards Code Activities of the National Institute of Standards and Technology, 1991.* Gaithersburg, Md.: National Institute of Standards and Technology, Department of Commerce.

Peach, Robert W., and Allen M. Wilson. 1980. "Product Certification and Its Potential Impact upon International Trade." In *International Standardization: Testing Certification and Related Matters, and their Implications under Trade Agreements Act of 1979,* 143–66. U.S. Department of Commerce.

Pelkmans, Jacques. 1990. "Regulation and the Single Market: An Economic Perspective." In *The Completion of the Internal Market: Symposium 1989,* edited by Horst Siebert. Tübingen: Kiel Institute of World Economics.

Pelkmans, Jacques. Forthcoming. "Governing European Union, from Pre-Federal to Federal Economic Integration?" Revised version in *Rethinking Federalism,* edited by Sylvia Ostry and others. Vancouver: UBC Press.

Pelkmans, Jacques, and Rita Beuter. 1987. "Standardization and Competitiveness: Private and Public Strategies in the EC Color TV Industry." In *Product Standardization and Competitive Strategy,* edited by H. Landis Gabel, 171–215. North-Holland.

Pelkmans, Jacques, and Niall Bohan. 1994. "Towards an Ideal GATT Technical Barriers Code." Revised version of paper for the CEPS/CSIS Conference on Technical Barriers.

Pelkmans, Jacques, and Jeanne-Mey Sun. 1994. "Towards an EC Regulatory Strategy: Lessons from 'Learning-By-Doing'." In *Regulatory Cooperation for an Interdependent World.* Paris: OECD.

Peltzman, Sam. 1975. "The Effects of Auto Safety Regulation." *Journal of Political Economy* 83 (August): 677–725.

———. 1976. "Toward a More General Theory of Regulation." *Journal of Law and Economics* 19 (August): 211–40.

———. 1987. "The Health Effects of Mandatory Prescriptions." *Journal of Law and Economics* 30 (October): 207—38.

Perry, John. 1955. *The Story of Standards.* Funk and Wagnalls.

Polinsky, A. Mitchell. 1979. "Controlling Externalities and Protecting Entitlements: Property Right, Liability Rule and Tax Subsidy Approaches." *Journal of Legal Studies* 8 (January): 1–48.

Polinsky, A. Mitchell, and Steven Shavell. 1979. "The Optimal Tradeoff Between the Probability and Magnitude of Fines." *American Economic Review* 69 (December): 880–91.

Poole, Robert W., Jr., ed. 1982. *Instead of Regulation: Alternatives to Federal Regulatory Agencies.* D. C. Heath.

Posner, Richard A. 1987. "The Constitution as an Economic Document." *George Washington Law Review* 56 (November): 4–38.

———. 1992. *Economic Analysis of Law,* 4th ed. Little, Brown.

Priest, George L. 1981. "A Theory of the Consumer Product Warranty." *Yale Law Journal* 90 (May): 1297–1352.

Redish, Martin H., and Shane V. Nugent. 1987. "The Dormant Commerce Clause and the Constitutional Balance of Federalism." *Duke Law Journal* (September): 569–617.

Regan, Donald H. 1986. "The Supreme Court and State Protectionism: Making Sense of the Dormant Commerce Clause." *Michigan Law Review* 84 (May): 1091–1287.

Revesz, Richard L. 1992. "Rehabilitating Interstate Competition: Rethinking the Race-to-the-Bottom Rationale for Federal Environmental Regulation." *New York University Law Journal* 67 (December): 1210–54.

Romano, Roberta. 1993. *The Genius of American Corporate Law.* Washington: American Enterprise Institute.

Rosman, Lewis. 1993. "Public Participation in International Pesticide Regulation: When the Codex Commission Decides, Who Will Listen?" *Virginia Environmental Law Journal* 12 (Winter): 329–65.

Rubinfeld, Daniel. 1987. "The Economics of the Local Public Sector." In *Handbook of Public Economics,* vol. 2, edited by Alan J. Auerbach and Martin Feldstein, 571–639. Amsterdam: North Holland.

Salop, Steven C., and David T. Scheffman. 1983. "Raising Rivals' Costs." *American Economic Review* 73 (May): 267–71.

Scherer, F. M. 1980. *Industrial Market Structure and Economic Performance,* 2d ed. Rand McNally.

Schmalensee, Richard. 1987. "Entry Deterrence in the Ready-to-Eat Breakfast Cereal Industry." *Bell Journal of Economics* 9 (Autumn): 305–27.

Shapiro, Carl. 1982. "Consumer Information, Product Quality, and Seller Reputation." *Bell Journal of Economics* 13 (Spring): 20–35.

———. 1983. "Premiums for High Quality Products as Returns to Reputations." *Quarterly Journal of Economics* 98 (November): 659–79.

Shapo, Marshall S. 1987. *The Law of Products Liability.* Boston: Warren, Gorham and Lamont.

Shavell, Steven. 1984a. "Liability for Harm versus Regulation of Safety." *Journal of Legal Studies* 13 (June): 357–74.

———. 1984b. "A Model of the Optimal Use of Liability and Safety Regulation." *Rand Journal of Economics* 15 (Summer): 271–80.

Shaviro, Daniel. 1993. *Federalism in Taxation: The Case for Greater Uniformity.* Washington: American Enterprise Institute.

Spence, Michael. 1975. "Monopoly, Quality and Regulation." *Bell Journal of Economics* 6 (Autumn): 417–29.

Steiner, Josephine. 1992. *Textbook on EEC Law,* 3d ed. London: Blackstone.

Stephens, Carlene E. 1983. "Inventing Standard Time." Washington: Smithsonian Institution.

Stigler, George J. 1971. "The Theory of Economic Regulation." *Bell Journal of Economics and Management Science* 2 (Spring): 3–21.

Sun, Jeanne-Mey, and Jacques Pelkmans. Forthcoming. "Regulatory Competition in the Internal Market." *Journal of Common Market Studies.*

Swan, Peter L. 1970. "Durability of Consumption Goods." *American Economic Review* 60 (December): 884–94.

Sykes, Alan O. 1989. "Review: Reformulating Tort Reform." *University of Chicago Law Review* 56 (Summer): 1153–70.

———. 1991. "Protectionism as a 'Safeguard': A Positive Analysis of the GATT 'Escape Clause' with Normative Speculations." *University of Chicago Law Review* 58 (Winter): 255–305.

———. 1992. "Constructive Unilateral Threats in International Commercial Relations: The Limited Case for Section 301." *Law and Policy in International Business* 23 (Spring): 263–330.

Tiebout, Charles M. 1956. "A Pure Theory of Local Expenditures." *Journal of Political Economy* 64 (October): 416–24.

Tillotson, John. 1990. "Fish, Please, but No Beef: Recent Controversial Issues Affecting Intra-Community Trade." *World Competition* 13 (June): 33–51.

Tirole, Jean. 1988. *The Theory of Industrial Organization.* MIT Press.

Tribe, Laurence A. 1988. *American Constitutional Law,* 2d ed. Mineola, N.Y.: Foundation Press.

Tversky, Amos, and Daniel Kahneman. 1974. "Judgment under Uncertainty: Heuristics and Biases." *Science* 185 (September 27): 1124.

U.S. House of Representatives, Committee on Science, Space, and Technology. 1992. *International Standards and Trade.* Hearing before the Subcommittee on Technology and Competitiveness. 102 Cong. 2 sess. (March 4). Government Printing Office.

van de Walle de Ghelcke, Bernard, Gerwin van Gerven, and Koen Platteau. 1990. "The New Approach to the Elimination of Technical Barriers in the European Community." *Brigham Young University Law Review* (Fall):1543–73.

Verman, Lal C. 1973. *Standardization: A New Discipline.* Hamden, Conn.: Archon.

Viscusi, W. Kip. 1979. *Employment Hazards: An Investigation of Market Performance.* Harvard University Press.

———. 1984. *Regulating Consumer Product Safety.* Washington: American Enterprise Institute.

———. 1993. *Product-Risk Labeling: A Federal Responsibility.* Washington: American Enterprise Institute.

von Heydebrand, Hans-Christoph. 1991. "Free Movement of Foodstuffs, Consumer Protection and Food Standards in the European Community: Has the Court of Justice Got It Wrong?" *European Law Review* 16 (October): 391–415.

Weimer, David Leo. 1982. "Safe and Available Drugs." In *Instead of Regulation: Alternatives to Federal Regulatory Agencies,* edited by Robert W. Poole, Jr. 285–309. D. C. Heath.

White, Michelle J., and Donald Wittman. 1983. "A Comparison of Taxes, Regulation, and Liability Rules under Imperfect Information." *Journal of Legal Studies* 12 (June): 413–26.

Wittman, Donald. 1977. "Prior Regulation versus Post Liability: The Choice between Input and Output Monitoring." *Journal of Legal Studies* 6 (January): 193–212.

Yarbrough, Beth V., and Robert M. Yarbrough. 1992. *Cooperation and Governance in International Trade: The Strategic Organizational Approach.* Princeton University Press.

Index